MW00532509

DB2 Handbook for DBAs

Ranade IBM Series

K. BOSLER • *CLIST Programming*, 0-07-006551-9

H. MURPHY • *Assembler for Cobol Programmers: MVS, VM*, 0-07-044129-4

H. BOOKMAN • *Cobol II*, 0-07-006533-0

J. RANADE • *DB2: Concepts, Programming, and Design*, 0-07-051265-5

J. SANCHEZ • *IBM Microcomputers Handbook*, 0-07-054594-4

M. CARATHANASSIS • *Expert MVS/XA JCL: A Complete Guide to Advanced Techniques*, 0-07-009816-6

P. DONOFRIO • *CICS: Debugging, Dump Reading and Problem Determination*, 0-07-017606-X

P. KAVANAGH • *VS Cobol II for Cobol Programmers*, 0-07-033571-0

T. MARTYN • *DB2/SQL: A Professional Programmer's Guide*, 0-07-040666-9

S. PIGGOTT • *CICS: A Practical Guide to System Fine Tuning*, 0-07-050054-1

N. PRASAD • *IBM Mainframes: Architecture and Design*, 0-07-050686-8

J. RANADE • *Introduction to SNA Networking: A Guide to VTAMINCP*, 0-07-051144-6

J. RANADE • *Advanced SNA Networking: A Professional's Guide for Using VTAMINCP*, 0-07-051143-8

S. SAMSON • *MVS: Performance Management*, 0-07-054528-6

B. JOHNSON • *MVS Concepts and Facilities*, 0-07-032673-8

A. WIPFLER • *Distributed Processing in the CICS Environment*, 0-07-071136-4

J. RANADE • *VSAM: Concepts, Programming, and Design, Second Edition*, 0-07-051244-2

J. RANADE • *VSAM Performance, Design, and Fine Tuning, Second Edition*, 0-07-051245-0

J. SANCHEZ • *Programming Solutions Handbook for IBM Microcomputers*, 0-07-054597-9

P. DONOFRIO • *CICS Programmer's Reference*, 0-07-017607-8

M. CARATHANASSIS • *Expert MVS/ESA JCL: A Guide to Advanced Techniques*, 0-07-009820-4

J. RANADE • *DOS to OS/2: Conversion, Migration, and Application Design*, 0-07-051264-7

K. BRATHWAITE • *Relational Databases: Concepts, Design and Administration*, 0-07-007252-3

B. JOHNSON, D. JOHNSON • *DASD: IBM's Direct Access Storage Devices*, 0-07-032674-6

M. MARX, P. DAVIS • *MVS Power Programming*, 0-07-040763-0

G. HOUTEKAMER, P. ARTIS • *MVS I/O Subsystem: Configuration Management and Performance Analysis*, 0-07-002553-3

A. KAPOOR • *SNA: Architecture, Protocols, and Implementation*, 0-07-033727-6

D. SILVERBERG • *DB2: Performance, Design, and Implementation*, 0-07-057553-3

R. CROWNHART • *IBM's Workstation CICS*, 0-07-014770-1

C. DANEY • *Programming in REXX*, 0-07-015305-1

G. GOLDBERG, P. SMITH • *The REXX Handbook*, 0-07-028682-8

A. WERMAN • *DB2 Handbook for DBAs*, 0-07-069460-5

R. LEFKON, J. KNEILING, P. SOMERS • *Understanding CICS Internals*, 0-07-037040-0

DB2 Handbook for DBAs

Aaron Werman

McGraw-Hill, Inc.

New York St. Louis San Francisco Auckland Bogotá
Caracas Lisbon London Madrid Mexico Milan
Montreal New Delhi Paris San Juan São Paulo
Singapore Sydney Tokyo Toronto

Library of Congress Cataloging-in-Publication Data

Werman, Aaron.
DB2 handbook for DBAs / Aaron Werman.
p. cm. — (J. Ranade IBM series)
Includes index.
ISBN 0-07-069460-5 : $49.95
1. Data base management. 2. IBM Data base 2 (Computer system)
I. Title. II. Series.
QA76.9.D3W46 1991
005.74—dc20 91-37128
CIP

1 2 3 4 5 6 7 8 9 0 DOC/DOC 9 7 6 5 4 3 2 1

ISBN 0-07-069460-5

The sponsoring editor for this book was Jerry Papke, the editing supervisor was Ruth W. Mannino, and the production supervisor was Suzanne W. Babeuf.

Printed and bound by R. R. Donnelley & Sons Company.

Contents

Acknowledgments

I would like to thank the many people involved in creating this book. Jay Ranade and Jerry Papke at McGraw-Hill helped get me going. Bob Thomas, Carol Hoag, and Ken Buerer at Thomas Publications (*Mainframe Journal* and *Enterprise Systems Journal*) and David Stoddard at *Data Base Programming and Design* encouraged my starting to write. Ruth Mannino patiently reviewed the material.

Many of my clients at Data Definition in the United States and abroad helped focus the ideas discussed here. Many coworkers helped me understand many of the issues as we planned, designed, developed, and tuned DB2 applications. Many colleagues — too many to list here — suffered through my talking about **what-if** scenarios and I appreciate their patience and helpful advice.

Several people read through preliminary versions of this book. I would like to thank Tim Hartley for his insightful comments. Roy Sacks provided many useful tips, especially on the day-to-day database administration problems. Many others have reviewed parts of the text. All errors are despite their best efforts, and are the responsibility of the author.

This book is dedicated to my wife Vicki, for her support, patience, understanding, and advice.

Preface

The premise of this book is that DB2 applications are different from others. The text focuses on the twin themes of the changing world of applications and the issues specific to DB2 in application development and management. The goal of the book is to make the reader think about these issues, which should make their next applications better.

Another way to look at this book is as a collection of advice. The most commonly asked questions in my DB2 consulting practice are answered here. These answers focus on the general issues in the industry. The discussion of the problems attempts to allow the reader to decide if the answer is suitable to the circumstance.

This book discusses significant architectural issues in developing DB2 applications. The topics relate to the broader logical design issues, the DB2-specific physical design issues, and standard characteristics taken on by the applications. The ideas are presented as explicit techniques. Several of these techniques will be used to develop each application subject.

The contents can be used in two ways. The book can be read in its entirety; this will present the variety of DB2 applications issues. Chapters can be read individually to review the issues as the reader confronts those issues in applications. The user can view this book as a handbook or cookbook when designing a specific type of system.

Obviously not all the issues discussed will apply to a given application. Some topics presented may seem obvious to many readers, as the book will present standard development options as if they were new discoveries. Some topics may seem esoteric, as indirect means to the goal.

The context makes the difference. It is hard to choose techniques without experience. The discussion will attempt to present both the positives and negatives in each option. The presumption is that the reader is sophisticated, and will pick out the techniques of interest. Once you understand the method, it is yours to use, change, or customize, but beware of those practices that you don't quite "get."

There are a large selection of books aimed at the DB2 novice. There are even several that address technical issues in this field. The difference is that this book focuses on the maturity of your use of DB2 services. A technically mature audience is presumed. The reader should have DB2 experience and general understanding of information processing issues.

This book is not for the novice. There is a review of DB2 function relating to each topic, but it is far from exhaustive. The contents address users with DB2 training and at least one DB2 application under their belt. More experienced users and designers will gain more from the issues as presented within. I am a DB2 designer and DBA and am speaking from that experience.

The perspective offered intentionally focuses on database issues, and favors long-term solutions over immediate corrections. The reader will often not have that luxury, but there should be evaluation of the appropriateness of the solution. Knowing the best-case approach helps to design even the quickest fix.

Anyone writing a book of this sort has an agenda, a desire to evangelize certain types of thinking about problems. There is an agenda here of understanding the DB2 concepts, of a relational perspective, and of strategic goals.

The focus is on application design and development. There is a strong emphasis on operational and security issues. This is because DB2 applications tend to have problems in this area. Furthermore, these issues are the central theme of our time: Why is central computing justifiable when decentralized processing is cheap?

Note that the review questions are serious questions. Often they do not reiterate issues from the text. In many cases they can help provide insight about the issues addressed. There are several significant issues that are addressed only in the question answers.

Writing this book has been an entertainment. Each chapter is an attempt to describe a technical issue subjectively, combining a technical review of the subject with my gestalt view of the topic. The chapters thus merge an essay on a topic with answers to the most common questions that arise in consulting on the subject. I hope this synthesis imparts meaning to the reader.

Aaron Werman

DB2 Handbook for DBAs

Chapter 1

How Mature Is Your Use of DB2?

There is a marvelous convergence of users of DB2 as their use of the software develops. It seems fascinating that most users go through the same phases in integrating DB2 into their applications. From the outside looking in, each user seems to repeat the same processes. In a way it makes sense — each stage of use is a reaction to the shop's past and a reaction to experience with DB2. It can be instructive for a DB2 user to review this maturing process as a means to plan for future changes.

The Early User

The early user of DB2 is clearly discernible and early users can easily identify themselves. The use of DB2 is experimental. Very early, shops must develop their DB2 standards and procedures.

Standards and procedures are the rules of how one is to use the system. These include:

- Operational procedures for starting and stopping the system.
- Setting up the DB2 start-up parameters (DSNZPARM).
- Developing naming conventions for the DB2 data sets. Developers need naming standards too, and guidelines for reasonable use of the DB2 facilities.

Small and large DB2 pilot projects

A pilot project is a common activity for the early DB2 user. In some more rational cases the pilot project is a low-profile

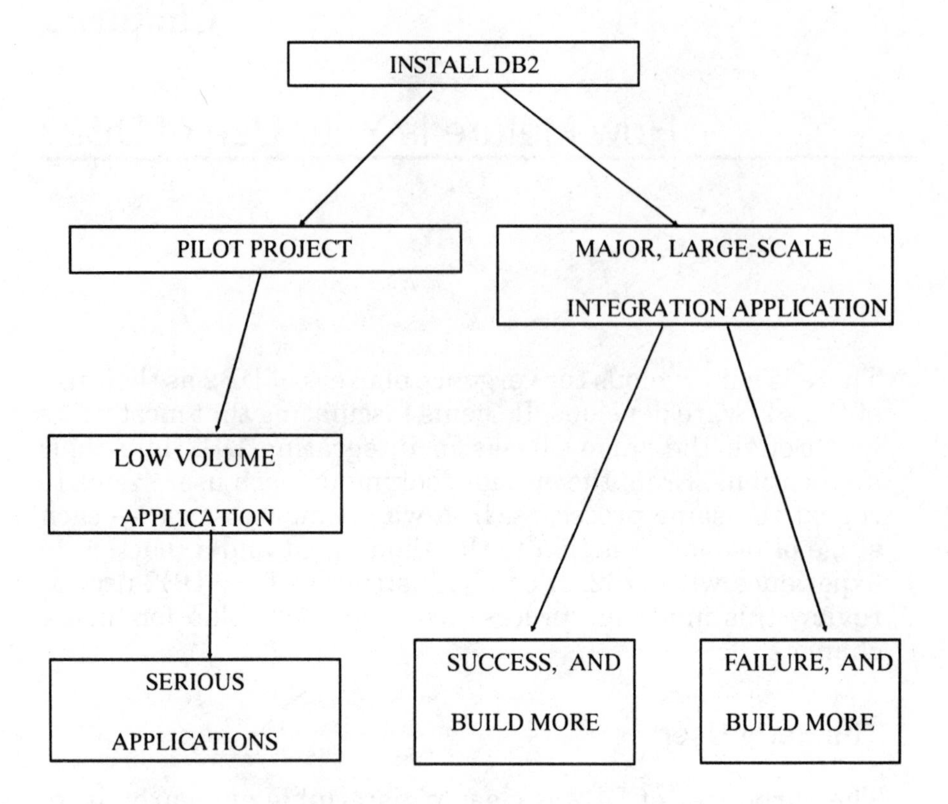

Figure 1.1 Pilot vs. strategic first projects.

application. A pilot project is an activity intended to steer future use of the techniques, and in which the application created is subservient to the training role. As such, a high-profile pilot project is a political rejection of the new technology.

The pilot application allows the shop to learn the issues and benefits of a new software tool. The features available need to be tested. Staff have to practice new ideas: Should we add new columns to tables in production while they are in use? What is a reasonable transaction rate DB2 can manage? How is the system tuned? How are DB2 applications migrated to production? Should secondary indices be used? How is DB2 different from our other software?

Sometimes there is heavy pressure to justify the expensive selection of DB2. This can lead to creating high-profile pilot applications where the requirement is both to evaluate the software and to produce an important application. (See Figure 1.1.)

The idea behind large-scope pilot projects is to gain the benefits of the new tool immediately. A common reason to purchase DB2 is that outdated data management facilities cannot provide flexible and quick application development. The most glamorous area in these new user requirements is providing decision support capabilities — creating reports that users can customize, allowing immediate access to data. Marketing is especially sensitive to this failing in older database applications. A common first application in DB2 is therefore a decision support system for marketing.

These are not the only examples of early intense use of DB2 in an organization. It is common to purchase DB2 as part of a spending spree involving radical systems changes. Conversion to MVS from other operating systems almost always includes DB2. Often, for scheduling reasons, these organizations have no choice but to use DB2 immediately as part of the conversion process.

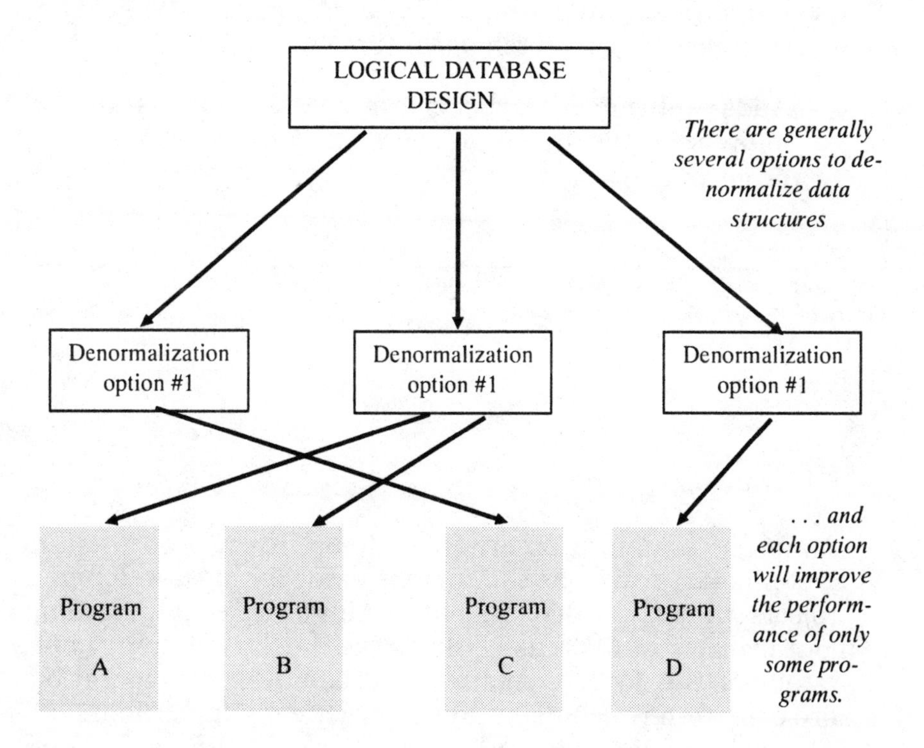

Figure 1.2 The importance of normalization.

A common method of row-at-a- time processing is:

```
SELECT COLUMN1, COLUMN2, COLUMN3
  FROM TABLE1
  WHERE COLUMNUNIQUEKEY = :value
```

in a loop, rather than getting a set of data in a statement like this:

```
SELECT COLUMN1, COLUMN2, COLUMN3
  FROM TABLE1
  WHERE COLUMNUNIQUEKEY
     BETWEEN :value1 AND :value2
```

selecting individual rows of a set of data to be processed:

- Is generally less clear programming style.
- Is inefficient in giving DB2 the information it needs to access and prefetch data.
- Adds additional overhead in processing each statement resulting in more complex and less efficient programs.

Figure 1.3 An example of single row processing.

The large application

A similar situation occurs in systems integration projects. (Systems integration is the current name for big development projects that span departments.) Most large-scale development projects in MVS use DB2 as the database management system of the future. Again the scheduling considerations here can often preclude building "practice" applications.

The risks in deploying a large-scale application based on a new technology are obvious. The technical issues should be

An example of noncolumn specific selection is:

```
SELECT *
  FROM TABLE1
  WHERE COLUMNUNIQUEKEY = :value
```

Rather than retrieving the specific columns the program needs:

```
SELECT COLUMN1, COLUMN2, COLUMN3
FROM TABLE1
  WHERE COLUMNUNIQUEKEY = :value1
```

Another common example is:

```
SELECT COLUMN1, COLUMN2,
       COLUMN3, COLUMNUNIQUEKEY
FROM TABLE1
WHERE COLUMNUNIQUEKEY = :value1
```

Retrieving extra columns in DB2 results in:

- Confusing the optimizer by implying that the additional data are needed in the application. This in turn can cause an inefficient data access path to be chosen.
- Additional overhead, since DB2 passes each column from the DB2 address space to the program. DB2 does not have to pass the entire row to the program!
- Poor programming style. A rule of modern software engineering is to only reference data needed by the program: *information hiding*. This reduces the risk of processing inappropriate fields.

Figure 1.4 Noncolumn specific processing.

fully understood before using database management features. This is particularly common in decision support applications where the application designers do not fully comprehend the performance implications of their design decisions. The resulting inefficient applications can often be less than optimal solutions to the user requirements. This in

User programs may retrieve data only to ignore it, e.g.:

```
   EXEC SQL DECLARE C CURSOR FOR
   SELECT COLUMN1, COLUMN2, COLUMN3
     FROM TABLE1
     WHERE COLUMNUNIQUEKEY
       BETWEEN :value1 AND :value2
* . . .
  EXEC SQL
    OPEN C
  END-EXEC
  LOOP:
  EXEC SQL
    FETCH C INTO :structure
  END-EXEC
 * program filter condition example
  IF column2 OF structure EQUALS variable
    PERFORM P999-PROCESS-DATA
  GOTO LOOP
```

Rather than simply:

```
  EXEC SQL DECLARE C CURSOR FOR
    SELECT COLUMN1, COLUMN2, COLUMN3
      FROM TABLE1
      WHERE COLUMNUNIQUEKEY
         BETWEEN :value1 AND :value2
         AND COLUMN2 = :variable
  END-EXEC
* now retrieve and process all the data
```

By embedding the filtering in the SQL query:

- DB2 access path selection can opt for a more reasonable path.
- We eliminate the overhead of passing extraneous data to the program.
- The program becomes shorter, clearer, and much more easily tuned.

Figure 1.5 Example of user program data filtering.

turn can lead to unfair disparagement of DB2 as being the cause of awkward and slow applications. (See Figure 1.2.)

Inappropriate denormalization causes even worse problems. Data structures are the most stable objects in a data processing environment. Programs can change rapidly, but data structures shared between applications rarely change.

Early attempts to make DB2 table structures more efficient often make incorrect assumptions and are slower than the normalized structure could have been. Tuning is inappropriate until the designer understands the tradeoffs. The denormalized structures are less flexible than the normalized ones. Trying to make a data design allow for faster processing thus puts at risk a major justification for conversion. Given a goal of ridding ourselves of awkward data processing structures from obsolete requirements, can we afford to start with new messy structures?

Inexperienced use of DB2 in large-scale applications tends to have a different sort of impact. The major problem in any large application is control. The advanced features of the new technology are very risky to use. These types of project send the developers a clear (but often not explicitly stated) message that they should not try anything different. Trying something new is of course risky, and risk is the one thing that very large projects cannot afford.

Massive projects are management challenges, with the technical issues only secondary in importance. In this situation, trying out new features in DB2 may jeopardize the schedule. Thus, these applications often do not make effective use of DB2. The applications design most resembles use of whatever data management facilities the developers most often used before.

If the shop converted from VSAM, the early programs using DB2 tend to access data in the same manner as VSAM accesses data. That includes processing individual rows instead of the sets of rows that DB2 offers. (See Figure 1.3.) Often the programs retrieve entire rows instead of just the specific columns the program uses. (See Figure 1.4.) Programs often retrieve extra data and filter it on a row by row basis. (See Figure 1.5.) Programs join data using program logic by retrieving the one table's row, and then matching it to the second table's data. (See Figure 1.6.)

As a result of these application programming techniques many early applications look like VSAM applications con-

Many program effect joins by program matching of data, ignoring DB2 facilities, e.g.:

```
  EXEC SQL DECLARE C CURSOR FOR
 SELECT COLUMN1
   FROM TABLE1
   WHERE COLUMNUNIQUEKEY
      BETWEEN :value1 AND :value2

LOOP:
EXEC SQL
  OPEN C
END-EXEC
EXEC SQL
  FETCH C INTO :structure
END-EXEC
* get corresponding records
EXEC SQL
  SELECT COLUMNAA, COLUMNBB
   INTO :structure
   FROM TABLE2
   WHERE KEY = :column1
END EXEC
```

Rather than simply:

```
 EXEC SQL DECLARE C CURSOR FOR
  SELECT COLUMNAA, COLUMNBB
   FROM TABLE1, TABLE2
   WHERE COLUMNUNIQUEKEY
      BETWEEN :value1 AND :value2
      AND KEY = COLUMN1
 END-EXEC
* now retrieve and process all the data
```

By allowing DB2 to join the data:

- The program becomes shorter, clearer, and much more easily tuned.
- DB2 access path selection can choose a more efficient path.

Figure 1.6 Example of user program join processing.

verted into DB2. The programs do not gain the benefits of DB2 processing. They only partially allow for future DB2 development. The data are available in DB2, but often in the awkward denormalized structures that are frequently the hallmark of VSAM processing.

Most early DB2 transaction processing applications are low-volume applications. The most common seem to be human resource applications with very low transaction rates or even running under TSO.

Another common selection for first DB2 applications is simple decision support applications. Decision support refers to flexible applications that allow users to generate customized reports. Often these applications are built to support marketing analysis. This type of system has enormous advantages: the processing requirements are not solid.

The users have no experience with this type of application and therefore have no level of expectation with which to compare the function or performance. Any decision support capabilities tend to be more sophisticated than the alternative of asking a programmer to develop a report.

These systems have the advantage of using the advanced querying capabilities of DB2. Ideally, this should be done in an area in which a level of expectation is not yet set.

The disadvantage of this kind of system is that it tends to grow out of control. The demand for this kind of service can be so high that the early system will become enlarged. New function requests can enlarge the application before the desired experience with DB2 can be garnered. This often results in awkward design of decision support applications while the designers are still learning how to develop them effectively.

Summary

The transition into use of DB2 involves assimilation of new technology. This includes both learning DB2 techniques and removing obsolete techniques.

Those involved in the transition should keep a clear view of their goals, specifically how much long-term change management can afford.

Use of nonrelational techniques will damage future applications. Use of DB2 techniques by inexperienced users can lead to a host of performance problems.

Review Questions

1. How fully has your shop assimilated the DB2 set processing facilities?

2. Can an inexperienced DB2 designer design effectively for performance?

3. Should an inexperienced DB2 designer design for performance?

4. When should the user simulate joins instead of using SQL joins in DB2?

Answers to Review Questions

1.

2. Yes, an inexperienced DB2 designer can design for performance. The effectiveness will be judged by future modifiers of the application. Often standard database design practices are valid for DB2. Often the same performance criteria as used in older systems are valid in DB2. Of course, the tradeoffs may be unclear to the early user. A presumption of potential error should be made in early designs.

3. It seems dangerous for an inexperienced DB2 designer to design for performance. A fundamental goal of early DB2 applications is to learn the tradeoffs of physical design. Either the experience will be acquired in the lower-volume early applications or else we have to practice on the later higher-volume programs.

4. Generally the user should never simulate joins instead of using SQL joins. The only exceptions are for join processing that cannot be done directly in DB2. An example is explosion processing that can contain a tree of arbitrary depth. SQL does not allow for recursive structures.

Sometimes it is easier to join data programmatically than it is to use permuted static SQL joins or dynamic SQL for this sort of processing.

Chapter 2

The Developing DB2 Shop

A major goal of any pilot project is as a test for the various operational requirements. System and application security is complex in DB2: there are many options and different levels of security within the product. Sometimes it is more appropriate to use security facilities outside DB2 to control access to applications.

This conflict between trial-and-error learning and the burden of delivering requested function is uncomfortable. Many early DB2 applications use a security strategy that differs from the final one chosen. It is a common desire to maintain a consistent level of security and consistent use of security features throughout a shop. Changing your security techniques early is often a better option than continuing with an uncomfortable security method.

DBA Role Development

The arrival of DB2 may be judged an appropriate time to initiate a central database administration function in a shop. An inchoate DBA function can use the early DB2 applications as a trial ground to determine its responsibilities.

Impediments to Early DB2 Applications

The new DB2 user generally should expect DB2 applications to cost more than traditional applications. Considering these initial applications as practice is often more realistic than considering them purely in terms of function.

The problems in early DB2 applications are generally caused by lack of understanding. The impediments are thus self-created problems. An early DB2 shop should focus on the efficiency of transferring the garnered knowledge to the next phase of DB2 development.

Developing DB2 Shops

As the use of DB2 increases, there is often a contagion stage of use of the database management system. DB2 use spreads, often so fast that it spreads the technical knowledge developed in the early use of DB2 thin.

Having tested the waters with early applications, the developing DB2 shop is now ready for some real applications. To most shops this means transaction processing. Because of inexperience with DB2, many transaction processing applications emulate the previous database management system.

In other words, if a shop is moving from VSAM to DB2, the first DB2 applications will not markedly differ from VSAM applications. In fact, the programs look remarkably like VSAM applications converted line by line to DB2. Set processing of data is a rare event. Joins and other DB2-style programming options are ignored. Instead, row-at-a-time and program controlled data selection is often the norm.

The reason for not using joins (or subselects, or UNION, or other sophisticated DB2 constructs) tends to be a combination of two factors: history and fear. The history factor is a simple premise — every program resembles the last application the programmer wrote. A programmer learning DB2 will only gradually adapt to the DB2 style of programming. The first few programs the programmer writes will carry a lot of baggage from the past.

At the same time, many technically oriented programmers will be excited to be provided a new "toy to play with." We would imagine that programmers would be tempted to exercise the new features immediately.

Fear of the Unknown

This exploration of technical features can occur in a few programs. The reason it does not become general practice is the fear of endangering the application program product. Most programmers do not have opportunity to try new features while being judged on their immediate productivity. Trying new features may produce programs that cause performance problems and so delay project completion. The alternative of developing unsophisticated programs is less risky.

In many DB2 shops, at this stage of development there are rampant rumors about DB2 features. Often we hear unsubstantiated or partial truths about how to develop DB2 applications. The most common one of these is: don't do joins in transaction processing. Another variant is: joins are inefficient; do the join processing yourself. The concept of set level processing seems dangerous and foreign.

DB2 Joins vs. User Programmed Match Processing

The fact behind these gross rules of thumb is that there is a reasonable amount of activity a transaction can process in a given period. A transaction query of any type that attempts 1000 physical reads cannot offer subsecond response time without a device that allows a read in less than a thousandth of a second.

A join is not inherently good or bad as a programming facility. A join that involves 1000 reads is probably unreasonable for transaction processing. But the programmer cannot do that kind of processing in transaction processing anyway, in DB2 or out of it. If the processing involves 10 reads, is it better for the programmer to join the data in a program loop or for DB2 to do it? In general there is little performance difference.

Often when there is a performance difference between DB2 complex queries and program-processed queries, DB2 offers the better performance. The reason for this relates to two factors.

The minor factor is the work DB2 does to transfer extra data. The major factor is that joins convey more information to the DB2 optimizer. The DB2 optimizer determines the access path for each SQL statement in a program independently of other statements.

The DB2 plan generation lacks understanding of statement context, since it has no way of telling the order in which the program will be executed. Thus, a SQL selection involving a two-way join can provide more information about the program activity context than two independent SELECT statements. The DB2 optimizer will then be more likely to access data more efficiently.

In general, DB2 is better at doing joins than programmers are: it has a clearer understanding of the tradeoffs in each path option, and can react to changes in data. More importantly, each new version of DB2 may be able to select a better path. Programmer-designed joins tend to make programs larger and less easy to maintain. DB2 joins are thus probably currently more efficient than user-programmed data selection, and will get better. User-programmed data selection simulating joins will consign the application to mediocre performance.

The common sentiment at developing shops that joins are inappropriate for transaction processing is a miscommunication. The rule probably starts out as something to the effect of "don't do joins in production without first verifying the performance implications" — which is reasonable advice about joins or any other processing. It is obvious how this type of statement can be misinterpreted, especially by those who are unclear on how to determine the performance implications.

Rare Use of Joins

Does your shop use joins frequently? An easy way to tell is by simply querying the DB2 catalog. Figure 2.1 shows how to identify how many joins your plans contain.

What Is Wrong with Not Using Joins?

DB2 as a relational system has a simple view of the world of data. In terms of data semantics, relational database management systems are intentionally less sophisticated than the earlier generation of network and hierarchical database management systems. For example, a network database system can embed more sophisticated interrecord consistency rules in the data than can DB2.

Relational systems intentionally do away with the interrelationships embedded in the data for the sake of allowing for flexible queries. This may be an advantage for decision support, but it can be a nuisance for transaction processing that tends to have very stable interrecord relationships.

The features DB2 offers to compensate for this are nonnavigational data access, including sophisticated management of complex queries and better operational support for large mainframes. Functionally, this means that users who do not use joins are buying DB2 to manage large buffers and do backups. This use of the form of modern data management without the content cannot be justified on technical grounds.

Obsession with Data Conversions between Applications

A hallmark of a shop that is rapidly moving to DB2 is the problem of coexistence with other means of storing data. Applications develop in DB2, but most of the data are somewhere else. The effort involved in moving data from other systems to DB2 and back again seems to be a major component of every application developed.

The conversion can be done using a program product such as DXT from IBM, or Focus from Information Builders, Inc.

```
SELECT 'number of selects involving joins: ', COUNT(*)
   FROM SYSIBM.SYSSTMT
   WHERE TEXT
        LIKE'%SELECT %FROM %,%WHERE%'  /* the
      comma is the  delimiter between joined tables */
   UNION
SELECT 'total number of select statements: ', COUNT(*)
   FROM SYSIBM.SYSSTMT
   WHERE TEXT
        LIKE '%SELECT %FROM%'
```

This statement will count the number of SQL statements in bound plans involving joins. If your shop frequently uses joins embedded in views, then you can get a more accurate figure by querying the appropriate PLAN_TABLE. Count the number of statements with the METHOD column equal to 2 or 3.

Figure 2.1 Counting the joins in a DB2 program.

(New York, N. Y.). More likely, the data conversion will be done by a user program. The advantage of the vendor program products is that these products maintain dictionaries that ease future conversions across systems. The advantage of user programs is that they may perform faster and are more flexible in converting data exactly as required.

Logging Transactions

A design problem similar to the conversion issue is the problem of consistency of the data in the disparate data management systems. If there is a system failure, will the data be recoverable? Will the data be consistent?

A common technique used by maturing DB2 shops is to log all transaction data changes to a table. The logged data allow undoing the change activity if a problem occurs. The data may also be used for bringing the DB2 data to a consistent state with the other data manager — the data changes can be applied to the other copy of the data.

Extract File Processing

A design strategy that has not stood the test of time is the use of an extract file produced from the operational data for reporting purposes. This technique is often called generalized extract file processing. These are extracts of data, based on very specific known reporting requirements. A paradigm of modern data processing is that requirements for reporting are constantly changing.

In the past, many large transaction processing systems based their report development on this technique. The rigidity of the technique makes it anathema for modern applications. Maturing DB2 shops can quickly learn the flexibility of extracting the data into DB2 decision support tables.

The Maturing DB2 Shop

As applications in DB2 become more complex, the use of DB2 gets more diverse. Some artifacts of the previous systems still allow for some generalization.

A common problem is coming to grips with decision support activities. Usually, understanding the issues of decision support is a signal of information systems maturity. An identifier of a maturing DB2 shop is the partial use of decision support systems. "Partial" in this context means that the applications are departmental in nature, often using processed (so-called active) data instead of immutable raw data.

Usually a shop with some 24-hour requirements will start implementing them in the maturing phase of use of DB2. Many maturing shops will attempt to use data-driven design techniques (but generally halfheartedly). A true data-driven design is an attribute of a mature database shop. Another, more basic, sign of understanding of DB2 processing tradeoffs is the use of the DB2 LOAD utility vs. mass insert programs where appropriate.

Transaction Processing and Decision Support Data Separation

A mature database shop usually makes individual application requirements subservient to a global architecture. The application programming savings in new systems development justifies the application development overhead. As the complexity of program function and number of programs increase, the highest cost in providing services is that of the interfaces between the applications. An architecture simplifies and reduces the overhead in interfacing between applications.

As the tangle of operational applications gets more complex, the combination of requirements makes using the same data for reporting unrealistic. Extracting the data into a sequential extract file is also unrealistic, since the data can be easily used only for reporting needs that the designer expected.

Reporting is where DB2 shines. Justifying use of DB2 can be an important issue to remember at this stage of development. Decision support is the way to go if your shop makes the justification of DB2 against more traditional database management an important political issue. Reporting using DB2 vs. older means of access is usually a major improvement.

This is not to say that DB2 is inappropriate for transaction processing applications. It is an effective tool for that purpose.

The problem with transaction processing DB2 applications is that there generally is not a qualitative improvement in productivity at this stage because of the cost of coexistence with data in other systems. This is often exacerbated by "overselling" of DB2, which causes these projects to be measured against unrealistic expectations.

We cannot use transaction processing data directly for decision support purposes in most cases. Reporting and transaction processing have different ideas of what data should look like. DB2 bufferpool use in decision support differs radically from that of transaction processing and conflicts with it. Reporting operational requirements and transaction processing operational requirements tend to conflict. Thus, maturing DB2 shops tend to learn that almost all data has to be kept in duplicate — one updatable copy for operational systems, and a read only copy for reporting.

The Growth of Historical Data

Traditional data processing concentrates on supporting immediate processing. The process-oriented concept of data deals with design issues in terms of outputs rather than the stable data. In a process-oriented world data are either active or irrelevant. As reporting and decision-making requirements get more complex, the picture generally shifts to a concept of active data vs. history data. This allows data to be aged out of the active pool of data into the historical data reporting transition area and finally into oblivion.

Most DB2 shops are attempting to get out of a bind that traditional data processing projects tend to cause. Many applications become so customized that it is unrealistic to attempt to change them; often we can add new function only by tearing the application apart. Data structures work the same way, and a database design customized to a particular application will often be unable to support a new application function.

Normalization is the major tool in providing application flexibility. Data denormalization is the primary means to customize data to a specific application. But denormalized data is not the only culprit. The major problem in integrating distinct applications is scheduling.

The issue of scheduling applications is that distinct applications can work on a different logical schedule of data updating. In this case, the data in the one system will not reflect the same state of processing as data in the other.

Often, data that seem at first sight to be shared between two applications in a replicated form are actually two slightly different variant copies. Often these applications cannot share data except after some complex administration of updates between the applications, such as happens in year-end processing. This activity synchronizes the disparate systems data, and hence is called synchronization.

Synchronization between applications is a complicated issue. It is the most common cause of application divergence. As new application requirements arise, the lack of synchronization becomes unacceptable. But what options do we have?

The most obvious solution is to rebuild all applications from the ground up. This new composite application will be based on a consistent batch update processing schedule. All data will be kept entirely consistent. No data redundancy due to inconsistency will be needed.

Tempting as it seems, a complete application rewrite is unlikely to solve the synchronization problem. Once the rewrite is done, some new requirement may come up demanding 24-hour availability, or another scheduling inconsistency. An application may be deployed at a remote site without the capability to pass updates to the central system on schedule. The appealing central premise of system-level consistency will be lost.

The problem with system-wide consolidation is that it is an artificial construct imposed on top of user requirements. Database architects tend to see data as a flow rather than taking the process view of data as a state in processing. This view provides a solution. We can allow application integration by eliminating the concept of current data.

The problem of active data is eliminated by abandoning all active data. Current data are in exactly the same format as history data. The data can be stored in a raw, unprocessed format. If changes are done by inserting modification records, active data will never be "out of synch" with an application. There will be no active data. Instead, there will be a process that creates the current status. Processed data changes may be relevant for one application but not for another; each would be best served by being offered the data it wants. All lack of synchronization in the system stays out of the data. This offers the database design freedom from data customization for any particular application or schedule (see Figure 2.2).

What Is Next?

What is happening at the leading edge of development? There tend to be two types of very mature shops. The ones with clear focus tend to concentrate most on business rules. The technology is well deployed, and the effective use of it becomes paramount. Others more concerned with technology tend to attempt to build very sophisticated applications.

As a shop becomes a more sophisticated DB2 user, whoever is making the long-term decisions has to consider the data as a global, rather than application-specific, commodity. DB2 maturity is meaningful only in the context of overall database administration.

early: *ACTIVE*
vs.
IRRELEVANT

middling: *ACTIVE*
vs.
HISTORY
vs.
DEFUNCT HISTORY

advanced: *RAW DATA*
vs.
PROGRAM VIEW OF THE DATA

Figure 2.2 A maturing view of data history.

Self-Assessment Quiz

This quiz is intended only as food for thought about your long-term database design and management strategy. The numbers intentionally do not consider industry or application type. The questions are not in any particular order. The numbers from specific applications may mean different things in a different context. The questions mix the issues of DB2 usage and database management issues because the issues are so intertwined. These figures should certainly not be used to imply any advice about what your shop should be doing. Choose the BEST MATCHING answer.

How Mature Is Your Use of DB2?

1. What percentage of SELECT statements in transaction processing reference more than one table?

   a. Under 1 percent
   b. Under 10 percent
   c. 10 to 20 percent
   d. Over 20 percent
   e. We don't do transaction processing

2. What percentage of SELECT statements in all processing reference more than one table?

   a. Under 5 percent
   b. Under 10 percent
   c. 10 to 25 percent
   d. Over 25 percent

3. Do you separate decision support data from transaction processing data?

   a. No
   b. No, but we extract some data for information center or reporting

c. Yes, but much of the operational data history is not reflected in the decision support data
d. Yes, most or all of our data are available for decision support

4. Are mass extract data summaries used for the bulk of your reporting?

a. No, but reporting currently is a major design problem area
b. Yes
c. No, but it is a common design strategy
d. No, almost never

5. Are there any round-the-clock applications in your shop?

a. No, and we have user requirements for them
b. No
c. Yes, but they are inquiry only applications
d. Yes
e. We have no 24-hour requirements

6. What percentage of your tablespaces containing over 10,000 pages are partitioned?

a. None, we have no tablespaces that big
b. None
c. Under 30 percent
d. Over 30 percent

7. How do you schedule DB2 utilities?

a. All utilities are scheduled by systems staff when they get around to it.
b. We have a standard fixed schedule for each utility.
c. We have a standard fixed schedule for each utility that we adjust occasionally.
d. We have a standard fixed schedule for each utility that we adjust regularly based on collected long-term statistics or utility scheduling software.

8. Do you have a DB2 production DBA function?

a. No
b. No, but there is a production control function
c. Yes, but it is a part-time effort
d. Yes

9. Do you have a DB2 development DBA function?

a. No
b. No, but there is a "system architect" function
c. Yes, but it is a part-time effort
d. Yes

10. Do you use application-independent data modeling techniques for design?

a. No
b. No, but there is a "system architect" function
c. Yes, but only for occasional massive projects
d. Yes

11. Do you use data modeling to design data structures for applications?

a. No
b. Yes, but it concentrates on data normalization
c. Yes, but it is done very late in the application design phase
d. Yes

12. What percentage of your total quantity of data in production is actually replicated? (Estimate this in terms of tracks of data, based on data redundancy between applications and denormalization; do not include data that are not updated and are only used for reporting.)

a. Over 50 percent

b. 30 to 50 percent
c. 20 to 29 percent
d. Under 20 percent

13. What is the weighted average row length of production data used only for transaction processing? The query in Figure 2.3 is a simple means of calculating the value.

```
SELECT     SUM(CARD * RECLENGTH)
           /
           SUM(CARD)
 FROM    SYSIBM.SYSTABLES
 WHERE DBNAME IN ('DBPROD1', 'DBPROD2')
    AND  TYPE = 'T'
```

Figure 2.3 Calculating average row length.

Choose only the tables updated by operational transaction processing. If there are any tables with unusual length or rarely populated VARCHAR columns, exclude them from the summary.

a. Over 200 bytes
b. 150 to 199 bytes
c. 100 to 149 bytes
d. Under 100 bytes

14. What percentage of active data is available in DB2?

a. Under 20 percent
b. 20 to 40 percent
c. 41 to 60 percent
d. Over 60 percent

15. How big is your biggest bufferpool?

a. Up to 200 buffers
b. Up to 1000 buffers
c. Up to 8000 buffers
d. Over 8000 buffers

16. How many bufferpools do you use in production?

a. More than one
b. One for most uses (we may have a BP32K which is occasionally referenced)

17. What is your production GET PAGE / READ PAGE ratio?

a. 2 or less
b. 4 or less
c. 6 or less
d. Over 6

18. Does your shop have a data administration function?

a. No, but one is under consideration
b. No
c. Yes, but it is mainly concerned with naming standards
d. Yes

19. Are requests for reporting or decision support data dealt with in terms of an overall data architecture?

a. No, they are dealt with in an individual manner
b. No, but requests are carefully reviewed for data duplication
c. Yes, on a project basis
d. Yes, on a global basis

20. Are there distinct data groupings for decision support vs. operational data?

a. No, data are rarely stored on-line for reporting
b. No, but a substantial amount of the data in DB2 is only intended for reporting use
c. Yes, but there are many cases of replicated reporting data that are inconsistent
d. Yes

21. Are all applications moved to production analyzed using EXPLAIN?

a. No
b. No, but many are
c. Yes, but the EXPLAIN output is only occasionally reviewed
d. Yes, and the output must be reasonable to accept a production application

22. Are codes tables shared?

a. No
b. Occasionally
c. Yes, most are
d. Yes, and centrally controlled

Calculating Your Score

For every (a) answer, give yourself 1 point. For every (b) answer give yourself 2 points. For every (c) answer, give yourself 4 points. For every (d) answer, give yourself 5 points. For every (e) answer, give yourself 3 points.

If you scored over 90 points, your shop is on the forefront of database use. There is clear focus on long-term planning. You have probably had DB2 for several years, and have a strong corporate commitment to its use, or initiated all development in DB2. Central database design techniques have been used long and well. Exceptional conditions have allowed you to manage your data most effectively. Keep up the good work.

If you scored between 75 and 90 points, your shop has a clear commitment to DB2 and database management in general.

You are probably progressing toward those goals effectively. You are doing better at achieving the database objectives than most DB2 shops. Review the questions and consider what external factors are causing your occasional lower scores.

If you scored between 60 and 74 points, your shop is typical of DB2 shops. You are probably slowly moving toward implementing DB2 as your main database management system. The time and effort it takes to convert or redevelop applications in DB2 is slowing the process. The sequential nature of this conversion limits the ability to do large-scale data modeling. There is probably some degree of mixed message about database management goals. Reviewing your answers may help identify the areas that should be emphasized.

If you scored under 60 points, your shop is probably not seriously using DB2. Any applications using DB2 tend to mirror non-DB2 application development techniques. The shop is also probably not committed to central database design. Most design is seemingly done on an application by application basis. Your shop uses DB2 as a very expensive file handler. In general, database designers cannot change the focus of a shop. If limited priority is given to central issues and your applications tend to be small and independent or you use canned applications, your shop may be taking a rational approach. (But why use MVS and DB2?) If you perceive a need for central services, it may help to act as a salesperson of those techniques to upper management.

Chapter 3

Application Considerations in DB2

Themes in DB2 Applications

When we design an application in DB2, there is an extensive unstated set of goals to be managed. These are not the design goals of the application itself; hopefully those goals are fully specified. There are directions in which shops are heading, motivations for using types of software, and pressures that direct our efforts.

By choosing DB2 as an application platform, we are usually making a long-term commitment to large centralized computers. More integration, more complex data structures, rigorous operational management, cleaner data, and more flexibility are ineluctable — or we are wasting our time.

We are also buying into the IBM view of the world. DB2 is growing into a *data warehouse* or *information warehouse* containing central data. SAA and distributed features will allow integration with peripheral computers.

New-Style Applications

In using DB2 instead of IMS or VSAM we are attempting to justify newer, flashier kinds of applications. There is a spate of new types of application that are painful to build on older platforms. Cooperative and distributed processing can be done more naturally against dynamic data structures in relational rather than network database structures. Expert systems and artificial intelligence applications are also well suited to a relational data structure and the power of a mainframe computer. The relational structure especially aids development of decision support and end user computing.

Business Issues Overriding

Business issues are the justification of any application development. In the past business justifications had become subservient to application issues. A justification for not providing a function was often the lack of ease we would have in implementing the requirement. The rules built into existing applications can effectively hamstring business by preventing change. (See Figure 3.1.)

We want to:	*integrate billing with inventory*
But:	*inventory is reconciled on Sundays*
	billing is reconciled daily
So:	*we can only integrate once a week*

Figure 3.1 Example of data-time inconsistancy.

The application platforms we deal with are usually webs of very tenuously connected applications. The weakness of the connection is a result of two things:

- **Parochial applications**. Applications built with immediate cost justification tend to ignore global factors. This tradeoff reduces the cost of specific aspects of the business at the expense of fitting poorly into the overall company picture. In turn, this forces the building of strange bridges to interface these applications (if this can be done at all).

- **Historical applications**. As company practices change, so do applications; but they typically take the path of least resistance. Thus, for example, many transaction-processing applications in production are actually batch applications with transaction-processing front ends attached. "Old software" is so pervasive that most company application inventory looks like it was designed to support company practices a decade old (and most programmers assume that it would take a decade to bring the application interfaces to today's needs).

This process freezes the business. Flexibility is impaired. Application support limitations curtail the business from pursuing new opportunities. The buzzword "flexibility" strikes a raw nerve. Flexibility is an expensive, elusive, and rare quality in today's world. This is the justification for systems integration applications; this is the rationale for data administration; this is the argument for CASE; this is the heart of all nonexplicit requirements. Can we provide a path for applications to change as requirements change? If we cannot, we are simply patching the pieces while waiting for a systems Armageddon.

Interfacing Systems

How should applications relate to each other? This question has two aspects: Is there an application architecture? Can we define the business rules and goals?

As an applications programmer in the 1970s, I had a theory that all application issues were a combination of perversity and artifact. Applications design issues seemed so trivial and repetitious, and all the complications were self-imposed. Every application seemed to have a variety of development options: a good one, understood by all, and the ludicrous one chosen for tactical reasons. This perversity of the application development process was based on the relative insignificance of long-term goals in the application development world. Every application design was based on paying lip service to the correct way to build the system. The final application development followed the path of least resistance in stringing together artifacts of historical applications. We would downplay the user cards in relation to the more significant jokers dealt by existing software (read: data update synchronization).

Today, the presumption must be that all data are constantly up to date and regularly synchronized. This is the only effective means to maintain consistency of data: not making it dependent on batch processes to be balanced. This objective is so far from the reality of most shops that we must attempt to build a bridge toward that aim. Even if your company has not provided you with a mandate to lay out an architecture, it is your duty as a professional to define the best long-term structure and evaluate the risks.

PCs, LANs, and Cooperative Processing

Applications are distributed for a variety of reasons. It is generally tactically easier to build applications on the platform the data are already on (this process can sometimes change; for example an overloaded mainframe can tempt development of new applications on any other available device). Cooperative processing and interfaces to other platforms are changing the way we look at this picture.

PC use is not typically based on reducing mainframe load; instead, the premise is providing extra function. Mainframe computing is a notoriously poor means of providing:

- Graphics
- Applications that end-users can easily customize
- Ease of use
- Highly tailored applications for small audiences

PCs allow cheap development of powerful applications, including graphics, user help facilities, and more. This opens the world of computing to a new audience: users who need the information, need to manipulate it, and are unwilling to train in computer skills.

Mainframes are a most effective means of providing centralized data, continuous operation, and sophisticated and stable applications. Cooperative processing is an attempt to merge these two strengths: giving us quality and controlled data and the flexibility to play with it on a cheap, user-friendly PC. This is not a means of reducing costs — rather, it becomes a way of painlessly getting good data to users.

Most of these smaller platforms are based on users doing quasi-programming activities. This is a powerful and profound idea. Users know what they want, and programmers are not needed as interpreters of the requests. There is a danger here that the users will misunderstand and misuse the data. A powerful argument for central computing is central understanding of the data and quality control. Many distributions of data result in extra overhead in the form of programmers in the distributed sites, while still producing reports that are in error.

CASE

CASE is a generic term for any product that simplifies the development of applications. In this context I will discuss application process (sometimes called "behavior") and data modeling tools. These are often called "upper CASE" — a pun used to distinguish them from the tools involving code development, which are called "lower CASE."

The fundamental aim of the process of application or business modeling is to capture the essence of the activity being done. The model produced is then presented for review through the tool. The tool tries to make the activities clear to allow the peruser to correct errors or design systems based on them.

These CASE tools allow one to build graphical representations of the activities and specify the procedures as they are analyzed. The tools generally build dictionary entries containing descriptions of the components. Usually this dictionary is the focus of the CASE effort, allowing the capturing of business rules and goals and lower-level data, and allowing the information to be used as the design is further refined.

Immature Technology, Unskilled Technicians

It is obvious that a first application built in a new technology or technique will be poorly done. The reasons for this include the misconceptions about the technology. The interest and desire to understand the innovations will motivate designers to learn how to use the CASE tool well. However, desire is no substitute for experience. The study of new facilities will distract the staff from the primary goal of supporting the business.

Most users of DB2 are still in the stage of technological immaturity. In fact, many writers of books on DB2 are neophytes to the issues. In many shops few staff members have sharp insight into the use of DB2. This lack of skill in the tools causes problems in applications that are built on fallacious design principles.

The Changing Application: Technology and Techniques

As applications change, so must we. Techniques that developed with different goals or with different cost structures cannot be justified.

I recently was attempting to cost a DB2 systems implementation. The project was in Indonesia, where many managers earn less than $6,000 a year, and programmers often earn significantly less. This salary structure seems appealing in a country where $3 a day is a reasonable wage, but it throws the entire cost structure of projects out of whack. This radical change in the cost of programmers changes all rules of thumb in determining project cost and value.

In the standard United States cost structure, a CASE tool that costs $150,000 seems highly reasonable. The value is in improving large project development. Can the same tool be cost-justified as a replacement for thirty-odd staff?

Every change in cost of hardware should result in a similar reevaluation of how applications are implemented. Cheaper hardware and new facilities will often make new types of applications reasonable. The rapid change of products means a constant reevaluation of hardware and software platforms and application choice is necessary.

These issues are confronting us daily. Should we be developing software on PCs or on the mainframe? Should we be developing software for PCs or for the mainframe, or both? Should we use CASE, a 4GL, an application generator, or COBOL for developing an application? Does this application actually cross departmental lines? Should the scope be bigger? Should we apply transactions from a foreign system nightly, or immediately?

The rationale for each of these issues is changing as costs change, requirements evolve, staff capabilities grow, and the audience changes. The long time it takes to deploy a new application means that the reasoning of today may not hold water over the life span of the application.

Summary

Applications are changing dramatically, and DB2 use often gets intertwined with the evolution. This process can make it harder to assimilate DB2 in a political environment.

Information services are frequently focusing on the business issues; a goal is to become actors instead of being implementers of decisions. Many existing systems provide a counterpoint to this. Parochial and short-term considerations built into applications limit a business's ability to change.

DB2 exists in a climate defined by these business considerations. The tools in this context read like an advertisement list: CASE, expert systems, cooperative processing, systems integration. Each tool attempts to facilitate building more powerful applications as quickly as possible. The easy problems have been solved, and the remaining problems are complex (and often caused by the previous solution).

Review Questions

1. What is the attitude of your shop toward new technology? Specifically concentrate on the relationship between application cost to use and interest.

2. Is DB2 used as an agent of change in your environment? To what extent are the costs of this change bundled together?

3. What is the advantage of DB2 over other IBM mainframe database management systems as an agent for change?

4. Is it feasible to adapt CASE tools without a rigid development methodology?

Answers to Review Questions

1.

2.

3. The advantage of DB2 over other IBM mainframe database management systems is the growth potential in DB2. There is far more new program development in DB2 than in other database management systems. This includes the enormous number of DB2 developers because most new mainframe applications use or interface to DB2.

This robust software growth and DB2's popularity position DB2 as the standard for database management. DB2 becomes a baseline for evolving technology and becomes an agent for change in traditional data processing shops.

4. CASE tools in the restrictive sense are means to automate parts of an application development methodology. Automating a nonexistent process is absurd.

Several vendors of software development tools have repositioned their products by marketing them under the CASE umbrella. If these tools are not part of a methodology, there is a relationship between them and the application development method. These tools do not need a methodology to be used effectively.

Chapter 4

DB2 Applications

Designing Integrated Applications

Integrating a shop's applications is a complex issue. Designing an application to solve a specific problem directly is clean; it is appealingly goal-oriented. We are given a specific problem, and we solve only that problem. Adding additional application issues makes a program more complex and harder to build.

This solution may in turn cause other problems. Without global considerations, applications are typically built very rigidly. Multiple applications of this sort can lock the business into a hodgepodge of unrelated automation components. A large business cannot afford many isolated systems.

Designing interfaces to other systems into an application is expensive, and complicates the design of applications. These interfaces are different from building a huge integrated application, but are far better than applications that "suboptimize" a narrow area at the expense of the general business. Systems that have defined interface schedules present another thought-out secondary approach to solving these interrelationship problems.

Attempting to design applications that reflect the goals of the business forces the designer to confront many conflicting philosophies, strategies, goal, and needs. If we succeed, we may be able to make the total business better, tune the balance between enterprise units, and do many other nice things. These applications are enormously expensive to build, and have a smaller function-to-price ratio than others. Clearly integrated applications are a ternary idea.

Given that full integration is a mature concept, too mature for most DB2 shops, can the database designer apply the ideas of integration (in the hope of greasing the wheels of change) without full company commitment? Sometimes it is possible.

The fundamental problem of integrating applications is the inability of data to work together. The reasons data may not work together are:

- **Location**: the data may simply reside in different places. Distributed processing technology is rapidly removing this impediment. The same problem occurs in data stored in multiple database managers that do not smoothly share data.
- **Cycle issues**: some data may be on different processing cycles than others. For example, one application may run a weekly reconciliation on Tuesday, and another on Thursday.
- **Concept differences**: often several applications will understand the business issues differently. Often a sales application will understand the field PROFIT completely differently from a shipping application. Often these are not rudimentary distinctions, but rather collections of hundreds of rules (e.g., apply refunds only at the end of the month). This type of difference in basic data will percolate throughout the application. Data modeling can have a valuable role in enabling data integration, and through that process integration. This is a political and strategic question for the most part: Is the company willing to pay for the current data modeling for its long-term benefit?

The twin of data modeling is the isolation and collection of business rules. The foresight to gather both well can aid any company's long-term application projects. Remember that these are long term projects requiring constant feeding; if abandoned or ignored temporarily, they will lose credibility and usefulness.

An integrated application is a wondrous thing to watch or in which to participate. These programs normally require collections of new and exciting tools, complex deployment of armies of staff, management of mounds of information and requirements, and balancing needs of many communities of users.

Often these projects are an order of magnitude larger than the types of application the shop knows how to develop.

The scale of these applications makes them more interesting from a management perspective. It is very common to farm out substantial parts of these projects to so-called systems integrators, contract houses with experience in this type of project.

The benefit of the system integrator's management structure is gained. This can be the most important issue in a shop inexperienced in this arena. Often the number of staff needed is too high for the shop to sustain. Sometimes contracting out portions of the project is an attempt to minimize the political issues inherent in a multidepartmental application. Using services should never imply relegating control to the provider. A service user should use the best provider, and work to keep the useful knowledge in-house.

The Role of DB2 in the Application Development Life Cycle

The Whorfian hypothesis states that the language we use defines what we can think. This is true throughout the computer field. I can often tell, by looking at a program, a lot about the programmer's history, the first language studied, or how old the programmer is. This is because programming styles and language components change very quickly and people change gradually.

Considering the computer environment as a civilization, DB2 defines a very strong culture. At the same time, it is embedded in a very stable and static context of IBM mainframes with their downward compatibility. DB2 is a strong definer of what we are doing, but we are resistant to change. It is instructive to review the context of what DB2 is telling us.

DB2 through the Application Life Cycle

Maintenance

DB2 applications change the application maintenance issues in some ways. DB2 has become entrenched in a world that understands maintenance to be the major activity of an information systems department. At the same time, no one knows how to do it well. It seems a collection of very different activity components, but are they? How can they be controlled? There are no clear answers in this regard.

The two solutions the marketplace has been offering have been *reengineering* and *object-oriented* ideas. The idea of reengineering is that we know how to develop applications, but don't know how to change them. Reengineering is a technique of converting the murky maintenance concepts into understood development issues. A reengineering tool attempts to draw the maintainer of the system away from the code, allowing the maintenance to be done as a form of design change.

Object-oriented issues are rooted in cognitive psychology. The theory of object-oriented is completely alien to relational techniques. Relational design is based on complete data flexibility. Semantic issues in relational design tend to be confined to referential relationships between data and domain restriction of data values. Object-oriented as a philosophy considers data to be a hidden ingredient in the defined behavior, where the behavior is paramount.

Implementation

Implementation traditionally refers to the activities required to move a tested application into production. This can be a minor effort or a major one, depending on the environment. A generic application consists of batch programs and transaction processing programs. There are underlying data structures (usually both DB2 and external files, and sometimes other database management system files), data, programs, security, schedules, and operational requirements and dependency lists.

Most of these activities are consistent to both DB2 and non-DB2 applications. In both cases there are standard actions to add to auto-schedulers, procedures to write, and training to provide. The surprise for most DB2 neophytes is the number of objects that are involved on the DB2 side. A typical DB2 application contains far more tables than there are files in a VSAM application.

Every DB2 table is in a tablespace, which is in a database. There are indices and views, synonyms, and aliases on the tables. The programs include DBRMs, plans, and packages. The teleprocessing monitor (IMS or CICS) interfaces to DB2 have to be reconfigured. Each component has DB2-specific security requirements.

This is the point where the status quo breaks down. The intrinsic interdependence between the DB2 components and their isolation from the rest of the system is an incredible effort to manage.

Summary

DB2 applications have a tremendous weight to bear. The change to DB2 implicitly implies rejection of many past practices. Any new DB2 shop carries the weight of ambivalence to change.

The rate of change is relevant here. If the transition is rapid, the use of DB2 is often poor. If the transition is slow, the systems have to coexist. Rapid transition means using bulldozers, and often results in serious design deficiencies. Slow change locks shops into the interfaces of the past.

DB2 applications have the same systems lifecycle as older systems, but they can seem very different. This is because the applications developed in DB2 tend to be different from more traditional ones.

Review Question

1. Why does denormalization imply future unintegrated applications?

Answer to Review Question

1. Normalizing data in a database design means to eliminating customization to a specific application. By definition, denormalization is a means to customize data for a specific type of use.

If we denormalize data, we assume that no new access patterns will be required. Integrated applications will generate new access patterns because of the diverse requirements of the users. Unplanned needs will crop up and conflict with the denormalization.

Chapter 5

The DB2 Objects

STOGROUP

A STOGROUP is an ordered list of volumes used to place DB2 indexspaces and tablespaces. DB2 uses this list to define the VSAM data sets needed for creating an object. The VSAM processing takes place within DB2. The list is simply serially searched for a volume with enough room for the object.

It is important to note that a STOGROUP is a completely passive facility. DB2 refers to the STOGROUP only when it invokes VSAM storage management services for the data set. This will happen when object is created. It will also happen when the administrator runs the utilities:

- LOAD REPLACE
- REORG
- RECOVER

against the STOGROUP-defined object. In other words, a STOGROUP can be modified using the DB2 ALTER STOGROUP statement without it affecting the associated data sets. If there is a problem with a volume, the procedure is normally to ALTER any STOGROUP referencing that volume to remove the offending volume. This will keep future data set allocations off the volume. After that, any data set on the offending volume must be re-created. If these objects are STOGROUP-defined, they can be found as shown in Figure 5.1.

The data sets can be re-created using the RECOVER utility. Since the offending volume was excised from the STOGROUP, the data sets will be re-created on the next available volume.

REORG will redefine data sets using the latest STOGROUP and data space definitions. STOGROUP-defined data sets are implic-

```
SELECT IXCREATOR, IXNAME, PARTITION
  FROM SYSIBM.SYSINDEXPART
  WHERE STORTYPE = 'I'
                              /* only STOGROUP defined */
     AND STORNAME = ?
                        /* choose appropriate STOGROUP  */

UNION ALL

SELECT DBNAME, TSNAME || ' (ts)    ', PARTITION
  FROM SYSIBM.SYSTABLEPART
  WHERE STORTYPE = 'I'
                              /* only STOGROUP defined */
     AND STORNAME = ?
                        /* choose appropriate STOGROUP  */
```

Figure 5.1 How to identify the users of a STOGROUP.

itly deleted and re-created by running the REORG utility against the object. This provides an easy means of moving objects.

The creation of a STOGROUP adds a row to the DB2 catalog table SYSIBM.SYSSTOGROUP, and a row to SYSIBM.SYSVOLUMES for each volume in the STOGROUP. The current information can be regenerated with a query:

This can be useful in identifying changes due to ALTER STOGROUP changing the associated volume.

Should You Use STOGROUP-Defined or VCAT-Defined Spaces?

In the early years of DB2, explicit definition of VSAM data sets was the preferred route. This allowed I/O-bound data access (we used to use far smaller bufferpools) to be more efficiently designed. Further, VCAT-defined tablespaces have the pleasant characteristic of not deleting the underlying data set. This simplifies recovery of objects accidentally dropped by database administration.

Reduced I/O bottlenecks and more confidence in DBAs (and perhaps better tools and procedures) have led to pressure to use STOGROUP-defined data sets. There is currently a very

```
SELECT STG.*, VOL.*
  FROM SYSIBM.SYSSTOGROUP STG,
                    /* relevant storage groups */
          SYSIBM.SYSVOLUMES VOL
                    /* volumes in that storage group */
  WHERE STG.NAME = VOL.SGNAME
      AND STG.NAME = ? /* appropriate storage group */
```

Figure 5.2 STOGROUP relationship to DASD volumes.

strong trend to simplify storage administration. STOGROUP use can both hurt and help here.

The DB2 system catalog identifies the relationship between the STOGROUP and the DASD volumes. Figure 5.2 shows a means of reporting that association.

STOGROUP use can ease the work of database administrators. It can reduce the effort needed to manage DASD. The IDCAMS jobs to define the data sets are not needed. The gain is that data design issues can be managed completely in the DB2 environment.

STOGROUP use is awkward in a large automated organization, resembling the problems in using DB2 security. The DB2 facilities are interesting, but do not integrate smoothly with the rest of the operation. STOGROUP definition is fairly incompatible with the efforts of most enterprise storage management groups. In particular, storage management tools are surprisingly not well integrated with DB2, and most do not have bidirectional interfaces to control DB2 STOGROUP definitions.

This limits the ability of storage administration groups to fine-tune data set placement. Sometimes shops use the regressive option of simply allocating large blocks of storage to the DB2 DBA, to be managed in the DB2 microcosm. This is generally an inefficient strategy in DASD performance and use. The strategy may be justified sometimes because DB2 is usually the most volatile and growing area of DASD use, but only accounts for a fraction of most shops' data.

The management approach in this case becomes:

- Use a general pool for all unstable applications.

- When an application reaches stable levels, return its DASD to central DASD management.

The STOGROUP issue is part of a larger problem. Automated or expert system consultative systems are becoming effective to control expanding DASD farms efficiently. STOGROUPs are an easy facility to use in relation to DB2, but can complicate the general DASD management issues. Use of STOGROUPs in *large organizations* is very much a strategic move based on DASD management plans and selected DASD management tool vendor direction. Sometimes VCAT definition is the best option in this larger picture.

In smaller organizations, STOGROUPs are a very convenient option. They simplify administration with almost no overhead. Many shops that opted for earlier releases of DB2 could not use STOGROUPs in production because of limitations in STOGROUP options. Many of these limitations have since been removed. These users are now trapped by inertia. The VCAT definition may no longer be necessary because of improvements in STOGROUP facilities. A major conversion and procedure change may be required to use STOGROUPS.

It is poor practice to mix both STOGROUP-defined and VCAT-defined data sets in a single DB2 logical environment. This may increase the effort required in systems administration. The only reasonable mix of the two is to define objects in production using STOGROUPs, then immediately to use ALTER . . . VCAT SQL statements to convert the tablespaces and indices to use VCATs rather than STOGROUP-controlled data sets.

Databases

A database is several things to DB2:

- A logical grouping facility, used to organize application data, data set defaults, and authority.

- A unit of START/STOP for operational management

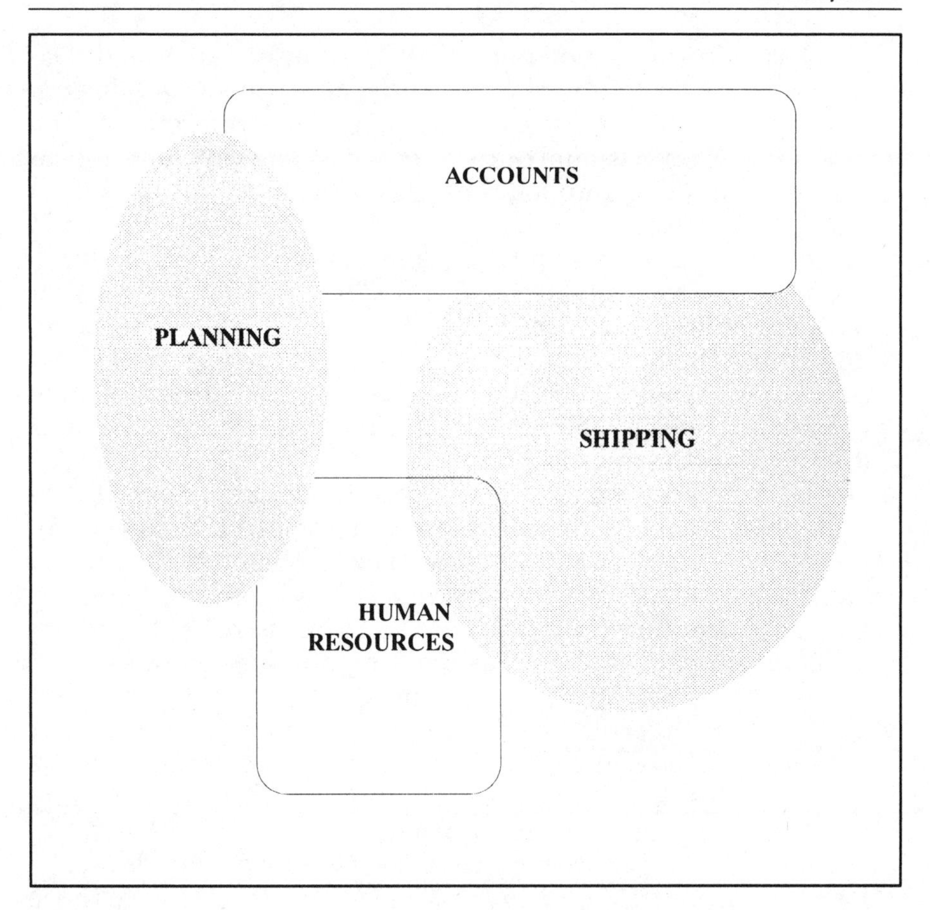

Figure 5.3 Applications tend to overlap.

- A run-time collection of objects, where each database serves as a label of each object belonging to it, and each object is described in a database descriptor directory entry.

The problem with this mixture is that each of these uses has distinct requirements. There are limits on how much we can effectively put into each DB2 database, and it seems like a convenient means of subdividing our data. Unlike some relational database management systems (such as OS/2 Extended Edition Datamanager), a DB2 database does not limit use of its data. We can merrily join a half dozen tables from as many databases. Without the limitations imposed by the system, we must decide what should be put into a DB2 database. How should we use databases?

The term *database* has horrendous semantic overload. Database means so many things to anyone involved in information systems. The most common usage is a reference to the interrelated operational data accessed by the various application systems. This implicitly partitions a shop's data based on application system function.

Figure 5.3 shows a Venn diagram of a typical suite of applications, several of which overlap. The overlap means that data are shared between them. The database designer has to determine the best collation scheme for these applications.

The tendency is to use the database to distinguish between the application components. In this manner we can have four distinct databases as in Figure 5.4.

This may seem like a clean logical division, but it has problems. It seems unappealing to associate a database directly with an application suite. The problem is that many applications overlap whatever logical divisions we build. To associate **database = application** seems to reject the premise of integrated applications crossing application lines.

This structure can still work in a slight variant. We can associate each table with an *owner* business function. A database can be defined for each business area. This database usage relates data, but does not imply that the data will only be used by a particular application.

A variation of this technique is to use a separate database for each corporate department. The issues are similar to those in the functional division. Many users shy away from this style because of potential awkwardness in the event of a business reorganization. The distinction here is that a fundamental business function seems a stable division, while organizational issues can be ephemeral.

DATABASE

ACCOUNTS
SHIPPING
PLANNING
HUMAN RESOURCES

Figure 5.4 Example set of related logical databases.

There is a complication to this format caused by operational issues. Some activity, such as data definition changes, has locking impact throughout the database. This can make it appealing to have some physical design consideration included in deciding what is apportioned into each database.

The operational considerations are very specific. There is a hierarchy of limitations imposed by database activity:

- Utilities lock the referenced data. Some utilities, such as STOSPACE, update catalog information as well.
- Dynamic SQL will must reference the catalog for structure and authorization information. If data are referenced, they are locked appropriately.
- BIND will reference the catalog for structure and authorization information, and update the catalog plan information.
- Data-definition language references the catalog for structure and authorization information, as well as updating structure information and authorizations in the catalog and structure in the directory.

There are also security considerations. These are most relevant in development environments, where programmers have high authorizations. For example, DBADM authority is commonly granted to developers who have private databases.

Tablespaces

DB2 provides three types of tablespaces: simple, segmented, and partitioned. The simple tablespaces can contain one or more tables, but are dealt with as a single entity by DB2 access processing. Segmented tablespaces can contain one or more tables. The file is logically separated into groups of a fixed number of pages. Each group of pages is processed independently in accessing the data. Partitioned tablespaces can only contain a single table, and consist of a distinct files for each partition corresponding to a clustering index key range.

DB2 (version 2.3) provides a logical data set close operation, allowing for specifying that the tablespace can be closed when not in use with only minor performance impact. This is a kludge added to DB2 because sites with large numbers of DB2 data sets were limited to the number of data sets that MVS would allow a single user to open. This forced large DB2 users to expend the extra overhead of CLOSE YES data space, repeatedly closing and opening the files.

The DB2 space allocation algorithm will preallocate extents when the amount of available space left is SECQTY/2. This should be taken into account when allocating secondary space quantities. A large secondary quantity will promote creation of secondary extents.

A traditional approach is to allocate in the primary quantity enough space for growth for three months. Secondary quantities of about 10 percent are used unless the data size is very volatile. Many shops use a minimum size for primary and secondary allocations. A common minimum is 1 cylinder. An allocation of less than a track does not make sense.

Tables

A page cannot contain more than 127 rows. This limit is due to the page header containing a row map with 127 entries. In a 4K page, this works out to 24 bytes per row; anything less will waste space.

If a fixed-length row size is over half the page size, the entire page will be allocated to the row. There is some wasted space in most tables because of inexact blocking. DB2 will never span a row across multiple pages. This issue is best completely ignored when tables have short rows (under 400 bytes) — the space to be saved does not justify the tampering.

As row size gets bigger, several considerations emerge. If the table is large and frequently accessed, the space loss is a double whammy. Accessing the entire table wastes storage and requires extra I/O. Moreover, bufferpool efficiency decreases if the amount of data kept buffered decreases.

For long rows, consider the possibility of splitting a single table in multiple *sibling* tables sharing common primary keys. This is a very effective strategy in cases where data are overly denormalized or where there are distinct access patterns relating to column combinations.

A common example is a CHAR "notes" column in a transaction system that is rarely populated. Even if it is not reasonable to use a VARCHAR to replace it, it may be reasonable to move the field to another table, and add a flag denoting the note field's existence. This saves space, reduces typical transaction cost, and also shortens the row.

Long fields of various sorts present a similar problem. They tend to be rarely updated, are often rarely referenced, and frequently have a maximal required length that is much longer than the typical length. Often they can be processed by maintaining them in some special manner, trading application complexity for performance improvement. Common strategies include:

- Creating a fixed-length column and accepting the overhead of wasted space for some efficiency in processing.
- Splitting a long column into a fixed-length column and keeping the excess in a spill table, if needed. This is very effective if the values are generally short.
- Keeping the entire column in a spill table. This is a preferred technique in a rarely populated field or in a rarely referenced one.
- Maintaining the variable-length column in a table as a linked list or logical array of fixed-length short columns. This strategy directly conflicts with the inability of SQL to process recursive structures. This processing often performs poorly and requires a great deal of application logic to maintain. The reason this approach is ever used in DB2 is either because there are data items too long for DB2 to manage in a 32K page (or because they will exceed the 4K page size and shop preference is to avoid 32K pages), or because of migration of logic or ideas from other non-DB2 applications.

Indexes

An index is used by DB2 to point directly to data to eliminate physical sorting. Indices can also allow some data access without reading the associated row, defining a clustering (default) order to a table to establish uniqueness of the data and to define ranges of cluster data.

DB2 maintains clustering indices, for which the index definition defines the expected table row physical order in the tablespace. Unique indices guarantee that no rows duplicating index entries can be inserted in a table. A partitioning index is a special case of a clustering index; it defines the key ranges of data in partitioned tablespaces, and the index entries for each partition are maintained in an individual file. Unlike some relational DBMSs, DB2 stores index data in separate files from the data.

Indices are limited to 64 bytes cumulative key length, or 40 for partitioning indices. They have no understanding of variable-length fields: DB2 pads indexed VARCHAR and other VAR fields to maximum length. There is no way (barring tampering with the execute channel programs for DB2) to compress the index entries.

The degree of uniqueness of the indexed data is a major consideration for the reasonableness of index processing. There is a very high overhead in dealing with duplicate index entries. A synonym chain is used to store the duplicates, and the chain has to be searched sequentially. All indices have 4K pages.

Index root, nonleaf, and leaf pages

The first data page on an index is called the root page. It contains an array in which each entry is a pair containing:

- **A pointer**, which normally points to the appropriate next level index page but, if there is only a single index page (an unusual occurrence only in indices on tiny tables), this points directly to the data page row in the tablespace. This field is 4 bytes long, consisting of a 3-byte relative page address and a single-byte page entry number.

- **A key,** which is a concatenated composite of the internal format of the columns in the index. For any nullible column (an unappealing index column characteristic from a logical design perspective), a null indicator is attached. Any VAR column (an unappealing index column characteristic from a physical design perspective), will be padded to maximal length.

The index structure attempts to partition the indexed data evenly. That is, if there are 100 entries on the root page, the range of data between any two consecutive ones should be approximately one percent of the data.

The final pages in an index structure contain leaf pages. These contain a similar structure to the root page. In fact the degenerate form of an index is a single data page containing a root-leaf combination page whose pointers refer to tablespace row entries. In any other case, the root page pointer points to something, which may be a leaf page. The leaf page pointers always point to tablespace rows.

In an index defined without the UNIQUE attribute, the leaf page may contain synonym chains. There is always a one-to-one relationship between the data pointers on the leaf nodes and the rows in the table. A nonunique index can contain fewer key entries than data pointers. The synonyms consist of an array of pointers to the appropriate tablespace rows.

Index leaf pages with synonyms

Most indices contain too many entries to fit into a two level index. Here there will be one or more levels of nonleaf pages between the root and leaf pages. These again have the same basic structure as the root pages. There are no synonyms chains here, of course.

A medium-sized index generally contains only a single nonleaf level, giving the index a total of three levels. A large table with very long index keys can contain many levels of nonleaf index pages.

This is a critical performance issue. In a typical DB2 access pattern of an index that is frequently accessed in a system with reasonable buffers, the index root page is always in core. Many of the first level of nonleaf pages will be buffered because of the access frequency. Other levels of index will have low buffering rates (except for data access hot spots and loci of reference of each program).

This means that a three-level index search data access may require two physical reads: the root page is typically buffered, the nonleaf page is gotten from the buffer, the leaf page is physically read, and the actual data in the tablespace are physically read. This is the most common access pattern in transaction processing. Adding a fourth index level (i.e., a second nonleaf level) will increase the reads by 50 percent to three, by adding another physical read of the additional non-leaf level page.

Bufferpools

DB2 provides four buffer pools as a place to stage I/O processing and as a means of decreasing the number of physical I/Os to be done. These include bufferpools BP0, BP1, and BP2, which are used for tablespaces and indexspaces with 4K pages, and BP32K, which is used for tablespaces defined with 32K pages.

DB2 was designed to use very large bufferpools, and performs poorly when the bufferpool size is small. Usually it is expected to use a single bufferpool, BP0, for all processing. There are, however, some exceptions.

When radically different types of activity are being processed in the same DB2 subsystem — for example, ad-hoc queries involving tablespace scans on large tables concurrently with transaction-processing — the ad-hoc processing can destabilize the transaction processing response time. Multiple large queries can flush the most valuable buffered resources: index root and nonleaf pages, and commonly accessed transaction data. This will slow the application to require worst-case maximal effort in transaction processing.

In this situation it may be appropriate to accept the extra cost in memory and buy another bufferpool (i.e., get enough real memory to support a new one), or else accept the performance impact of dividing a specific bufferpool, knowing that we can keep our transaction processing response time stable.

In very high throughput systems, a similar situation can arise. If the system is dealing with large amounts of data, the tablespace and index I/O may compete with each other. The tablespace access can force the index buffers or frequently accessed table buffers such as translate table pages to be flushed too quickly. Again the competition prevents meeting the capacity goals. In this rare situation, the vital index buffers can be isolated from competition in a distinct buffer pool.

Summary

STOGROUP is the DB2 facility for internally allocating VSAM files. It is recommended for use usually as a convenience. Some users prefer VCAT definition to STOGROUP because of the conflict with central DASD management or to protect data sets from being deleted by an accidental DROP.

The DB2 DATABASE has operational management issues, since it can be started and stopped, and DDL or DCL processing can lock out other users of the same database. More commonly databases are allocated early by application, and later in vague subject areas. In most cases there is dubious relationship between the DB2 grouping of DATABASE and the logical data design database.

Tablespaces are the means of allocating storage for tables. They can be simple, segmented, or partitioned. Simple tablespaces are rarely justifiable unless multiple tables will be interleaved within — a tedious process. Thus, almost all tablespaces should be segmented.

The advantages of segmented tablespaces include more detailed space management bit maps and the ability to mass delete all rows efficiently. Partitioned tablespaces can contain a single table, with one tablespace VSAM file (partition) corresponding to a key range in the clustering index. Partitioned tablespaces are a powerful tool for managing large tables or complex operational issues at the expense of having more files to manage.

DB2 tables closely resemble the logical data design. There are some tradeoffs resulting from the access and storage mechanisms of DB2. Tables can be reformatted if the row size is awkward in relation to the page size, there is some rarely accessed data, or there are variable-length data that often expand in size.

Indices have the same storage characteristics as tablespaces. Unique indices prevent duplicate single entries for each key value. Clustering indices establish table order during reorganization. Secondary indices should be created judiciously. Indices with many duplicate values tend to be useless.

Review Question

1. If a DBA accidentally drops a production database (perhaps when intending to drop a development database), what has to be restored?

Answer to Review Question

1.

DATABASE
    TABLESPACES
        TABLES and their data
            INDEXes
        VIEWS
        SYNONYMS
        ALIASes
        Referential relationships

The objects identified above all have to be re-created. All plans that referred to any of the aforementioned tablespaces, tables, views, or indices have to be rebound. Security has to be restored for each of the objects.

Chapter 6

Decision Support, Reporting, and Executive Information Applications

Decision support systems (DSS) do not have inherent differences from reporting systems of the past. The difference is an issue of style. Decision support systems tend to have more complex data design and more frequent data refresh than the older systems. Decision making implies allowing the easy customization of the data produced for the reports. This is a significant change to end-users, offering them fast access to reports. DSS is the reason that many users have opted to use DB2.

DSSs can be looked at as an umbrella-term for reporting systems that can generate new reports quickly. A type of DSS is the executive information system (EIS), which we can look at in two ways. The first is as a marketing tool: adding brand credibility to a slick and colorful DSS. This is, sadly, a major rationale for EIS development; these systems can often be identified by looking at the function lists. A system whose functions replicate other IS activity or include seemingly randomly chosen bells and whistles should be cause for concern.

Second, EISs may be looked at as a means to quickly *and directly* deploy data for fine-tuning corporate activity. As such, this can be looked at as an extension of managerial trends of the past decade. For example, management by exception can be automated on many EIS systems. Parameters can be set up to identify company activity that deviates from plan.

SQL Generating Front Ends

Decision support applications often have a homemade back-end SQL generator. Be careful of these types of applications. They may force you either to perpetually upgrade the SQL generation capabilities, or else live with a system that produces slow and inefficient queries. Vendor products from successful players have the potential advantage of improved code generation.

Many vendor products demonstrate this issue, tremendously improving their performance after the first product releases. Currently most of these tools do not completely use SQL selection processing. The report generators often overselect data and then filter the appropriate data from the selected rows. This process guarantees horrendous performance degradation.

In many complex query situations, DB2 retrieves the data row by row, usually applying some filtering (this is called *stage 2 predicate processing*). Additional filtering by the query tool means that DB2 will process the original query poorly. The tool is simply not passing enough information to optimize the query effectively. Overselection means that indices will not improve performance. This processing incurs additional CPU and I/O costs. Buffer pool resources will be wasted on inappropriate pages. The overhead in FETCHing the rows from DB2 to the query tool is significant.

Reporting Issues in DB2

Large-scale data processing applications have traditionally consisted of front-end systems dealing with granular data, and back-end systems dealing with segmented collections of data. The back-end systems often consisted of a periodic procedure extracting data from the operational files, producing an extract file. The extract file would be used to create reports.

This process has many advantages. The primary one is performance. The extract procedure is a one-pass process, with minimal impact on the batch window. The report generation process also minimizes the number of passes to read the data extract, typically involving excerpting appropriate data to a collection of reports. In more sophisticated applications, the data would be dumped to a collection of temporary files to be sorted and formatted into reports.

This procedure evolved as fourth-generation languages came into vogue. Some vendor packages attempted to report directly from the operational systems data, but these never achieved great popularity. The major successes of the 4GLs were due to the ability to produce reports quickly from the existing extract files. The existing data could be formatted in nicer ways and data reduced for specific purposes.

This was the data processing world at the arrival of DB2. The problem in this structure was becoming obvious: if the appropriate data was not extracted in the right order, the systems would not help. After the initial success, these systems could only reformat existing reports.

DB2 was often sold in the past with an implication that operational data could be used for reporting purposes. Experience shows that this is an uncomfortable mix.

Occasionally applications developers in DB2 attempt to produce reports directly from operational systems. These have problems due to the complications in bufferpool management and stabilizing operational resources. Most sites tend to reject this approach because of the intractability of the locking conflicts between operational and reporting activities. The poor match between the data structure designed to support operational systems and the data structure that could best support reporting activities causes more conflict.

The justification of the migration to DB2 looks (from the viewpoint of this discussion) dubious: continuing a theme without a major improvement in product. Reporting systems in DB2 have been incredibly successful. The older reporting systems using 4GLs and report writers became constrained by the limitations of the technology.

Restructuring data in complicated ways can break the back of these report writing systems. Limitations built into tools often preclude a desired activity. Data in report writing systems are often incomplete. Performance problems can make many activities unreasonable. This inability forces developers to build extract files with specific functional reporting directions built in. The limitations of the data design can be perceived as the limitations of the technology.

This means that DB2 systems used for reporting have to preserve the data in a more orthogonal form. A single flat file, or the table equivalent will not do. Fully normalized data are typically not a reasonable option either: a major selling point for decision support systems is that quick reporting will allow informed judgment. Third normal form data typically will force a report process to join five or more large tables, resulting in slow response time. The data design has to allow both for fast reporting and for easy reporting on unplanned grouping of data.

DB2 can provide facilities to do this kind of processing very well. The main feature is the sophisticated and scalable data manipulation engine.

Data Analysis and Decision Support

The tendency to discuss performance aspects notwithstanding, the problems of extract data are primarily analysis and data administration issues. Too many decision support applications are implemented before the data issues are fully understood. Generating reports from misunderstood data is the garden path to losing credibility.

This is an important point in understanding our industry. Programmers have a tendency to want to produce results. Users have a tendency to view the results as gospel. The result is that programmers often produce reports very quickly, ignoring the subtleties of the user's request. The programmer expects the user to validate the result, and the user expects the numbers to be right. The programmer will quickly go from hero to goat if a misunderstanding is embedded in the report. The business need is unfulfilled, a potential error was caused, and no one is satisfied.

Data analysis in all its aspects is the key to effective decision support data. Standard naming conventions help the users understand the data definitions. Data quality review can help determine if the data are valid. It is amazing how many of the errors in operational data tend to be concentrated in particular segments, which can cause bizarre reports to be generated. Of course, there is a tremendous risk that users can develop queries answering the wrong question.

Data Quality Issues

Source system data correction is an absolute must. We can consider a DSS as a means to fix data quality by reporting on the data to validate it. Here it is imperative *not* to deliver the data to the users until they are correct. Stage each piece of the data, and scrupulously verify it with users, preferably tying any data back to standard company reports.

Data quality problems have been the root of almost all problems in DSS applications. The problems have to be addressed at their source. As systems get older, they often become less restrictive. Odd requirements will cause data edits to be removed. Fields go into partial disuse, and extraneous fields can be used as storage bins for new data or flags.

Merging Extracts: The Dilemma of the Unintegrated Data Sources

Attempting to merge data from several applications seems tempting. It would be nice to have an integrated reporting facility. This approach can be very powerful, but is very prone to error.

The problems are an artifact of the reason the systems are not implemented in an integrated fashion: it is hard to build an integrated system. Integrating the data can require as much analysis as would be required for redesigning the application itself.

A key to this process is the degree of implicit integration existing between the systems. Hints that the applications work together can be found by checking:

- The application cycle time, especially relating to strategies such as reconciliation to other systems, or points of synchronizing all applications data. Look for batch programs that merge data between systems; these are called *bridge* or *apply* programs.

- Shared data elements. If much data are shared between the systems, it might be easy to integrate their data. It is even more likely to be feasible if the shared data include many desired data keys. It is vital to do a comparison of data between the systems to validate data quality. Any significant mismatch probably implies differences between the systems' understanding of their *private* data.

- A tightly related set of business rules relating to the applications. Applications deviate from each other as designers attempt to reconcile incompatible business rules. This is why separate divisions', or companies' databases can rarely be integrated, unless there is an overriding list of explicit requirements (such as compliance to statute).

Summary

Decision support applications are flexible reporting facilities, usually with front ends allowing end users to generate reports themselves. Executive information systems are more complex DSS systems with more bells and whistles, more frequent data refresh, easier use, and exception processing facilities.

Decision support can be done with an application developed completely in-house using a third-generation language. More often these applications are built using report generation tools. Examples of these tools include QMF (Query Management Facility from IBM) and FOCUS (from Information Builders, Inc.).

Reporting systems based on file extracts can be replaced by decision support applications because of the additional flexibility. Extract file reporting could produce reports easily only on queries that were expected.

Review Questions

1. What distinguishes a decision support system from reporting programs?

2. What is an executive information system?

3. What are the impediments to a corporate data decision support system?

Answers to Review Questions

1. A reporting program will format reports from data. A traditional reporting system would not easily allow many new requests. Decision support systems allow users to change the data selection parameters. Decision support systems range from slightly more flexible report programs to systems allowing sophisticated user-generated reports. Often decision support systems tend to allow more user-friendly reports, including graphical representation of data (charts).

2. An executive information system is generally a means of adding cachet to a decision support system. From a database point of view, most executive information systems look exactly like decision support systems.

The externals of executive information systems can be very different from decision support systems. The major aspects of the divergence are:

- Flashy front-end software allowing easy use by nontechnical staff (presumably executives). This is an attempt to entice the user to play with the system.
- Disguising the "ugly" mainframe panel-oriented interaction with a paradigm of interaction with which the user is more comfortable. This is a means to reduce user resistance to computers.
- More reduction of raw data than in typical reports. The reduction can be a summary of overall data as in an enterprise-wide sales total. For example, the entire sales of a company can be distilled to a single pie chart. Another common reduction is to report on changes on an exception basis. In this approach the user sets limits and is notified of data that exceed these limits.

3. The impediments for a corporate data decision support system include these problems:

- It is generally impossible to put all data in a decision support system.
- It is an enormous effort to identify the true meaning of data. The work in cleaning data makes it unreasonable to put too much data in decision support.
- Most businesses have unintegrated applications. These applications tend to contain data that are resistant to integration.

Chapter 7

The Frequency of Extracting and Refreshing Data

The computer cost of operating a DSS is directly proportional to the frequency of refreshing the data. There is a direct tradeoff between the frequency of capturing, reconciling, and downloading data into a decision support system and the cost of the processing. Users defining their DSS requirements generally have a very murky picture of their data needs.

After any application is in production, the requirements become clearer. Commonly this results in demand for more frequent refreshing of the data. Whatever frequency is chosen will likely become a political issue.

It most strongly behooves the refresh application designer to make the cost tradeoffs clear. This generally requires more thorough analysis of the data sources. Experience shows that this extra research will have an enormous pay back.

Decision Support Reporting Using Operational Data

An option many neophytes in DB2 consider is using the same data for both operational systems and decision support. This can be a valid action in some very restricted circumstances. For instance, the data may be shared when the transaction rate on both the operational and reporting sides is low. As the application requirements get more sophisticated, it becomes very hard to share data.

The problems in using operational data include:

Locking

- **Reporting**: often gets very broad locks, often tablespace level, locks in shared mode. The duration of these locks is very long.
- **Transaction processing**: will usually acquire exclusive or update locks on small amounts of data, lasting for very short periods

The conflict results in reporting applications preventing concurrent transaction processing. Deadlocking between applications cannot be predicted or managed in this environment. DB2 awkwardly chooses the application that logs the least as the preferred candidate to roll back in a deadlock, guaranteeing reporting programs will never complete.

Bufferpool sharing

- **Reporting**: the same bufferpool has to be used on a given shared tablespace. This sharing will cause the typical activity of reporting, tablespace scanning, to flush the bufferpool of any cached transaction processing data.
- **Transaction processing**: the problem can be mitigated somewhat with large buffer pools and by using separate bufferpools for indices associated with transaction processing (though there is no guarantee that DSS activity will not choose those indices as well unless the designer hides the indexed field from the ad-hoc querier).

The conflict causes frequent flushing of buffer pools. This means that transaction processing may exhibit worst-case behavior at any time.

Indexing

- **Reporting**: needs many complicated indices. Extra indices cause minimal performance degradation, since updates are rare and the indices can improve performance. There are many justifications for indices with long composite keys. Indexed fields are not expected to be random. Most applications rely on index merge and alternate indices.

- **Transaction processing**: each table should have very few, very short, very unique indices that are very evenly distributed. Most applications rely on matching scans of the clustering index.

The conflict is that extra indices cause tremendous performance degradation on updates, and dramatically increase the chance of lock contention in the mixed environment. Too few indices guarantee tablespace scans by reporting programs.

Data structure

- **Reporting**: denormalizing is reasonable, since there is little update processing. The data structure should match the reporting needs, and keys should be logical rather than arbitrary. Data should be decoded wherever possible. Data summaries should be kept and maintained by the updaters. Never use any sort of compression on the data, since it is accessed sequentially.

- **Transaction processing**: the data structure usually matches the transaction requirements. Keys should be short and random, and often are arbitrary numbers. Data are stored in encoded format. Compression is a tempting alternative, since the data are accessed randomly. Denormalization should only be done in specific situations where:

  - ☐ The performance requirements demand a radical solution.
  - ☐ The update processing pattern can be analyzed as not causing data inconsistency.
  - ☐ A reasonable expectation exists that no change conflicting with the denormalization will occur.

The conflict is that logical data design means different things in a reporting environment than in an operational application. Thus, there is little likelihood that the logical design for one will satisfy the other.

Physical design for transaction processing likewise conflicts with reporting. A transaction processing application running on decision support data may be crippled. Conversely, the physical design of a hybrid application will exacerbate the previously mentioned problems.

Data Propagation

The IMS data propagator is a means to keep your DB2 and IMS data reasonably synchronized. It also provides a facility either directly through the exits, or indirectly by using DB2 distributed database support, to propagate the data further.

The early release of the Dprop product allows for convenient *synchronous* distribution of data: as each IMS work unit completes (reaches a SYNCH point), the data become available for downloading to DB2. Further releases will enhance the facility with better support of asynchronous processing. This will allow a fully loaded operational application to run without the additional overhead (chances are your users could not query the live production data during peak hours anyway) and then extract the data for processing. Later facilities will allow propagation of data from DB2 to IMS (and conceivably other database management systems).

Summary

Decision support data are extracted from transaction processing systems. How often to refresh the data is a critical decision in the design. It is expensive to frequently refresh the data. Usually users are incapable of analyzing or adjusting to data less than a day old.

This refresh frequency has become a glamour issue, where users will often demand data to be available almost immediately. Sometimes it is reasonable to provide the data to allow for future business development. More likely, a gradual process of increasing currency and availability of data for reporting will serve users' needs.

Data extraction is an impediment to transaction processing. The source has the option of logging updates to allow the data to be retrieved to be copied to decision support. Changed data can be marked with time stamps to allow new data to be retrieved. Sometimes ascending keys and a decision support "high-water mark" can identify new data.

Extract designers should minimize the impact between extraction and transaction processing. This can be done:

- By scheduling extracts when the corresponding transaction processing is not running
- By extracting data in small and short work units
- By the unpleasant option of logging relevant data to a log file.

Application of the extracted data into the decision support tables should be designed to avoid conflict with decision support queries. Usually this is easier than extracting the data, since DSS is less time critical and has less volume. The best means of applying the data is to design a pause in queries to insert new data.

If requests involve very long running queries the user will almost surely acquire table-wide shared locks, which prevent any updates. The options of preventing this processing from locking out updates are:

- By further replicating the data for the queries (a rare option)
- By deferring scheduling the updates
- By breaking a large query into multiple small queries

Most data in DB2 decision support systems come from non-DB2 source files (or combined DB2 / non-DB2 sources). This forces deep consideration of the interaction between the two. The IMS data propagator is designed to allow for data extraction from IMS transaction processing into DB2.

Review Questions

1. What are the advantages of immediately available decision support data?

2. How can DB2 operational data be used for immediate decision support purposes?

3. What are the disadvantages of immediately available decision support data?

Answers to Review Question

1. The enterprise decision-making processes can be fine-tuned interactively. This is a significant idea, in that the entire premise of a business activity normally involves very slow change because of insufficient data. Quickly available data can change the way some businesses function.

2. DB2 has limited ability to immediately capture updates.

- Data can be captured through a transaction that copies data marked with an appropriate timestamp or flag.
- Programs can log updates to a DB2 or external file that is polled by a data copy routine.
- There are some systems programming solutions; the data can be dumped through use of the DB2 logs or through the EDITPROC or VALIDPROC exits.

3. There is generally a tremendous cost to increasing the speed of propagating data to the decision support system. Most users of the data cannot react quickly. In other words, even if they can identify a problem the users can not do anything about it.

Each decision support system tends to receive data faster than they can be properly used. The refresh cycle time tends to decrease as businesses learn how to react to new data. This often requires a very different business approach — which is hard to do.

Chapter 8

Managing a Decision Support Environment

The database industry ignores support issues until products are very mature. DSS applications tend to ignore management issues in their design. Staff is rarely available to manage the data sets involved, and the constantly changing structure of the DSS applications often scare the traditional DBA into avoiding these applications.

Ideally, a DSS design should include facilities for:

- Centralized control of the major components. These include the history files, company code and translate tables, and summary and test extract tables.

- Conjoint management of any user-created "semipermanent" extracts. These are shared tables or ones used for long-term analysis.

- User-managed temporary tables. The system should provide facilities to automate this process, giving the user options to DROP unneeded extracts, automating archival of nonreferenced data, and so forth. The degree of compliance here is dependent on the quality of the facilities. For example, a function of "DROP, but you have a week to unDROP the object without assistance" will often result in cleaner environments.

Utility management is vital for effective control of decision support environments. There is always a temptation to abandon the standard protocols of the various utilities. This changing environment seems from a system perspective very much like a development environment.

This must not happen. A useful DSS is a production application and must be maintained as such. Standard backups should be taken, objects should be sized correctly and REORGed when necessary. This allows better control of the surroundings, but also can have tremendous performance implications.

Oversized indexspaces or simple tablespaces involved in scans can waste I/O. Index structure in many DSS applications is poor, and this tempts the optimizer to use scans instead of searches. A DSS is the area where column-level RUNSTATS statistics can be most valuable — but the end users can rarely determine which columns to analyze.

Decision Support and Planning Systems in a Transaction Processing Environment

Planning systems are a cross between traditional operational transaction processing and decision support systems. These applications tend to use much operational data to perform simple "what-if" analysis for the future. As such, they combine many requirements of operational systems, especially the data requirements, with many aspects of decision support ad-hoc query processing.

Mixing the two makes for a combination of the problems we find in each separate environment. Planning systems generally are built in a transaction processing environment in which they are considered low-volume transaction processing. This is typically done in order to simplify the differentiation between transaction processing and TSO accessed data.

In a transaction processing environment, the normal emphasis is to stabilize transaction size. This allows the building of stable and consistent transaction throughput. Adding decision support capabilities will destabilize the environment and can easily lead to erratic response time.

Management and Design Issues in DSS

A DSS is a changing beast. This is of necessity: it is a tool for exploring the company. Locking users into their initial expectations of the application, which is a major goal of standard application development, must be looked at as a means to sabotage a DSS application. The users don't know what they want. Use of a DSS is a means to prototype applications, some one-time reports and some long-term reports.

This implies building a DSS in only a rudimentary fashion. Design the application as a prototype, let the users use it, and then develop the complete application based on user feedback. The DSS will develop into:

- Stable reporting applications
- A customizable reporting application
- A new application development platform

This is the case with almost every accepted DSS. The reasons for this are obvious. Users do not know what to expect initially from a DSS, since most have never seen one. This leads to both too high expectations and too low ones.

For developer convenience, the front end to a DSS can easily become a flexible tool. In this case, remember that an easy means to alienate users is to change the application rules. The flexibility allows the application to prototype itself, and evolve into the system the users want.

This strategy is more realistic for decision support than for traditional applications. The users of decision support applications are generally sophisticated. The hardest part in designing a decision support system is to capture the data intelligently. The front-end issues are relevant only if they are poorly or exceptionally well done.

Understanding the Data — What Does Your Query Mean?

The scariest aspect of decision support is quality control. If we develop an application, we plan to have users analyze the results and validate the report. I have never seen a DSS with a built-in quality assurance mechanism.

A decision support application can have a user who is not familiar with the system or data create dozens of reports in minutes. Some of these reports will be correct, some less so, and others completely inaccurate. No one will know which is which — and no credibility can be attached to these reports.

Some natural language tools, such as Intellect and SAA LanguageAccess, attempt to paraphrase the query. This can help, especially if the reiteration includes the data definition and the query is simple enough for the user to understand. After the query gets to a reasonable state of complexity it becomes laborious to follow the paraphrase.

In most of these systems the user selects an initial set of data, culling and combining them with other data, until satisfied. There is no obvious means to clarify the meaning of data like these. It is often the combination of several distinct queries manually edited, joined, and correlated with other data without painstaking review.

IS and DSS — Supporting a DSS Application

There is a common tendency for central IS to be bewildered by decision support. The goals are in such conflict with traditional applications that there may be resistance to DSS. This is clearly a poor strategy.

The major data processing strategic mistake of the 1980s was the loss of control of the information center. Many shops were unable to manage reporting applications; users responded to the backlog by simply hiring their own report programmers.

DSS may have nonmainframe front ends, but their core processing is generally mainframe. DP has to swallow its losses and reintegrate with the information center to support DSS.

The support of DSS processing has to include effective operational support, ability to recover data, effective refresh of DSS data, and reasonable security management. DSS comes in with a new set of expectations; a central IS group has to think carefully about when it is appropriate to say no to a DSS request. These problems are different from the problems in traditional operational systems.

DSS applications must be designed to support an operational structure. The environment should easily support this type of processing. Standards, if not too intrusive can make it easier to build DSS applications. In particular, isolate and generalize tools built to support each DSS application so that the next application can use them.

Be very careful about new DSS tools. There is a tradition of choosing bizarre and inappropriate nonstrategic tools for use in DSS processing. The cost of managing, training in, and supporting these multiple tools makes this a destructive approach.

Controlling a DSS

Decision support applications have an enormous capability to consume resources. It is hard to verify how effectively these resources are used. It is often trivial to generate a query that takes *days* to run.

Is a query that runs for days good or bad? It is impossible to say without careful analysis. In most cases there should be control to prevent applications from unintentionally running too long, and allow any special processing that requires enormous resources.

DB2 contains some facilities to prevent runaway queries. The DB2 Resource Limitation Facility (RLF) has the ability to abort queries that consume too much CPU. QMF contains a similar facility, the query governor.

These facilities have a fundamental problem. They let requests through, but abort them after they have wasted a significant amount of resources. The user waits, and sees only a "query was cancelled" message.

The only other alternative is to predict how much the query will cost beforehand. DB2 provides two means of doing so. In dynamic SQL, after preparing a SQL statement DB2 returns a TIMERON value (in SQLERRD(3) in the SQLDA) that contains a number somehow relating to the query cost. The SQL EXPLAIN statement can be used to determine the statement path.

TIMERONs are the means QMF uses to predict the relative cost of a query. Like the QMF prediction (which is derived from the TIMERON value), this value cannot be considered an accurate predictor of cost.

The EXPLAIN statement output can present a more accurate picture, but requires programming to get the output data from the PLAN_TABLE. This also requires a good understanding of DB2 to understand. The EXPLAIN statement results also are available from the DB2 instrumentation facility (IFI), but using this facility requires understanding of both DB2 and systems programming issues.

Dedicating Programmers to DSS Applications

DSS programmers are different from most others. There tend to be two major categories: data analysts who attempt to solve data meaning and access issues, and frontware developers who work on the user interfaces. Traditional DP developers tend to work on the back-end processing.

Even after completing developing an application, programmers should be involved in the project. DSSs tend to be a developing and changing application, and need much more resources than traditional application maintenance.

Data analysts are important too. There is a high risk of simply misunderstanding the data or what a query means. There is a significant issue of data quality even inside the DSS.

Educating the Users

Users tend to be even more confused about DSS facilities than developers. Mostly DSS is not directly used as planned. Plans for DSS tend to relate to solving report backlog problems. Implemented and stable DSS can best be a means of researching issues.

Users who know how to use the facilities tend to adapt to them well. DSS is different from standard IS applications in the complex training requirements involved. A strategy that seems to work best is to have short regular training sessions that involve use of the tool. A one-hour weekly session for eight weeks will be much better than a one-day training session. Remember that the level of sophistication of DSS users at *their jobs* is much higher than that of the application developers or trainers. This is very different from traditional data processing applications where the users are often very naive.

DSS Database Design

DSS design issues differ from those in other types of applications. There is minimal update activity in DSS. The DSS database designer therefore can take more liberties than for an operational system.

The cost of queries in a DSS can be enormous. Mostly there is no means to predict the queries in advance. The danger of update anomalies resulting from denormalization is eliminated in a system where the data is all derived from other sources.

Normalization is an awkward concept in decision support. Decision support data is typically minimally updated, which removes much of the justification of normal forms to prevent update anomalies. The idea of decision support itself makes normalization more problematic. How can we model data for physical design without knowing how they will be used?

The designer is caught in a dilemma. On the one hand, the data inconsistency justification for normalization is lost. On the other hand, denormalized data will make some queries simpler and some much more complex. The data design will have a profound influence on how the data will be used. Even completely normalized data will favor some queries in performance and ease of development over others. Normalization has profound performance impact on the finished application.

In practice, most DSS data are only rudimentarily normalized. It behooves the designer to normalize DSS data fully and then denormalize them in line with performance and use requirements. This allows the designer to at least understand the data structures involved. Data structures have an annoying tendency to freeze into place under the weight of applications.

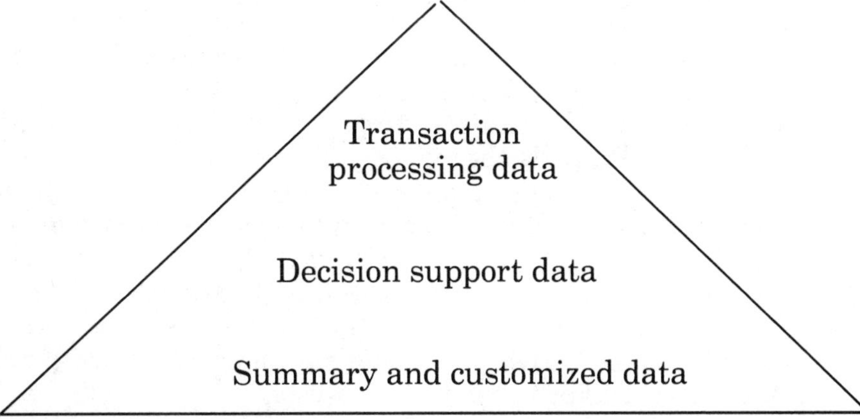

Figure 8.1 Three-tiered data pyramid.

Directing Traffic

Computer applications can be compared to Skinner boxes. For the readers unfamiliar with behavioral psychology, a Skinner box is a training device for pigeons. Birds performing the appropriate behavior are rewarded. The pigeons will quickly train themselves in the behavior. Computer applications likewise reward some actions, and punish others.

A DSS in its flexibility seems intended to train the user more than most applications. Users querying the data will be able to find some things very quickly. Other logically equally available data will be less accessible; either the path to find the data is not obvious or performance issues make the direction unwieldy. The structure of the system constantly directs users in some fashion.

This mutability has a profound impact on the way we design these types of applications. In particular, denormalization through physically joined tables or data summaries will influence the direction of the search. Because of the dangers of leading the users inappropriately, behavioral psychology has more relevance to DSS design than do the standard application design methodologies.

Tiers of Data: Atomic and Summarized Data

Decision support issues tend to force data into a three-tiered structure. (See Figure 8.1.)

The data requirements for transaction processing conflict with decision support. Very early on, any attempts to use the two simultaneously are abandoned. Transaction processing and decision support have very different views of data. If nothing else, decision support requirements to maintain historical data will divide the two.

Decision support detail data are significant for decision support processing. Often reports repeatedly summarize the same data repeatedly over time. Many reports replicate the same reductions of data. The means in DB2 to prevent repeating the same processing is to summarize the data into a smaller table and report from the summary data. Data are also summarized for individual analysis.

Encoding

Encoding takes various forms in a DSS. It seems tempting to compress the stored data with an EDITPROC exit. The data are:

- Mostly character, and compression will reduce the size dramatically
- Accessed less frequently, making the cost of storage significant
- Rarely updated, so utilities slowed by compression become less significant
- Less urgently needed, so performance degradation because of compression overhead becomes less relevant

Encoding in the sense of a DB2 data compression exit is inappropriate for most reporting purposes. Most DSS systems do so much tablespace scanning that the overhead of data compression works poorly with scanned data.

Encoding in most DSS thus refers to use of corporate abbreviations and the like. In many cases, this encoding can be expanded by a join with a codes table.

Compression of character values in large tables can reduce the size of the data set significantly. At the same time, it might make use of the data awkward if the codes are not in standard forms known by all potential users.

DSS Maintenance Issues in Data Administration

Data administration of a DSS can be an uncomfortable topic. Use of DSS tends to expand to more than the initial set of users. Corporate homonyms (names that have different meaning to different users) may confuse new users. DSS can often bring out all the data administration problems very quickly.

Data quality administration is imperative, whether it is done distinctly and formally or as part of the DSS development process. A DSS will bring out all problems when misleading reports are created. These problems must be addressed fully as soon as the issues are identified. Proactive analysis (done by a combination of developers and user data experts or data owners) should help reduce these situations.

This data administration information should not be hidden inside the DSS. The source systems must be corrected. The DSS can be used as a test bed for data analysis for operational systems.

Growth Patterns

Cycles of use by community

Each DSS data component generally has several distinct user communities. Usually these users have different needs for the data. It is useful for DSS developers to analyze the use of the data by each group.

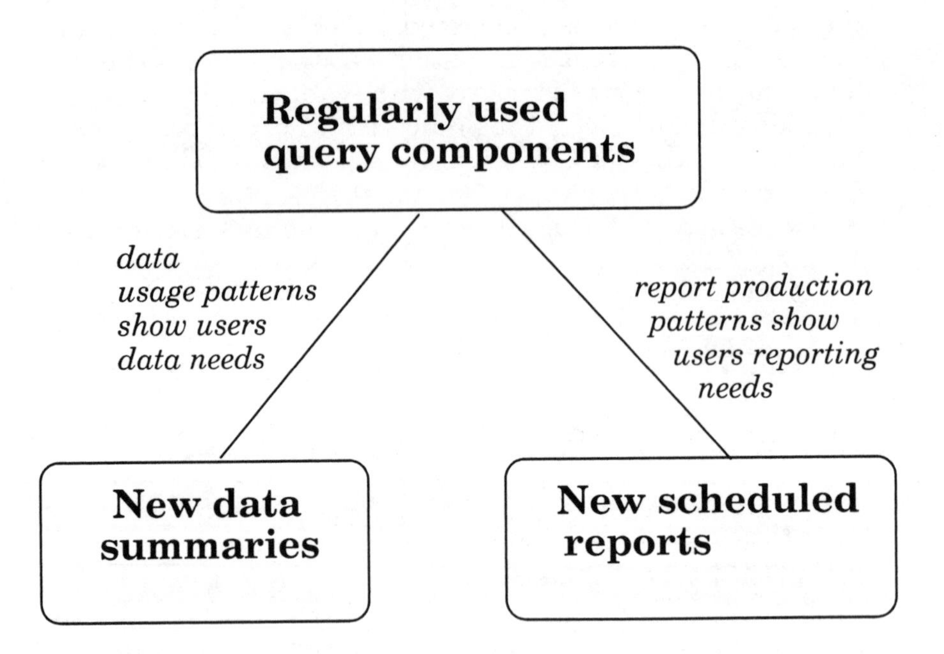

Figure 8.1 A DSS changing with business needs.

These data can be found in various chargeback systems, or else by reporting through SMF data or through DB2 trace historical summaries. The use analysis can help in capacity planning, and in identifying relationships between the data and use. The faster users are notified of the cost of their actions, the easier they can develop cost-effective DSS behavior.

Planning for growth

DSS planning generally consists of:

1. Identifying the desired data.

2. Choosing an arbitrary amount of history to be maintained.

3. Multiplying **1** by **2** to identify the amount of total storage that will be needed.

4. Asking users for sample short, medium, and long queries and how many of each they will submit.

5. Predicting a typical cost of each and multiplying by the counts to get the processing cost.

This approach is the traditional planning strategy. It never works accurately in early DSS because use cannot be predicted. Data tend to grow as new requirements develop (and the premise of a DSS is easy development of new requirements). Performance figures have only the vaguest basis in reality, since users cannot identify their requirements until they become very experienced DSS users.

Developers must also realize the sales issues in a DSS. Effective promotion of an application can increase interest. Early success can increase use.

This vagueness forces planners to embed huge "fudge factors" into any planning figures. This will allow for future growth. Sometimes use far exceeds the plan. Sometimes use falls far short of prediction.

Flow of growth in a DSS

As the users are doing regular reporting, periodically analyze their efforts to select useful reports to be regularly scheduled and disseminated, and remove obsolete reports from production.

Periodically review data summaries (and data and data structures) for use patterns, and compared with analysis of actual query activity. This leads to design of new summarizations and removal of unnecessary ones, as shown in Figure 8.2.

Systems Programming Issues in DSS — DSNDB07

DSNDB07 is the database DB2 uses internally for temporary storage — typically for sorts or for results tables that do not fit into the bufferpools. The database is managed by the administrator creating several tablespaces. The storage thus allocated is available to any DB2 process that requests it.

If the pages involved are from 4K indexspaces or tablespaces, any tablespace allocated to BP0 can be used. If the pages involved are from 32K tablespaces (there ain't no such thing as a 32K indexspace), this will require tablespaces allocated to BP32K.

The typical configuration is a single tablespace allocated to BP32K, because few sites ever have much activity involving wide rows. Joins creating extra wide rows needing sorting will need this tablespace.

The real activity of the temporary work area is in the 4K tablespaces. Most sites have far too few tablespaces. The advantages of multiple tablespaces are numerous. If there are multiple users requiring sorts, the multiple spaces can allow DB2 to allocate separate DASD and reduce DASD contention.

If a user needs more DASD than is available currently on the first DSNDB07 tablespace, DB2 will continue using space on the next available tablespace. Multiple tablespaces will not reduce the maximal amount of space available for a query.

If all DSNDB07 tablespaces are filled, DB2 will use VSAM space management to extend an underlying VSAM file. This process includes a message sent to the DB2 (MSTR) log and to console, which can be a nuisance. This facility can be used to advantage as a means of identifying when heavy processing activity is going on, or even to control the activity via an auto-operator.

DB2 uses database DSNDB07 to store intermediate data in the form of large results tables that do not fit into memory and as a sort work area. DB2 will use DSNDB07 tablespaces as spill files for any sorts it does, for merge scan joins, and for subqueries.

DB2 sort is efficient for about 1 million rows or less. This holds true even for very wide rows. For a much larger sort consider using an external sort. It is better to allocate DSNDB07 tablespaces on different (fast) noncached devices, and more tablespaces are better than less. Even a small DB2 subsystem should have at least three 4K tablespaces. For a large shop with multiple users requiring intermediate data, a larger number (six or more) is more reasonable.

In most environments the space is arbitrarily allocated. The size of the sort work area is often a confusing issue. In most decision support situations the size required is unclear. In some large-scale batch situations the size of the DSNDB07 tablespaces can be carefully calculated. More likely the sizes are completely guessed at.

A strategy to identify the appropriate size is to allocate a minimal amount of space, and a small secondary quantity (e.g., 1 cylinder secondary). As users require more space, secondary allocations are done, and the amount of total storage is easily determined.

A problem with this method of temporary storage allocation is the runaway query. In most decision support systems it is possible to generate queries that generate enormous amounts of data. This may be due to rational queries that simply produce huge reports caused by erroneous queries. A single query can consume enormous amounts of DSNDB07 space. Allowing secondary extents can prevent DSNDB07 from being the limiting factor causing requests to fail.

It may be worthwhile to get rid of the extents (an easy procedure) iteratively and check growth. It would further help if the cause of the growth can be determined. This allows the manager to ignore the growth which is due to errors. The typical considerations are the amount needed per user and the number of overlapping queries.

After quantifying the amount of storage needed, it may be appropriate to resize the DSNDB07 tablespaces to the selected primary quantity and a secondary quantity of 0. The premise of this technique is that the most likely reason for a demand of a huge increase in sort space is a runaway (erroneous) query. If the sort space size forces these to abort, everyone is happier.

A user or system administrator sees the -904 SQLCODE error, denoting query failure due to a VSAM inability to extend to temporary file. When this occurs, the user or administrator will hopefully review the query to see if it is correct and if it can be simplified. If actual work is prevented by the size restrictions, new DSNDB07 tablespaces can be created. It is reasonable and proper to allocate additional temporary tablespaces for special circumstances such as month-end processing or for an application conversion.

Summary

In the flurry of adding features to decision support applications, operational management can get lost. Applications should be built to ease management of this type of system and protect users from operational problems.

Planning applications that straddle the fence between transaction processing data entry systems and history-minded decision support are particularly awkward to manage. These systems need the flexibility of DSS and the stability of transaction-processing environments.

Review Questions

1. How is decision support summary data managed in your shop? How can the management be improved?

2. How can backups be done for user data in decision support data?

Answers to Review Questions

1.

2. DB2 image copies can be done, but if users can create their own tables, the logistics can be complicated. Often each user can simply be provided with a segmented tablespace in which to stuff all tables. This allows a single image copy to back up all the user's data.

In many cases this will not work because of software limitations in decision support tools. A common approach is to simply use DASD volume backups and ignore DB2 facilities. This method can work for decision support data since the data are rarely updated, and DSS does not normally involve referential integrity.

Backup copying of DB2 DASD volumes or data sets outside the auspices of DB2 should only be performed after all buffers have been written. This happens after a DB2 checkpoint or when the appropriate object is closed.

This means stopping the appropriate tablespaces by one of these options:

- Stopping DB2
- Stopping the tablespaces
- Stopping a database containing the tablespaces

When recovering data from non-DB2 backups, the tablespaces should be stopped. If a table is recovered, be careful to recover the indices as well.

Chapter 9

DB2 and Transaction Processing

Transaction processing relates to two data processing concepts. Frequently processed simple programs which interact with many users at computer terminals are often considered the heart of data processing. Many consider this to be transaction processing.

Transaction processing can also refer to a tight interrelationship between the actions taken within a transaction. This is the notion of transaction integrity, also called a logical unit of work.

Thus the central issues in DB2 transaction processing are to sustain a high transaction rate at least cost, and to keep the data values consistent. DB2 supports the high transaction rate issue through a series of architectural choices discussed in detail in Chapter 13. The transaction integrity is guaranteed by saving changes in the DB2 log. This chapter will review the DB2 work unit.

DB2 and High Transaction Rates

DB2 thrives in an environment with large bufferpools and fast CPUs. In these circumstances, DB2 will use the bufferpool as an I/O cache to reduce the number of repeated I/Os to the same page.

Furthermore, DB2 converts slow synchronous writes that are, by their nature, random into faster, relatively ordered, deferred writes. DB2 does this by waiting until a DB2 checkpoint to write the changed page to the file. Since many writes in that period can refer to the same page, the total number of writes decreases.

DB2 can protect the transaction program from losing updates due to computer failure by journaling the changes into the DB2 logs. This is normally not an impediment, since the writes to the DB2 log are sequential. In a system with a tremendously high number of updates, the log can become a bottleneck.

IBM has designed a feature of the 3990 controller that allows writes to done to a very reliable semiconductor cache. This cache *stages* writes by responding to a write request, notifying MVS that the data have been written as soon as they are in the controller. The speed of this process (a logical write can be done in under 3 milliseconds) assures that the log should not be a bottleneck even on the largest applications.

DB2 Logical Units of Work

DB2 uses these same log mechanisms to support logical unit of work consistency even after a system failure. This process is part of the DB2 start-up processing. As DB2 starts, it can detect whether it was cleanly shut down the previous time. If

```
       EXEC SQL
          COMMIT
       END-EXEC.

       IF SQLCODE EQUALS ZERO
      *      the work unit has been successfully commited
```

Figure 9.1 Completing a DB2 work unit.

not, DB2 will read back through the log files to process all updates that were not yet applied to the appropriate tablespace files.

The DB2 work unit management controls this process. The DB2 work unit commit procedure guarantees that the changes will take effect if the work unit successfully completes. Under TSO or the DB2 call attach mechanism, this is literally a COMMIT statement (Figure 9.1).

Under CICS or IMS, the SQL COMMIT statement cannot be issued. This is because both of these transaction processing managers have the option of managing their own data files, and the work unit integrity would be violated if the data could become inconsistent between the non-DB2 and DB2 data in a

```
EXEC CICS
    SYNCHPOINT
END-EXEC
```

Figure 9.3 CICS work unit synchronization.

transaction that updated both.

For the sake of brevity, the examples in this chapter will be in CICS, with IMS architectural differences pointed out. The individual CICS and IMS issues will be dealt with in subsequent chapters.

```
EXEC SQL
    ROLLBACK
END-EXEC
```

Figure 9.2 DB2 work unit roll out in TSO.

Since the transaction processing manager is functioning as a logical operating system, DB2 is a passive participant in the process. The transaction processing manager coordinates the action and notifies DB2 when to issue phase 1 and phase 2 commits or to roll back. DB2 simply reacts to the external command and notifies the coordinator when it completes. The transaction processing manager notifies DB2 when the logical unit of work ends. The program can explicitly request an end of a logical work unit, as in Figure 9.2.

```
EXEC CICS
     SYNCHPOINT ROLLBACK
END-EXEC
```

Figure 9.4 CICS roll out of a work unit.

But more often the work unit completion is a side effect of ending a pseudoconversation. Whenever a CICS transaction returns to the user in pseudoconversational mode, both in CICS and DB2 will commit their data. If a program successfully completes without ABENDing, DB2 will implicitly commit the last work unit.

There is a corresponding back-out procedure to roll out the action done within a unit of work. Under TSO or the DB2 call

Transfer $100 from SAVINGS to CHECKING

	CICS SAVING ACCOUNT	DB2 CHECKING ACCOUNTS
***time 1*:**	subtract $100	
***time 2*:**		add $100
***time 3*:**	SYNCPOINT	(coordinated COMMIT)

If data are saved in CICS but then DB2 loses its data the customer has lost $100 when transferring funds.

Figure 9.5 DB2 and CICS data coordination.

attach mechanism this is done with an explicit ROLLBACK statement, as shown in Figure 9.3.

In CICS or IMS the rollback statement cannot be issued, and is replaced with the transaction processing manager equivalent. In CICS this can be done as shown in Figure 9.4.

This is a very rarely used statement typically used only after the program detects an error. If a program or the system fails, DB2 will roll back all noncommitted work units.

Two-Phased COMMIT

When DB2 is interacting with another data manager, they cannot update data independently of each other. Even if CICS notifies DB2 to commit when it processes a SYNCHPOINT, what if DB2 encounters a problem, but CICS succeeds? The result would be two inconsistent data sources. (See Figure 9.5.)

Therefore, DB2 interacts with CICS and IMS through a mechanism that coordinates commit activity and recovery from system failures. This is a process of handshaking and verifying that the other has logged the updates appropriately. The procedure is called a two-phased commit.

A two-phased commit is a relatively simple process. Phase 1 involves:

- Writing the updates to the appropriate journal log files
- Appending a *phase 1 succeeded* record to the log
- Notifying the coordinator that phase 1 successfully completed

The coordinator is the originator of the request, which is either CICS or IMS. The coordinator can then initiate phase 2, which simply involves both parties writing a *phase 2 succeeded* record to their respective logs. If either or both parties fail, the data can be synchronized after they restart.

If the *phase 1 succeeded* record is not in the log, the database manager can assume that the work unit aborted before completion. The database manager can then roll back all the work unit's activity. If the *phase 1 succeeded* record was in the coordinator, it will query DB2 to verify that phase 1 succeeded, and if so both can commit. If either missed a complete phase 1, both will roll back. After both have completed phase 1, there is no reason not to commit the entire transaction.

The Second Stage of Commit Processing and System Independence

Why do we need the second-phase records at all? The phase 1 records identify the work units that succeeded. Shouldn't that be enough?

Consider a hypothetical single-phased commit relationship between DB2 and CICS. A problem would occur if the system failed, and DB2 was restored before CICS. In that situation, DB2 would not know the disposition of any of the data that only completed commit processing through phase 1. CICS may decide to keep or dispose of them — it is not under the control of DB2.

Without the phase 2 records, DB2 has to assume that all work units are in a transient state (called *in transit* in DB2). DB2 has to lock these data until CICS restarts because the data may be inconsistent.

By having phase 2 log records, DB2 understands that CICS will be capable of completing the work unit successfully. The point of the two-phase commit is to allow each data manager to restart without waiting for the other. If each has some processing that can be done independently of the other, this is to their significant advantage. Consider the consequences of DB2 being tied in knots by a CICS system that rarely uses DB2 services.

Automated Conversion to DB2

There are several products on the market that automate conversion from another database management system (including VSAM, IMS, and IDMS) to DB2. Both application and database are converted. Most of these products can convert a network database design into third normal form. This type of product is tempting from a theoretical point of view or as a management tool, but is problematic from a technical viewpoint.

The problem in this type of conversion is that the data structures do not work well in the converted form. Generally, data design will show its age after several passes of maintenance. Conversion is a radical form of maintenance. Except for the oddball application data design we find in fully normalized form, most data structures to be converted are:

- Very customized to the original DBMS facilities
- Physically designed to make use of specific environment characteristics
- Maintained enough to justify redesign in any case

This makes these conversion tools less appealing for mainstream applications. There are niche environments where they can be interesting. These include:

- Fairly new applications — for example, a shop that started conversion to IDMS and changed horses in midstream to DB2 conversion.
- Peripheral applications — the size of the entire program inventory of most shops is enormous. Most activity takes place in a small proportion of the programs that obviously must be reimplemented. But there are some applications that are rarely used, and the cost of reimplementation is unpleasant. A conversion tool can allow faster complete migration from another DBMS by converting these programs. Be careful about overlapping database structures. If shared data are involved, automated conversion can be a destructive choice.

DB2 and Other Database Management Systems

DB2 (version 2.3) has the ability to interact with other database management systems capable of two-phased commit. As of the writing of this book no products have demonstrated the capability. The same issues in DB2 interacting with CICS apply to the work units shared with the other database manager.

There are many ways in which an external (typically local area network) server can connect to DB2. The most prevalent means in use are the server connecting to DB2 using TSO or CICS and processing transactions emulating terminals. This allows the process to use the same facilities as the more traditional applications, simplifying use. The application can use LU6.2 or any of the host connect protocols to interface.

As the number of users and sophistication of the servers increase, we are seeing many problems with this approach. The overhead of TSO is significant, and it is not a reasonable platform for high transaction rates or high numbers of users. CICS adds some additional overhead of its own; additional, extraneous display services and the overhead of the CICS commit can have some impact on the application. The alternative is to write a server application that connects to DB2 using the call attach interface. This is unacceptable for anyone unwilling to get in the business of systems software manufacture.

Summary

Transaction processing attempts to support simple interactive processing as cheaply as possible. DB2 and transaction processing make an interesting pair. DB2 applications raise the ante and tend to be more complex than many traditional applications.

The initial DB2 design concentrated on support of conversational processing, where the programs run are more complex. It now supports most transaction processing applications. The strategy it uses is reducing the number of I/Os and converting I/O from random to sequential. The large buffers reduce the number of reads and writes. Processing data writes asynchronously at system checkpoints will reduce transaction delay.

DB2 is designed to support two-phased commits coordinated with another database manager. The two phases each consist of a record written to the log file and handshaking with the other participant. The two-phased commit allows each participant to restart without the other.

DB2 works with the transaction processing monitors CICS and IMS. Distributed requests from other DB2 or SQL/DS systems also can be considered in the same way. In all cases the initiator of the request, called the *coordinator*, is responsible for initiating all activity and correcting problems during recovery.

Thus, CICS or IMS will be the coordinator of DB2 transaction processing, and DB2 will commit and roll back based on commands from those systems. In a distributed database request, the originator of the request is the coordinator of the work units.

Review Questions

1. Can a SQL COMMIT be issued in a DB2/CICS program? Why?

2. Why is a two-phased commit needed in a DB2/CICS program? After all, a single phased commit would allow reestablishing consistency after a problem.

Answers to Review Questions

1. No, a SQL COMMIT cannot be issued by a DB2/CICS program. DB2 and CICS include a fixed protocol for their relationship in which CICS was designated the coordinator.
A DB2 program running under CICS has the option of updating CICS VSAM data. If the DB2 work unit was independent of the CICS work unit, their data could become inconsistent.

2. If they are synchronized by a two-phased commit, the coordinator of the request (CICS) can identify the status of the work unit on restart. Otherwise, DB2 as a participant could only defer all phase 1 completed work units until CICS restarted. This interdependence is unreasonable in many applications.

Chapter 10

DB2 and CICS

The DB2 interface with CICS is designed to manage two problems. First, CICS is the *client* for the data from the DB2 *server* and must coordinate processing. Both DB2 and CICS manage data, and a two-phase commit protocol is required. Second, CICS manages users as internally managed non-MVS tasks. DB2 deals with users on an MVS task basis. The CICS — DB2 attachment thus requires both a CICS task and a DB2 task to manage the connection. (An MVS task is a MVS system task coordinated with the CICS main task and scheduled by MVS, while a CICS task is scheduled by CICS itself.)

A CICS unit of recovery is implicitly completed when the transaction returns control to CICS. The transaction can explicitly end the unit of recovery by issuing a CICS SYNCPOINT command. Most transactions use the implicit option.

The ROLLBACK option of the SYNCPOINT command will undo the work in the unit of recovery. This can be used if an error is detected.

The normal SYNCPOINT operation can be useful in a high-concurrency environment. A CICS data query transaction can be logically grouped in three parts:

- Get data
- SYNCPOINT
- Process data, display results, and complete

This allows the transaction to release locks at the earliest possible point, allowing other users to update the data.

Some transactions use both CICS VSAM data and DB2 data, but only update data in one side. SYNCPOINT may be useful to increase concurrency in this fashion:

- Get CICS data
- SYNCPOINT
- Get DB2 data, update it, display results, and complete

The fact that the CICS data are not being updated may allow updating without harming data consistency. Be careful in this situation to analyze whether there is a cyclical indirect update. Thus, if the CICS data are updated by a transaction that reads DB2 data, SYNCPOINTs, and then updates the CICS data, the two transactions can together produce inconsistent data. If the updating is in one direction, this is not a problem.

The Resource Control Table (RCT) defines the parameters of the CICS DB2 connection. When the CICS attach facility is invoked, the RCT is instantiated into an internal CICS data structure, the Communication Control Table (CCT), containing a slot to store each possible DB2 connection.

CICS interacts with DB2 through *threads*, which are associations between transactions in CICS and activity in DB2. The connection between the two is established by a CICS *program list table* (PLT) definition, or by issuing the CICS DSNC STRT command in an active CICS region. The CICS region RCT entries define the available threads.

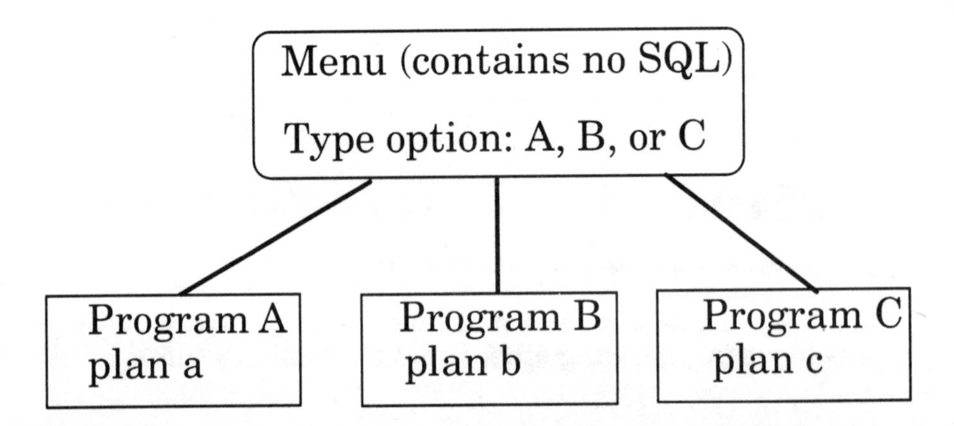

Figure 10.1 Plan selection in a menuing program.

A typical RCT will contain a few ENTRY threads dedicated to specific transactions and many POOL threads shared between various transactions. Another type of thread is a command (COMD) thread, used for the DSNC (operator command) transaction.

Threads may optionally be protected. CICS will reuse an unprotected thread only if a transaction is waiting for processing as the thread completes. A protected thread will wait for another transaction request.

DB2 offers the CICS application designer the option of dynamic plan switching. Dynamic plan switching allows a program to select the DB2 plan to use after a CICS SYNCPOINT. This is a convenient mechanism for simple menu applications, as shown in Figure 10.1

Dynamic plan selection allows the menu transaction to choose the program and plan to be used. This is useful in many circumstances, but is not appropriate for high-transaction-rate applications. DB2 cannot reuse threads for dynamic plan switching. High-transaction-rate applications involve over 10 transactions a minute.

Another option is to bind all programs into a single plan. This is a reasonable approach for transactions containing only a few programs. If the architecture of your applications seems to imply that only a few large plans will be used, be very careful. Plan size can be enormous. When many plans include the same program, the program skeleton plan will be copied repeatedly in the EDM pool, unless the shared components are in a shared PACKAGESET.

CICS: A Brief Review

CICS is the generic transaction processing manager for MVS. It requires no strong central control and no careful planning. It is easy to develop applications in CICS. Often CICS applications have database structures that are extremely denormalized to customize the data for a specific application. This often correlates to the type of fast development done in CICS.

With this legacy, anyone in the early stages of DB2 use in a traditionally CICS environment should worry about data customization.

The CICS connecting mechanism to DB2 associates a single DB2 subsystem to the CICS region at any given time. The association is managed through a CICS table, the Resource Control Table (RCT). CICS tables are parameters the systems programmer sets up which CICS uses to manage internal resources. The CICS tables have no conceptual relationship with DB2 tables, which are means of storing arbitrary formatted data.

There are two modes of establishing threads to DB2 from CICS. The RCT identifies these as ENTRY threads dedicated to a specific transaction or as POOL threads that can be shared. CICS will keep entry threads between invocations of the associated transaction, eliminating the overhead of thread creation. Pool threads can be reused only when an associated transaction is waiting for a thread just as a previous invocation of the same transaction completes.

The standard practice is to allocate ENTRY threads to those transactions that run repeatedly (many times a minute) for as many threads as are typically used. The entry threads are expensive in memory and system performance, and it is generally not advisable to keep threads without activity to justify them.

Entry threads may be used in exceptional cases where the transaction rate is lower to reduce the cost of thread creation. This is especially prevalent in early use of DB2. Usually this approach is unjustified and acts as an impediment to general system performance.

Once used, entry threads will maintain their connection to DB2. This allows *thread reuse*, where another transaction will be processed without the overhead of establishing the connection to DB2. The gain is significant in small, frequently used applications, such as high-volume data entry applications.

QMF as a CICS Conversational Application

There has been much user demand for QMF under CICS. IBM has questioned the wisdom of this. QMF is not by any stretch of the imagination a transaction processing application. In most shops it has a relatively low-volume use. Performance characteristics of these users fluctuate wildly. Most applications built in QMF are inexorably linked with TSO facilities, intermixing QMF with CLISTs and ISPF. QMF version 3.3 requires REXX to perform the calculation functions.

There are several reasons for wanting QMF under CICS. The most common problem is the unavailability of TSO in most production systems: the systems configuration (i.e., the way the system is defined and corporate culture) prevented use of QMF. Other reasons have included the overhead of TSO, the problems in managing TSO security, and the performance control complications in TSO.

The conversational QMF facilities provide the worst of both worlds for most environments. Conversational CICS applications are not greyhounds; they are slow and cumbersome, with high overhead. The performance diversity of the applications is much harder to control in CICS than under TSO. The system is best for those shops that need it for cultural reasons.

Conditionals in Procedures

From a technical point of view, the enhanced procedure facilities in QMF are more interesting than the CICS interface. They would have been trivial to add in the past. Perhaps this has not been done to prevent unfavorable comparison with other query processing or decision support or 4GL tools.

Conditional processing in QMF procedures is necessary to allow CICS applications to be processed. Under TSO the same processing can be done using a CLIST and the QMF command interface (CI) facilities.

Summary

DB2 and CICS interface through the resource control table (RCT), which is a CICS table. Each CICS region can only interface to a single DB2 subsystem at a time.

The RCT identifies the plan associated with each transaction. CICS developers have the option of using dynamic plan switching, in which the RCT identifies a program which will select the appropriate plan. Dynamic plan switching programs choose a plan for transaction processing and can change plans at each CICS SYNCPOINT.

The RCT is where CICS threads to DB2 and their numbers are defined. ENTRY threads are dedicated to a single transaction and are intended for the (exceptional) high-volume transaction processing. POOL threads can be shared between transactions and constitute the bulk of all CICS threads.

Most CICS applications are pseudoconversational. It is possible to develop conversational DB2 CICS applications. Conversational CICS is an awkward option. The CICS — QMF product is an example of this.

Review Questions

1. When should ENTRY threads be defined? How many should be created?

2. What are the DB2 options for structuring an application that consists of a menu that is used to select one of a dozen distinct application functions?

Answers to Review Questions

1. ENTRY threads are appropriate for high-volume transactions where the transaction rate is at least one every few seconds. In the case of very high-volume transactions, enough entry threads should be allocated to support normal concurrent load.

If peak demand is much higher than normal load, a combination of ENTRY and POOL threads should be used. If the overhead of thread creation is unreasonable, more ENTRY threads can be allocated. This final rationale is used more often than justified in practice.

2. The plan for a menu application that can select from among subfunctions can be either a plan for the entire application or a dynamic plan selection program. A final alternative is to use PACKAGESETs within the program.

Chapter 11

DB2 and IMS

IMS is a complicated environment. It has evolved in a haphazard way over its long history. Often, the facilities available seem arbitrarily chosen. IMS has a data communications and control component (IMS/DC) and a database management system (IMS/DB).

There is a unifying principle. All the facilities deal with centrally designed high-volume applications. The facilities are hard to use, but offer many design options to manage systems sustaining very high workloads. IMS database and application design is usually carefully thought out. IMS shops tend to have aggressive central database administration. (This type of database administration is closer to systems programming, whereas DB2 DBAs tend to be more aligned with programmers and users.)

IMS/DC programs are either message processing programs that are purely on-line, or batch message processing programs which are batch programs that have the option to interface with terminals through IMS/DC. There is a high-performance variant for transaction processing called IMS fast path. Another option is IMS batch, which runs IMS/DC independent jobs in standard batch queues.

DB2 will support all these environments. IMS batch and batch message processing programs have the capability of updating nonlogged files. This option allows generating data results that are not recoverable in the event of a system failure and cannot guarantee synchronization with DB2. Not logging can be a valid option for some batch jobs that never commit, and for which when a problem occurs, the data can be regenerated and the job restarted.

IMS programs have an awkward capability of accessing multiple DB2 subsystems (but only one at a time for each transaction). The common use for this is logging updates to a decision support subsystem, but doing the updates in another DB2 transaction processing subsystem. The availability of the IMS data propagator product reduces the justification for this processing.

IMS and Threads to DB2

IMS message processing regions will normally not reuse threads, but can coincidentally if a transaction is waiting just as another completes. Wait for input (WFI) and fast path regions process only a single transaction each. As long as there are queued input transactions, the thread can be reused.

IMS Dprop

It has always been axiomatic that a dual database strategy is a last resort. Multiple databases are a tactical solution that would cause enormous effort in replicated work, and enormous cost in duplicated function. This environment was forced on many larger shops in the 1970s and 1980s. The multiple DBMS were used because of a lack of function in the initial database management system selected, a required application only running on another DBMS, or various forms of corporate consolidation.

The bitter lesson these companies have learned is that a multiple-DBMS shop is indeed an expensive and unwieldy organization. The shop pays for extra overhead in:

- Less integrated data, limiting application functionality
- Extra staff costs in preserving the technology
- In general, sabotaging the data control function

Multiple database management systems will offer the user the worst of both worlds, while forcing that user to pay for both.

Ever since IBM decided to develop a follow-on to IMS, the question of how to deal with smooth migration from IMS to DB2 became a fundamental issue. The major problem is how to simplify managing a mixed environment with both IMS and DB2 controlling parts of the central data. This is a vital requirement: these shops are the most committed to IBM strategy. IBM has to keep these users happy.

Furthermore, if a DB2 migration will not solve those application backlog and cost issues that initially motivated the migration, downsizing and alternative architectures become very appealing. IBM clearly needs a means to ease the problems of a dual database strategy.

The problems of maintaining dual database management systems include hardware and software effort issues, staff coordination issues, and integration issues.

Hardware and software work increases in this environment because of the replication of effort. Multiple DBMSs will tend to perform less well than a single large one. The effort to control those DBMSs in relation to each other (if they reside on the same machine) is a significant overhead of the multiple-DBMS strategy. Since the size of the machine determines software costs, we do not just pay twice for the duplicated function, but we pay more for the larger CPU involved and use the DBMS services less well.

Staff coordination issues become complicated with extra software function. Training is expensive, and expertise only slowly achieved. Multiple DBMSs result in a lower cumulative level of expertise in each, and enormous scheduling problems in assigning area experts to each environment. This results in lower technical merit of applications and often forces shops to completely "de-specialize." Expertise in a particular area of business function may not be feasible when staff is not allowed to specialize on a particular business function.

Integration issues are the heart of the problem. Whenever multiple DBMSs are in use, some data are sure to reside on the wrong one. The simple division between the DBMSs also creates other discontinuities.

Often there is a reconciliation between the DBMSs — perhaps nightly. We poorly manage data shared by both DBMSs. Each DBMS stays consistent within itself, but is consistent with the other only immediately after reconciliation. Correcting this problem can typically require significant modification of all involved applications.

IBM clearly needs to ease the effort of its customers caught in a dual database strategy between IMS and DB2. This is necessary not just to reduce the overhead, but to allow the migration. Most users of both IMS and DB2 have the great majority of their operational data in IMS, and use DB2 more for peripheral and decision support activities. This is because we use operational data in multiple applications, and mixed DBMS applications have serious flaws.

CASE tools, or any other sort of sophisticated development software, rarely (and poorly) support mixed applications. The power of each facility negates the other; we cannot do a logical join between DB2 and IMS data. The number of components increases and the likelihood of failure increases. Logistically, it combines the weaknesses of both DB2 and IMS. This constraining of DB2 due to the awkwardness of IMS serves neither well.

This problem has continuously led IBM to attempt to find a means for natural coexistence between IMS and DB2. The initial IBM attempt to build an MVS relational database management system (the Eagle project) attempted to build a relational front end to an extended IMS DBMS. Later, IBM developed a program product for its Japanese customers that propagated data from IMS to DB2. This was a different product from the IMS Dataprop facility developed to deal with the same problem.

The problems in propagating data are the costs. These overheads include duplicating the data file size to store data in both DBMSs, and the double overhead of processing the data update requests for each transaction on both systems. IBM is acutely aware of these; the VSAM transparency product, which has similar goals and even less DASD overhead, has had little success. The basic problem is that to keep both DBMSs synchronized, all processing must take place during the transaction, in effect doubling the cost at the point of peak demand. With this amount of overhead, users may choose dangerous shortcuts that cause later problems.

To allow close integration between DB2 and IMS, the requirements are:

- Propagation of data within the unit of work (synchronously) from IMS to DB2. This is the major first step, since most operational data are in IMS. Synchronous data propagation is expensive, but guarantees the consistency of the data.

- Propagation of data on a when needed basis (asynchronously) from IMS to DB2. This reduces the cost of the propagation. The work can be bundled into blocks to reduce the total amount of CPU and I/O needed. The machine effort can be scheduled for low-demand periods.
- Propagating data from DB2 to IMS both synchronously and asynchronously. As DB2 operational applications grow, and as pieces of operational applications begin migrating to DB2, applications need to access data from existing IMS applications. This is not a functional improvement but rather a means to convert parts of applications with no impact on other parts.

Summary

IMS applications are notable for their rigidity and strong central design. DB2 is generally not a significant enhancement in this type of environment, but can reduce the cost of application development somewhat and add significant decision support capabilities.

Combining DB2 and IMS requires much money, planning, and strategic consistency. The IMS Dataprop facility allows data transfer from IMS, but is a program, not a solution to the complex problem of managing two database systems.

Review Question

1. Can an IMS to DB2 conversion of an entire shop be done one application at a time?

Answer to Review Question

1. An entire IMS shop can be converted to DB2 one application at a time, but there are problems in this approach. The basic issue is whether the applications are being redesigned or converted. Simply being able to coordinate recovery between DB2 and IMS is not enough.

In most cases, an information services department is justifiably unwilling to do an expensive conversion unless there is added value given to the user. Thus, most conversions include a large degree of *reengineering*, or redesigning the application.

Redesign generally involves radically changing the interfaces between applications. The one-at-a-time approach makes this awkward. The new design has to include one of the following.

- Using the same interfaces, an option that severely restricts the redesign.
- Adding temporary (so-called scaffolding) code to the old applications to allow them to interface with the new ones. This option can require enormous amounts of code changes and retesting.
- Adding temporary scaffolding code to the new applications to allow them to interface temporarily with the old applications. This option may generate enormous amounts of code intended to be thrown out after the conversion.

A particular problem with this approach is a changing database design. In many cases the premise of the logical design changes, the schedule of processing differs, or use patterns are inconsistent. All of these options create conflicts between the new and old; often the scaffolding code grows to become the bulk of the new application.

In this common situation, the redesign can be partially abandoned. Another approach is to admit the problem with the phased change. This strategy calls for building a temporary replacement application (presumably with some recoverable code) and planning to reimplement it after the set of interfacing applications is completed.

Chapter 12

DB2 Application Techniques

Integrated Applications without Data Modeling

Data modeling is a powerful technique to provide a coherent organization for your data. Most applications are built without the benefit of data modeling support. This has profound implications in terms of our ability to provide an effective long-term platform for applications. Consider the fact that most applications built in DB2 reimplement existing function with enhancements, and the reason for migrating the application is poor data structure support for the functions.

It seems that we are caught in a bind: expected either to reiterate the mistakes of the past or to model our business surreptitiously. There are flaws in both these directions. Ignoring the external issues is too parochial, and modeling without high executive mandate is untenable. The answer is to design in the capabilities for growth.

Consider denormalization as a symptom of this problem. Denormalization is an attempt to optimize data structures to support a specific process at the cost of reducing flexibility and increasing the potential for error and inconsistency. For each particular application, denormalization has enormous appeal; in the long-term life of a data structure it looks like an ugly adulteration. This is a metaphor for the general process of data structure design: Balancing the local and short-term issues with the commonweal. This also shows the problem that when we lack of a useful data model, we are left guessing what is the context.

At this point many of you are probably saying to yourself, "Sure, we don't have a data model, but I know who's using what and where — I'm carrying a data model in my head." Not having a data model clearly does not imply operating in a vacuum.

What a data model does is to externalize these decisions, making some choices explicit, where otherwise they would not be voiced. The model is a means of communication. It facilitates the informed election of the appropriate alternative by those who should be making the decisions. In lieu of this apparatus, many of these decisions are made late in the design phase, at ad-hoc crisis meetings.

This design-in-crisis pattern is a data processing tradition for smaller applications. Development of larger applications includes more early design effort, and more concern for the underpinnings. Smaller applications tend to avoid modeling because many aspects of data modeling have a fixed overhead, making modeling a small project cost as much as a big one.

Smaller and medium-sized applications have very strong justifications for modeling as well. Their common problems are:

- Interface issues
- Maintenance problems

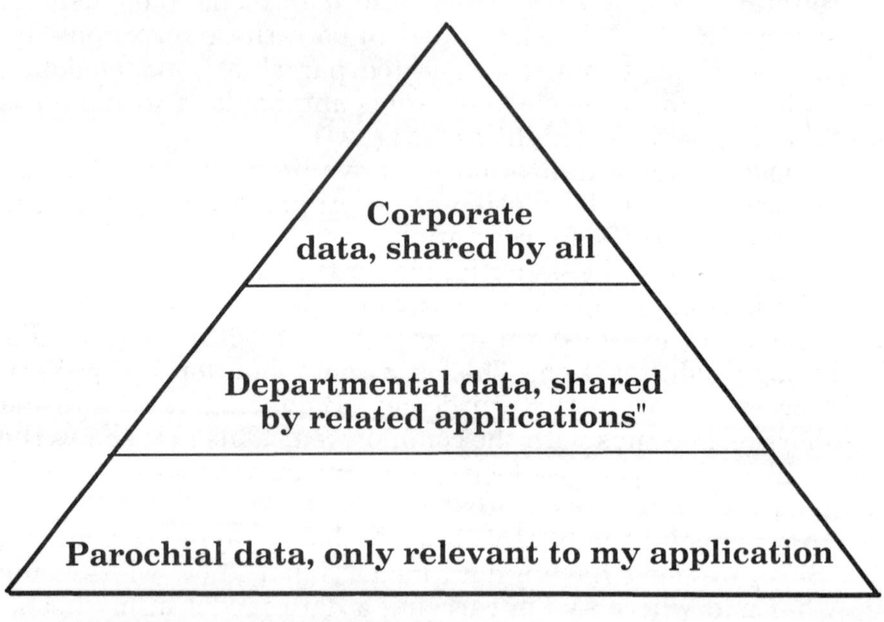

Figure 12.1 Three-tiered data use division.

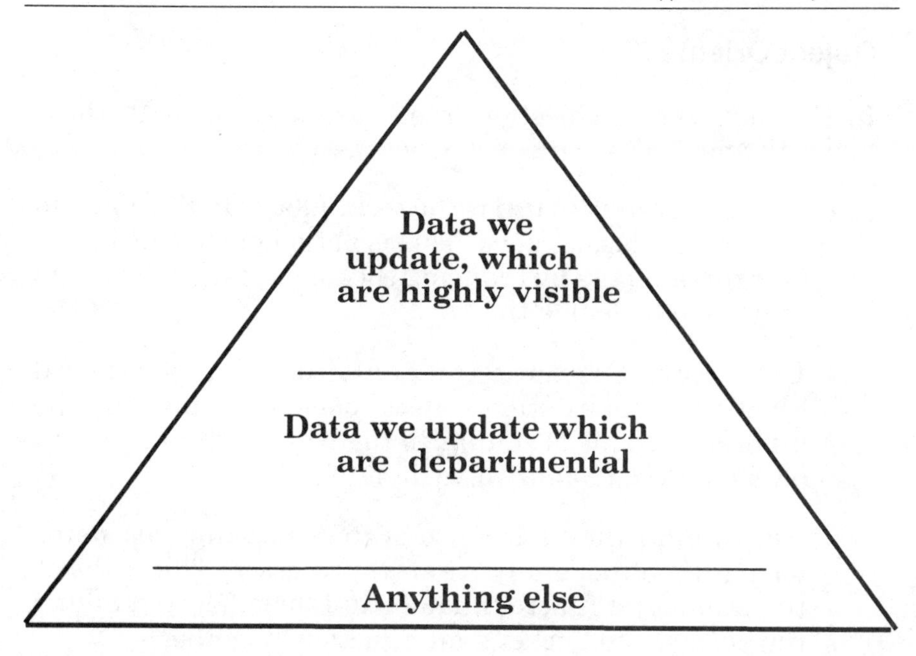

Figure 12.2 Update hierarchy: who changes what.

These considerations are exactly those which modeling attempts to correct. There are some aspects of data modeling that are less arduous, justifying their use in almost any scale new application development.

There is a lot that can be done without comprehensive full-scale data modeling. Almost any application deals with data in tiers, based on a logical hierarchy. There are several hierarchy options to choose from. Figure 12.1 shows an example of the default alternative. A similar diagram based on the degree of interrelationship between the application components is shown in Figure 12.2.

The advantage to the approach in Figure 12.2 is that we can disengage from any data that we are not directly responsible for changing. Data structures containing data changed by many applications in this kind of environment are very stable: no one has the resources to change them if the risk is having the entire pyramid collapse on them.

This means that we can concentrate our efforts of the top tier of the pyramid (and use any extra time to analyze the second). The third layer is the least sensitive; whatever we do to it will offer the least amount of overall benefit.

Object Oriented?

In the pure sense, object-oriented systems deal with three major themes.

- **Data encapsulation** is the technique of hiding data an application doesn't need. This isolation makes life easier for programmers by reducing the amount of information they have to deal with.
- **Inheritance** is the technique of deriving specialized functions from existing general ones by noting only the differences. This is similar to the way we think: a *small brown* dog is a qualified variant of a dog.
- **Polymorphism** is the use of the same function name for multiple (hopefully similar) processes. This reduces the number of function names to remember and allows the designer to bucket similar actions together.

Object-oriented systems attempt to present the data in the context of the data's *behavior*. This is a powerful idea in presenting a functional view of the stored component of systems.

This seems, at first glance, to be an enhancement of the relational model of data, adding more semantic context to the data. In practice, the models seem in direct conflict.

The conflict stems from the tight interrelationship that shows up in some resultant models. The result of most pure object-oriented design is a network model database design. It may be argued that this network model is based on the usage semantics of the data rather than an attempt to customize the data to an application, but the design will clearly not be relational.

Cooperative Processing Applications Concepts

The premise of cooperative processing is that corporate data belongs where it can be centrally managed, and local processing is the best means to interact with the user. Cooperative processing (also called coprocessing) is a form of client-server architecture.

Types of facilities

Any type of computer applications programming is limited to the development tools available. Cooperative processing is defined by the programs used to allow application development. As such, it still falls short, as of the writing of this book.

It is much more expensive to develop and manage applications in a coprocessing mode than on a single machine. This overhead is mostly due to the inadequacy of most existing tools. Most available software only partially solves coprocessing application development issues.

Screen scrapers

Screen scrapers and *frontware* are names for the front-end tools that can take standard mainframe computer interfaces (typically 3270 screen maps) and allow smaller computers to reformat and reprocess the data. These tools allow parsing out the data, and act as general-purpose application development tools that use these data. Typically the front end runs on a personal computer.

In conjunction with the processing facilities of a local processor, these products allow putting new faces on old applications. The front end can be fixed without tampering with the mainframe application. The user interface can be made more flexible. Application front ends can be customized for each user. An example product of this type is Easel (Easel Inc., also sold by IBM).

Simulated application integration

A fun use of frontware is to merge data from multiple applications. A single front end program can concurrently log into an IMS application and a CICS application, issue query transactions to both, and combine the results. Sometimes this can offer the function of an integrated application. These applications require very careful analysis to see if the different system's data can work together. In many cases data incompatibility makes the results blatantly inaccurate.

Knowledge worker applications

Most data entry applications solve their problems effectively using simple terminal interaction. IS is moving to provide applications for more sophisticated users. These users have more complex and dynamic requirements than simple data entry or query transactions.

An example is a stock analyst with a half dozen terminals in front of him or her. The analyst has several data sources, both within the company and from external data vendors. This forces the analyst to integrate the data manually. A frontware application can integrate the data, and only display the exception data. Exceptions can be defined by the analyst. Data can be displayed in a graphical format.

This type of application is ideal for coprocessing. The application needs the quality of data provided by central services and the interaction provided by the PC.

SAA: Fitting Pieces Together

Concepts, definition, and rationale

SAA, the IBM Systems Application Architecture, was developed when customers convinced IBM that the inconsistencies in the computer environments were unacceptable. Open computing, the desire to move applications between different (IBM manufactured) computers, and the need to develop applications with pieces running on different types of computers require standards. IBM acknowledged the need, and set out to define those standards.

Platforms and their characteristics

SAA is an umbrella containing operating systems, database management systems, and communications and application environments. The SAA operating systems are:

- MVS for large central corporate computing
- VM for central timesharing computing
- AS/400 for central departmental, office, and factory floor automation

- OS/2 for local workstation, small office automation, and graphical computing
- Presumably AIX will join the collection for technical computing

SAA includes features for several of the standard processing requirements. CPIC (Common Programming Interfaces) allows for remote procedure calls, shipping requests in a more sophisticated manner than CICS *function shipping*. LU6.2 is a standard means of communicating between these platforms where no platform is in control (*peer-to-peer*).

The first major influence of SAA is the user interface. Software following the display standards

- CUI — the Common User Interface for character mode displays
- GUI — the Graphical User Interface for bit-mapped displays

is already commonplace.

Summary

DB2 is part of a mix of new products, technologies, and techniques. Data modeling is a long known process that has gained tremendous impetus recently. Data modeling is the best means to allow for integrating applications.

Cooperative processing is a design strategy where the data are mainly stored on the host (presumably in DB2). Most nondatabase processing takes place on a local computer.

Object-oriented design attempts to build applications from components in ways we can easily visualize. Unnecessary data are hidden. Functions develop from basic building blocks in a natural progression.

Review Question

1. What application problems may arise from integrating an IMS and a CICS application by having a coprocessing appli-

cation act as a front end connecting to both and merging the data?

Answer to Review Question

1. The applications involved may have data that are not well integrated. This may mean that the designers have to analyze the data more thoroughly than in a standard application. The applications may also have data that simply cannot be combined.

If data consolidation between the two source systems is inconsistent, it may be ludicrous to merge their data. In many cases, analysis for such systems demonstrates such inconsistent data that the results would be useless.

In some cases, data inconsistencies can be detected and managed by the application. An example would be data that are time stamped when changed. In some other cases the consistency is less significant, especially if much data are summarized.

Chapter 13

The Design of DB2

The definition of the DB2 architecture came about in the late 1970s. At that time IBM was losing IMS sales in direct competition with IDMS (then from Cullinet, Inc.) This posed a threat to the IBM sales strategy of controlling client accounts, since users of non-IBM software applications had more available migration options to other hardware platforms.

At that point interesting things started to happen on the hardware side. Memory was getting much cheaper. CPU cycles were getting much cheaper, and CPU speed was increasing rapidly to the point that designers worried about reaching the theoretical limit of processor clock speed. DASD was getting faster, but at a significantly slower rate than semiconductors. Mainframe users were increasing capacity needs by almost a third every year.

At the same time, traditional database management systems would not be able to compete well in this changing hardware environment. Most standard application designs for IBM mainframe computers are attempts to make the most of a constrained environment. Rules of "good citizenship," "minimizing working-set size," and such were enforced very well. When applications were optimized for a restricted environment, they would react poorly to adding more resources. Most applications were I/O-constrained, and adding faster CPUs would not help. Adding additional memory would often hurt performance by increasing the length of chains to be searched.

A follow-on to IMS had to be designed in that environment. The hardware considerations demanded huge multiprocessor mainframes. I/O-bound programs do not benefit from additional CPU capacity. In particular, random I/O speed cannot significantly improve. But memory was getting cheaper.

IBM was developing the guts of an IMS follow-on product before beginning developing the actual DB2 program. The product's major I/O characteristics were the same as those of DB2 today, which is not surprising since they have been incorporated into the DB2 product. The major innovation of the software was the ability to exploit enormous amounts of real memory. Efficient memory management algorithms prevent additional memory from adding overhead. How can the memory be used?

Memory can best be used to reduce I/O delay. DB2 uses buffer pools to allow for three performance advantages:

- **Buffering:** Simply having a large buffer containing many pages that are kept in the buffer and aged out in a least-recently-used order allows frequently accessed pages to be logically read repeatedly without repeating the physical read. This is especially useful for frequently accessed data such as data "hot spots," index root and nonleaf pages, and space map pages.

- **Read ahead** (also called *prefetch* or *asynchronous reads*): If the application is reading forward in a file, DB2 can simply continue reading beyond the bounds of the application request. The next request can be fulfilled from memory. Also, DB2 can read large multiple page blocks of data, which is more efficient in I/O and CPU time than many single-page reads.

- **Deferred write:** Updated pages are often updated again both by the initial updater and by others. Each update is recorded in the DB2 log. The log is always sequentially processed. DB2 will normally delay writing updates until it reaches a system checkpoint. By deferring writes, DB2 accomplishes two things: frequently updated pages are only written occasionally, and even then the pages are written in sequential order asynchronously to the application.

This design for large bufferpools reduces the I/O delay of programs as long as DB2 has very large bufferpools. DB2 intentionally converts random I/Os, synchronous to the applications, into sequential I/Os processed asynchronously. Random I/O is mostly dependent on the slow disk seek time. Sequential I/O minimizes this I/O bottleneck, and can often be made faster by providing faster I/O channels with faster transfer rates, which is a simpler technical challenge.

The entire architecture of DB2 is thus based on the premise that a database management system must not have limits. A traditional rule of thumb is to allow about a third of the machine cycles for a database management system. Older software configurations could not absorb much more capacity because they were intentionally I/O-bound. DB2 lacks such worries. DB2 frequently surprises (but rarely delights) new users discovering how efficiently DB2 can exploit hardware. This is not because it is inefficient. The opposite is true.

The goal of the design of DB2 is to exploit all available resources effectively. Add more memory to DB2 — and DB2 performance increases linearly. Add a faster CPU, or more CPUs to DB2 — and DB2 performance increases linearly. The system seems to absorb whatever is offered.

This is a profound philosophical point. DB2 is intended to use the available resources most effectively. This clashes with traditional designs based on minimally affecting the system.

DB2 Address Spaces

The minimal configuration of DB2 has three private address spaces. Two have a prefix of the DB2 subsystem identifier, a code of up to 4 characters stored in SYS1.PARMLIB in the DB2 installation process. The default identifier is DSN (DSN lacks meaning; IBM centrally establishes a three-letter combination unique to each product with which to prefix names, preventing name conflict between software components). The two major components are DSNMSTR and DSNDBM1. DSNMSTR is the heart of DB2, dealing with the world as a relational database management system should. DSNDBM1 is a database file server controlled by the master program.

The third component, the IRLM, is not a DB2 subsystem per se. IRLM stands for IMS Resource Locking Manager. The system was built to allow multiple IMS subsystems to share resources at a finer scope of granularity than the MVS GRS (Global Resource Serialization) could provide.

There is a fourth, optional address space, the distributed data facility (DDF). This is the DB2 network file server management program. The program acts a coordinator of resources and as the manager of access to VTAM. This separation into separate address spaces is partially an artifact of the 16 megabyte limit of MVS/SP, and partially a means for IBM to internally manage its developers.

DB2 Function Division

DB2 was designed as a collection of interacting discrete functions which manage most processing internally. In many ways, this design resembles an object-oriented system design. The large collection of *agents* operate as internal functions or as discrete MVS tasks. This design structure is typical of the more recent design methodologies within IBM (remember that DB2 was completely rewritten for version 2). The advantages of this structure are:

- Simpler use of *more processors* as multiple-processor configurations become the norm.
- *Isolating separate DB2 system development functions*, which interrelate through completely defined data interfaces and task rendezvous.
- *Damage control*. Since any internal failure will be compartmentalized, this eases the effort required to make the total system resilient to failure of a component

Some of the general idea of agents can be seen by reviewing the list of DB2 error codes in Figure 13.1. In IBM style, DB2 return codes are a fullword (it has to fit into a single register), containing two halfwords. The IBM *DB2 Messages and Codes* manual lists the codes in hexadecimal format. The first halfword contains an agent identification, and the second contains a sequentially assigned error code for that agent. The figure shows some examples of the error codes, and their function identifier.

Error code	Function	Error Number
00E2 0001	Storage manager	0001
00D9 3012	Recovery manager	3012

Figure 13.1 Sample DB2 error codes.

DB2 Interaction with Application Programs

DB2 functions as a formal MVS subsystem, making it act as an imitation operating system. This is important because the threads connecting DB2 to application programs have to be resolved if the application fails. MVS notifies all formal subsystems of task ABENDs. When DB2 sees that an application has failed, it can roll the last work unit back, and cleanly terminate the application's connection to DB2.

There are many address spaces involved in even the simplest of service requests. DB2 interfaces across address spaces using cross memory addressing for transfer of large quantities of data. Smaller amounts of data can be more simply transferred using MVS SRB services.

DB2 operates in different address spaces than the application programs accessing DB2 data using SQL. The programs are attached by *threads*, which are logical interrelationships between DB2 and the application program.

For every thread created, two interrelated tasks are built. DB2 will create an MVS task called an *allied agent* for every thread created. The task simplifies the interface between DB2 and the DB2 service user in several ways:

- The thread becomes a mechanism to *charge back* activity to the associated task. All processing done synchronously by the application will be done by the allied agent and charged to the application. This simplifies the management of DB2.

- Because of the chargeback, the allied agent task runs at the *scheduling priority* of the user task. This allows user interaction with DB2 to be consistent with their other activity, and limits the need for the DB2 product to include operating system and queuing facilities.

- The task independence isolates one application's problems (such as application ABENDs) from other applications.

EDM Pools

DB2 uses the Environment Description Manager (EDM) pool to store the access plans to the data and the structure of the data. The DB2 directory (DSNDB01) is the secondary storage area for these objects. DB2 uses its standard access methods to read the data into the bufferpools (the tablespaces are defined in buffer pool BP0). From there, they are moved to the EDM pool, and managed by a separate least-recently-used algorithm to age out objects.

Cursor tables

The access paths are stored in objects called cursor tables. Table in this context does not refer to the DB2 table; the objects are not stored in true DB2 tables. The objects are stored in a base format called *skeleton cursor tables.* Each access to the plan by a new thread causes creation of an additional (initially blank) copy of the data portion.

Early versions of DB2 generated plans as true object code. This was efficient, but the DB2 designers were planning a system that was less a transaction processor and more associated with batch jobs and interactive, dynamic SQL queries. They did not expect a high number of static SQL paths to be referenced concurrently. Early DB2 users would constantly hit the wall of enormous EDM pools taking over their systems (and would frequently reach a limit of plan size that has since been eliminated).

The design changed to a threaded interpretive format, somewhat similar to the Pascal language P-code or other interpretive languages. This code is not available to the user (except as hexadecimal dumps for the curious). The access path refers to access methods such as tablespace scan, literals embedded into the queries, variables passed to the query from the allied agent when the program is executed, and database objects that are referenced through the DBD.

Database Descriptor

The Database Descriptor, or DBD, consists of data describing objects in DB2. The DBD content replicates data in the DB2 catalog (SYSIBM.SYSTABLES, etc.). The difference is that the DBD is a tree structure (from the database down) of objects in the database.

The DBD is used by plans to refer to the objects contained within it. DB2 uses the DBD for internal management of its data. It is often more efficient to keep this data in memory in the DBD in the EDM pool, rather than to replicate parts of the information many times in the plans or to access catalog data frequently.

A DBD can be re-created from the catalog information through the REPAIR DBD utility. This is significant if the directory or catalog has to be reconstructed because of system problems. The REPAIR DBD TEST option will validate the DBD against the catalog information. A DBD corresponds on a one-to-one basis with a DB2 database. The repair process can be repeated for each database that may be damaged.

Summary

DB2 was designed to use large bufferpools to convert random and synchronous I/O activity into more sequential asynchronous I/Os. This is done to use the benefits of cheaper hardware and to alleviate the languidly slow increases in I/O processing speed.

Review Questions

1. What conditions would make a smaller bufferpool reasonable in DB2?

2. Why doesn't DB2 embed plans into application programs?

Answers to Review Questions

1. If processing is so random in nature that buffering is not useful, the bufferpool size becomes almost irrelevant. A case in point is certain types of transaction processing.

If the triggers DB2 uses to select appropriate data for asynchronous reads err, the large bufferpool will not help. A smaller bufferpool will reduce the amount of data read in a single prefetch. This can help if the amount of data the reader is interested in is less than the maximal size of read ahead.

A transaction processing program generally does not want prefetch enabled. If the application does not intentionally disable it, unintentional read ahead may occur, wasting system resources. A program can reduce inappropriate prefetch by using the SELECT statement FOR FETCH OF 10 ROWS qualifier or by restricting the qualifying data rather than making the buffers small. A very small bufferpool can cause many indirect problems, such as making it hard to read plan skeleton cursor tables into the EDM pool.

2. DB2 does not embed plans into application programs mainly as a convenience for the IBM language developers. There is a security or database consistency issue if there is risk of malicious or erroneous changing of the data access paths. Otherwise, there is no reason not to have the plan as part of a program.

In fact, there would be many benefits to having the plan as part of the program. There is no reason to control storage management for both parts separately (but the EDM pool would still be needed for DBDs and cursor table initiations). Importantly, the combination would simplify optimization of database access and program compilation.

Chapter 14

How Many DB2 Subsystems Are Needed?

DB2 functions as a formal subsystem of MVS. It is possible to install multiple complete DB2 systems in a single MVS. Each is referred to as a *DB2 subsystem*.

The number of DB2 subsystems at many sites seems arbitrarily chosen. In earlier and smaller machines, CICS or IMS regions were created reluctantly and only after extensive research. DB2 became popular as these regions tended to proliferate.

CICS is very sensitive to new applications, and requires significant tuning (involving stopping and restarting the re-

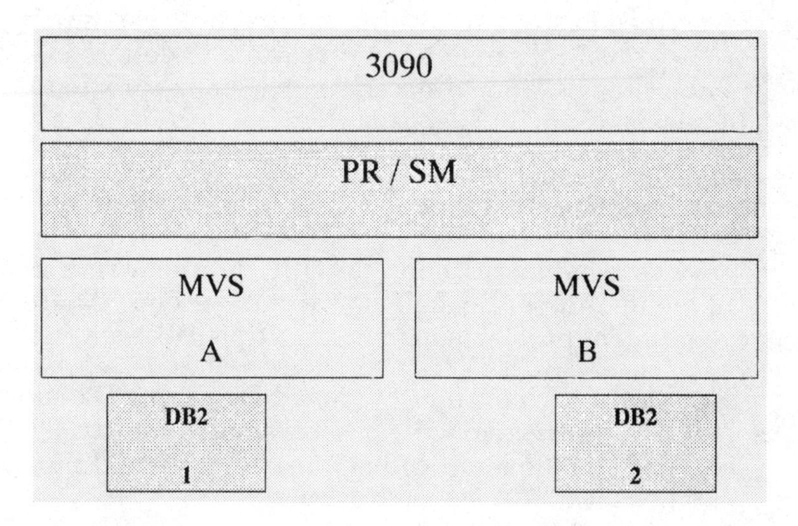

Figure 14.1 A powerful mainframe divided. A partitioned mainframe under PR/SM. Multiple MVS systems can also run under VM as guests or, in Amdahl machines as domains.

gion) whenever applications change. IMS must be cycled to make any changes. These are ample justifications for the proliferation of CICS and IMS regions. If resources are available, sites are tempted to create more regions.

DB2 does not offer as clear a rationale to build more subsystems. The temptation to add new CICS regions may carry over into being the reason for the number of DB2 subsystems at some sites.

Multiple DB2 subsystems have inherent disadvantages in their partitioning of the data between them, and add system overhead. They allow some advantages in management over a single DB2 subsystem. We are currently experiencing a trend of logically partitioning large machines into smaller ones (see Figure 14.1). This "divide and conquer" strategy is useful for some specific system management. It is unpleasant to pay the additional cost for very large mainframe MIPS, only to partition them.

Notice that partitioning may be creating multiple MVS systems or multiple DB2 subsystems. The focus of this discussion is to try to convince system administrators to give as much weight to creating new DB2 subsystems as they would to creating a new MVS system.

Creating a new DB2 subsystem is a political act. The cost of changing an existing environment is enormous. New parts can be defined easily but nothing created ever goes away.

There are good reasons and bad reasons to define multiple DB2 subsystems. Unfortunately, subsystems are too often created for no compelling reason.

Multiple DB2 Subsystems

It is easy to have more than one DB2 on a machine. Many environments support a half dozen subsystems. There are some significant problems in using multiple DB2 subsystems:

- There is a high system overhead for each DB2 subsystem. The subsystem will absorb a small quantity of CPU, an enormous amount of both real and virtual memory, and also some DASD and tape overhead.

- There is significant logistics overhead in maintaining data in separate places. The implication of multiple subsystems used for production is that some data are not where you want them. (The option of using a distributed database is available, if the current distributed database limitations are not incapacitating.)

- There is a high human resource cost in controlling and administering each DB2 subsystem. This effort includes not only system administration, but also duplicated operations staff, duplicated activity, and additional security administration. There are systems programming complications in dealing with more system components. Also, there is an enormous amount of DBA activity required in managing multiple subsystems. The DBAs have additional work in copying objects across subsystems. Applications can add complex needs to integrate the various subsystems. Having multiple production DB2 subsystems makes it hard to integrate schedules and data. (See Figure 14.2.) Often this integration is not well done.

- There is a major philosophical conflict between the premise of a logically centralized database, with all the associated costs, and building multiple production DB2 subsystems. Central databases are expensive but can be

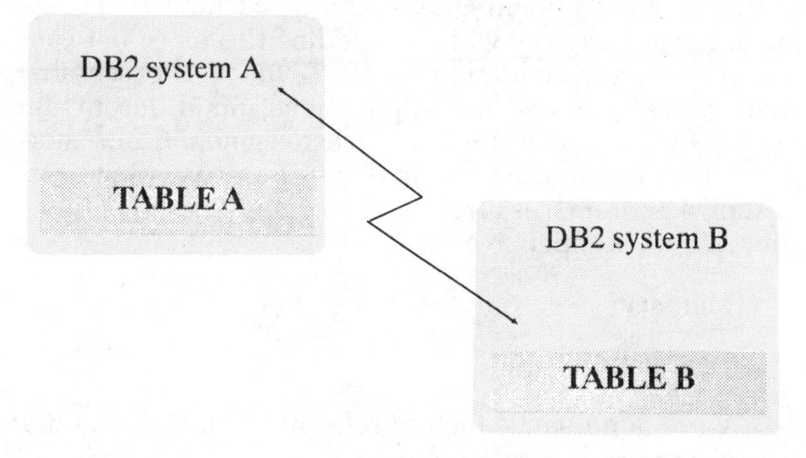

Figure 14.2 Needing data from two DB2 subsystems is messy. DB2 versions 2.2 and 2.3 will not allow a transaction to update both tables A and B directly. User code can update both, but must manage data recovery.

justified in their integrating an enterprise. Decentralized databases can use cheaper hardware. Adding DB2 subsystems effectively decentralizes a central resource. Multiple DB2 subsystems provide all the disadvantages of departmental applications, and cost more than centralized computing.

What Circumstances Justify Creating Multiple DB2 Subsystems?

The most basic justification for creating multiple DB2 subsystems is the need for application isolation. If you have important production work in DB2, using the same subsystem for development can be risky.

The major goal in most production environments is stability and delivering a consistent product. A development environment is typically a fermenting cauldron of apparently random activity. Even a stable software environment such as DB2 can allow production to be affected by development activities.

Also, having production running in the development environment constrains developers. A GTF trace against DB2 is a reasonable action in a low-volume development environment. The same trace can wreak havoc in production.

The same argument can be made to further and further refine the environments: Let's have a distinct DB2 subsystem for decision support (which straddles the fence between development and production anyway), for 4GL processing, for client-server, for distinct applications, for different departments, etc. These arguments are reasonable, but miss the point. DB2 can manage normal environments very well.

From a system resource vantage point, adding new DB2 subsystems is expensive in:

- Memory
- Task activity
- Various nuisance factors relating to tuning and managing the complete system

Using the same resources for fewer systems will make those systems look very good. Additional production DB2 subsystems are totally destructive to systems integration. From the standpoint of logical systems design, adding a new DB2 subsystem is sabotage, as shown in Figure 14.2. As decision support begins to merge with transaction processing (and it will) where do we draw the line?

A single application can consume the resources of a top-of-the-line CPU complex. In this situation there is little option but to have a dedicated DB2 subsystem. The alternatives are messier, and the data can rarely be shared in this situation because of the performance impact.

These issues dictate the basic method of dividing up active DB2 subsystems:

- One development subsystem.
- One production subsystem.
- All special-case applications have to be reviewed to decide if their requirements justify an independent DB2 subsystem. This type of application includes very high volume transaction processing. They may have special complications, such as waiting to log updates. Very high availability applications can strain system capabilities enough to make conjoint applications too complex to manage.

Almost all environments using DB2 do not need more than two DB2 subsystems. A strong case can be made that most shops with more than two active subsystems are wasting resources. The waste includes the CPU and memory overhead required to maintain multiple subsystems, rather than using them where nature and IBM intended: in creating larger bufferpools. Also, creating multiple subsystems is almost never associated with additional staff to monitor the subsystems. This in turn results in much worse management of the total DB2 resource.

Running Out of Capacity — The Multiple Machine Problem

There is a problem if the amount of DB2 required overlaps machine bounds. This can happen as a result of an existing inventory of smaller machines or acquisition of cheaper smaller machines, or when the DB2 requirements overwhelm large MVS capacity.

DB2 prefers faster processors. Applications running on smaller machines with the same total MIPS will have lower cumulative DB2 capacity. The cost of DB2 and licenses for software related to DB2 is high. The application integration cost between the machines is high. The overall cost of management is higher.

Ideally if there are multiple machines in a single environment, DB2 should run on the fastest and largest processor. The same issue is true for most MVS software also prefers fast machines. Therefore, we may be forced to run DB2 on smaller processors.

If the DB2 activity requires multiple local machines, minimize the number involved. CICS function shipping and other similar means of distributing the workload may, in the short term, be more expedient options than using multiple DB2 production subsystems.

If there are multiple machines which are not at the same site, more unpleasantness ensues. DB2 distributed processing is not a tempting choice for integrating applications. The needed function is not available. The capacity is fairly low. Other options, such as replicated data or client-server applications, may still be better options.

What Do Extra DB2 Subsystems Cost?

The typical memory overhead per DB2 subsystem is approximately 22 megabytes of real storage. The minimal CPU overhead is approximately 1 percent of the system. A typical DB2 subsystem needs at least 3000 tracks (based on 3380 track size) for each DB2 subsystem, excluding user data. Most sites should plan about 5000 tracks unless they are scrupulous in cleaning up installation verification procedure tables and other artifacts. In most large sites the overhead is closer to 10,000 tracks because of various support tools that maintain some data in DB2 tables.

The typical least manpower overhead in managing a DB2 subsystem is about 10 hours a month; but plan for a potential of many more. Usually where there are multiple DB2 subsystems substantial work in replicating and transferring data is needed. This is true both in production and development.

The price in performance is trivial in comparison to the cost in application functions. Every dividing line added will have tremendous cost. Any new DB2 subsystem is clearly divisive.

Almost every DB2 shop with real DB2 activity should have a separation between development and production. In early DB2 use, where there is no critical production activity, there might be no immediate requirement for a production subsystem. Often in this situation it is still worthwhile to implement two distinct subsystems by the time applications start migrating to production. This would allow for practice for the future and may catch security and procedural problems.

Smaller 4GL and DSS shops have a hard time distinguishing between production and development. This type of user is noted for small, less urgent applications, and often has applications in perpetual development. This style of environment can make do with a single subsystem. This is reasonable in the context of the culture: the systems structure must reflect the management structure. If this type of environment is embedded in a larger structure, a more complex decision has to be made.

An example is an infocenter department. If the group lacks requirements for controlled production application, it can coexist comfortably with a development subsystem. The problems arise when the applications overlap between production and development styles.

Fluctuating demands for many of these applications will tempt system administrators to bucket them in with development. But often much of the data resides in production. We are caught in a dilemma: we can proliferate systems for control, or minimize systems for a clean design.

Normally the only resources shared between multiple applications separated by different bufferpools are the logs and the hardware. Sometimes it is simpler to run distinct applications on separate machines. In some rare cases, the design of distinct applications will make the logs a bottleneck. This can be justification for separation if — and only if — capacity planning reveals this as a limiting factor.

A strong case can be made for a quality assurance subsystem or a systems programming subsystem if large enough applications or migrations are involved. The caveat here is that these should be very tightly controlled environments. In the normal course of operations, these subsystems are stopped — guaranteeing that there is no temptation to use an available subsystem for any other use. The requirements for quality assurance of a new system and the need to test newly changed systems software are the sole justifications for starting this type of subsystem.

Summary

Most shops should have two DB2 subsystems. The standard dividing line is by data. A development subsystem does not typically contain live data, while production does. Decision support activity can be isolated from operational systems by use of distinct bufferpools.

Review Question

1. Can a production DB2 subsystem be used for application development?

Answer to Review Question

1. In most cases it is unrealistic to use the same subsystem for both development and production. A development environment may destabilize production, an unappealing thought in an environment that avoids risk. The stability requirements of the production environment will restrict development ability to make changes or try new facilities.

A early production environment, with no urgency of application availability, may be reasonably used for development.

Some types of shops merge production and development into a "continuous development" flow, where all applications are constantly changing. These shops would have a hard time distinguishing between the environments. Until the culture factors change, these shops may not be ready for multiple environments.

Chapter 15

DB2 Bufferpools

DB2 provides for three bufferpools for the common 4-kilobyte page tables and all indices: BP0, BP1, and BP2. At least one bufferpool must be allocated to access data, and to allow DB2 to access the system catalog and do other standard management I/O.

The internal algorithms for buffer memory management in DB2 are inherently very stable. There is no limit to the amount of memory that can be allocated to any bufferpool, except the MVS/ESA limit of 2 gigabytes total real memory, which several DB2 shops have reached. Buffer searches do not involve actually addressing the pages themselves, so buffers are stable in a virtual memory environment. This is reasonable in a decision support application that sporadically requires a large buffer.

The more memory allocated, the better the performance of the application. DB2 design assumes that there is enormous bufferpool space available. Conversely, DB2 will surely perform poorly against a reasonable load with small buffers. The buffers are sensitive to several markers, based on the percentage of allocated storage in use. These markers, such as the *deferred write threshold*, should be avoided in practice.

Each bufferpool's pages are divided into three chains.

- **Never used pages**: The entire pool starts as never used; as applications access data, never used pages are the first allocated. This pool rapidly depletes.

- **Available pages**: If a page has finished processing — for example an updated page written to disk at a DB2 checkpoint — the page is considered *available*. Prefetched pages are immediately available. This allows DB2 to steal the page if it needs one. The reuse is based on an oldest out, least recently used (LRU) order. The most frequently accessed pages, including index entries, data *hot spots*, and *space map* pages, will rarely be stolen if the bufferpool is a reasonable size for its use.

- **In use pages**: When a page has been updated, it is in use, and remains that way until written to the data space it belongs to. After being written, it is transferred to the available queue.

How Should Bufferpools Be Allocated?

The standard recommendation is that only BP0 should be allocated. DB2 is better at coordinating the disparate needs of different applications than programmers. Furthermore, the DB2 bufferpool size can normally be changed only by stopping and restarting DB2 with a different start-up parameter, although BMC Software (Sugarland Tex.) sells a product that can dynamically change bufferpool size.

The converse change can be made by moving a data space to a different bufferpool by using the SQL ALTER statement, stopping and restarting the object. The single large mass of buffers is in many cases more easily managed than are multiple ones.

In almost all cases BP0 should be the only bufferpool allocated, and it should be created the largest size reasonable. Of course, there are situations in which multiple bufferpools should be used. Let us review some situations that would justify this activity.

There are applications that conflict in use of buffers. An example raised before was decision support access of data that uses buffers mostly for large-scale asynchronous reads. Transaction processing uses buffers mainly for reducing reads of index nonleaf pages. Most of the time the conflict between these application types can be easily resolved by simply using distinct bufferpools for each application type.

A typical configuration for this type of user is BP0 containing:

- DB2 catalog tables
- DSS data
- Transaction processing

This can be reasonable if the transaction processing application will function adequately without data being buffered. Many conflicts between reporting and batch vs. transaction processing can be resolved by simply using MVS priority and standard tuning methods.

Different Transaction Rates

If transaction processing includes several disparate application types, it seems tempting to separate the applications into distinct buffer pools. This could allow individual tuning of the buffering of the applications, and allow for relative tuning between them.

Very high transaction rate applications process several hundred transactions per second. If your application involves fewer than dozens of transactions a second, it is likely that techniques intended for very high transaction rate applications can impair system performance. In many cases, these techniques are used when the system planners do not understand the application requirements.

In an environment with minimal capacity planning or unclear performance issues (for example, the first major DB2 application), there are justifiable worries about performance. If there is early management pressure to assure high performance rates, often tuning options will be used too early to maintain confidence in systems control.

Typical configuration for the early high volume DB2 transaction processing includes BP0 containing:

- DB2 catalog tables
- DSS data

with BP1 containing

- Transaction processing data for application A

and BP2 containing

- Transaction processing data for application B

There is generally minimal conflict between applications A and B in this configuration. The overall system throughput is probably less than if a single bufferpool the combined size of the three is used. When application A requires 100 times the work of application B, this may be the easiest means to stabilize processing time.

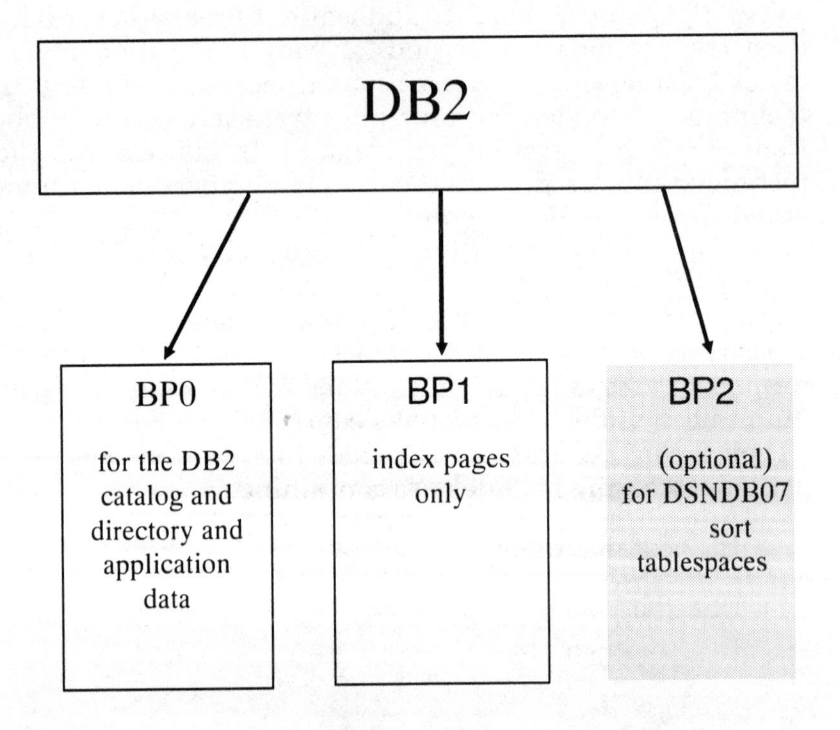

Figure 15.1 A sample bufferpool organization.

The most common configuration for this type of application actually involves BP0 containing

- DB2 catalog tables
- DSS data

with BP1 containing

- Transaction processing data for application A and application B

This allows a reasonable amount of buffering for the transaction processing applications.

Very high transaction rate applications

If there is an application with a very high transaction rate, it is often isolated to a distinct bufferpool. This may be the only way to guarantee fast response time by assuring that the buffer contains most of the referenced data.

The application can be isolated to a separate single bufferpool, or into multiple ones. The rationale for multiple bufferpools is that index data hit rates are often very high. It seems reasonable to favor those frequently referenced pages over the less accessed tablespace pages.

Thus, it is common for the highest transaction rate DB2 applications to use a small tablespace buffer that will be a staging area for table I/O, and buffer the occasional data access hot spot. The index bufferpool is made enormous, making the index buffer effectively a copy of the index cached into real memory. If any sorts are done, they may be interspersed with tablespace I/O or separated into yet another bufferpool. This is done by appropriate buffer pool selection for the tablespaces in the DSNDB07 database. Figure 15.1 shows this configuration.

In many cases of very large applications, an entire MVS system (and machine or logical partition) is dedicated for the application. This is justified by the traditional lack of integration these major applications have with other applications, and the convenience in tuning and operational management that a separate system provides.

Summary

Multiple DB2 subsystems are expensive. As few as necessary should be created. The instability of the development environment and DP tradition makes it tempting to split development from production. In most cases those two subsystems are the only ones needed on a day-to-day basis.

Many shops separate decision support from transaction processing. In most cases they will be better served by sharing a single subsystem and using separate bufferpools.

Some legitimate justifications for more DB2 subsystems are:

- Very high rate transaction processing applications that are completely isolated from the rest of the data processing world
- Multiple machines
- Subsystems that are temporarily turned on for use in quality assurance review of large applications or for testing new versions of DB2 software

Review Question

1. Are there operational management gains in having *more* DB2 subsystems?

Answer to Review Question

1. In some cases it is easier to charge back total application cost. In shared DB2 subsystems it is hard to charge for activity that is not associated with a specific allied agent (but there are tools that allow for this).

There are some shared resources in DB2. Logs are shared. Checkpoints are shared. Management of internal errors and one application's problems can slow processing of another application. If some applications need to be protected from this interference, they may more easily managed separately.

Chapter 16

Operating, Managing, and Planning for DB2

It is not enough to write programs that do what the users want at reasonable speed. Function and performance are vital but may be irrelevant if the application data cannot be recovered if there is a data set failure. An application must be able to restart after problems occur, and in a reasonable time based on user requirements.

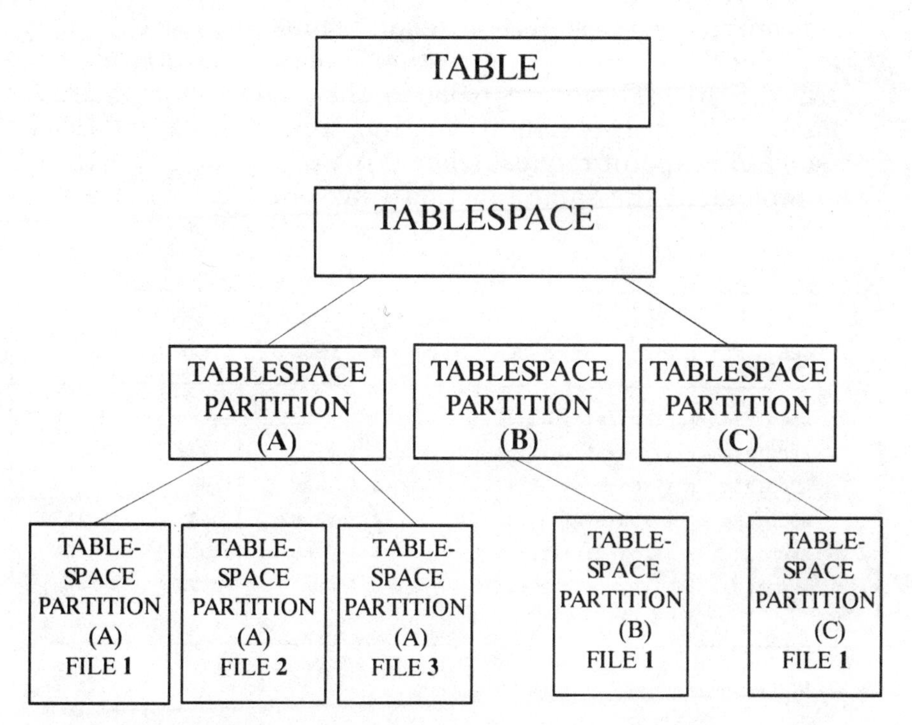

Figure 16.1 The underlying structure of a table.

DB2 functions as a proper MVS subsystem, being notified when applications ABEND. In many ways we can consider DB2 as an extension of MVS, functioning as a higher-level operating system server (or to be "datacentric," we can consider MVS as a DB2 file handler).

Recovery/Restart in DB2

If DB2 or the system crashes and DB2 is then restarted, the data are restored to the last successful commit point before the restart. (There are certain exceptions to this, which will be discussed later.) Applications can be made to restart and continue processing the data.

Batch applications tend to need the most thorough restart strategy, since the repercussions of complete rerun are high on system resources and batch windows are often constrained.

MVS provides a checkpoint/restart capability, implemented through system macros and involving copying data sets. This facility can be used in certain situations, but the overhead and complicated design requirements make its use the exception. The MVS checkpoint/restart functions do not support DB2 directly. There are tools in the market (for example Batch/+™ from Intex Solutions, Inc.) that will automatically issue a checkpoint request when COMMIT is issued. It is trivial to implement the same function yourself. This is not a com-

JOB_NAME	DATE	TIME	SEQUENCE	OBJECT	TYPE	POSITION
ABCD1234	11/03/91	21:11	1	FILE1	qsam	21300
ABCD1234	11/03/91	21:11	2	FILE2	qsam	1211
ABCD1234	11/03/91	21:11	3	VSAM1	esds	14
ABCD1234	11/03/91	21:11	4	VSAM2	esds	183119
ABCD1234	11/03/91	21:11	5	CURSOR1	db2A	14
ABCD1234	11/03/91	21:11	6	CURSOR1	db2B	banana

Figure 16.2 Example of an application restart table.

plete solution, since there is incomplete coordination between the system checkpoint and the DB2 work unit.

This implies that any batch program requiring restart capabilities should have them designed in. A common strategy is to use a restart table. (See Figure 16.1.) This table is used to control all batch jobs using DB2. A shop standard determines the protocol used and all programs following the protocol should be automatically restartable. An example of a restart table is shown in Figure 16.2.

An example protocol for restart is:

1. All jobs will accept as parameter a logical run date. This is not necessarily the current run date, since a job may be deferred.

2. At the beginning of each batch job, a SETUP procedure is invoked. This procedure will query the restart table for an existing job matching both job name and date.

If a match exists, COMMIT. Then open and position each of the identified files to the specified record.

If no match exists, insert appropriate rows into the restart table for any object that has to be repositioned. COMMIT to release locks on the restart table.

3. Now the application can continue processing. Instead of COMMITting (at the shop standard interval), the program will invoke the SETUP procedure to update the position rows for the table, and COMMIT.

This procedure works for standard batch processing, such as a batch-apply transaction. The procedure works for sequential files, such as sequential data sets and the VSAM equivalents. Design cursors to be reopenable (note that in Figure 16.2 the CURSOR1 object restart information includes both 14 and "banana" — it is a parameterized cursor with two parameters). Information to coordinate with other database facilities also can be kept in the same kind of structure, as long as the protocol is maintained.

This works nicely in many ways. Since the restart table is shared between applications, it becomes a tremendous convenience — it can be used to see if predecessor jobs were run, to pass information between steps, and to serialize application processing. The window of time for accessing the table is very short: get the data, update if required, and commit. Therefore, the table should not be a bottleneck to the system.

This procedure allows for batch applications that are now smart enough to be easily rerun. If the application bombs because of non-application-related problems, the operations staff can be requested to automatically rerun the application with no new parameters. This requires no complicated setup, and minimizes risk. This results in higher availability of applications.

The caveats in using this type of procedure are the standard problems in work unit management. If any activity is processed out of the scope of the DB2 work unit (e.g., a BDAM random file update), the process should be either repeatable or correctable. Repeatable in this context means that when the program is restarted, and the same update applied, no harm is done. Correctable implies that the DB2 work unit activity can be "unapplied."

Undoing the work can be managed by logging each action in the work unit to a DB2 *undo* file that can be used to pull back any updates. Non-DB2 files are inappropriate, since there may be a problem in the unrecoverable file. Another method is to restore the file from a backup copy.

The availability of this structure can also reduce the number of operator restarts of applications. The application can react to standard problems such as a SQLCODE of -911 (deadlock has destroyed your current work unit) by invoking the restart procedure and continuing. This will reduce the number of jobs that bomb, and again further simplify production management.

Batch processing against direct files can present difficulties. Usually, simply restarting the rest of the application will implicitly reposition the direct access processing correctly. In other cases, special case restart logic has to be written.

HOLD cursors

The availability of *hold* cursors, such as

```
DECLARE mycursor CURSOR WITH HOLD FOR
SELECT column1, column2
  FROM TABLE
   WHERE column3=:v
```

is a tremendous nuisance in restart processing. Using earlier versions of DB2 (before version 2.3), our applications had to commit periodically for restart purposes. COMMITting will lose position information, obliging the programmer to reposition the application cursors appropriately.

```
PERFORM .... VARYING I FROM 1 BY 1
COMPUTE FCOMMIT =
                      I /   ITERATIONS-PER-COMMIT
                  *  ITERATIONS-PER-COMMIT
IF FCOMMIT IS ZERO THEN
     EXEC-SQL
               COMMIT
     END-EXEC
```

Figure 16.2 Example of arbitrary COMMIT points.

Given the existence of the cursor hold facility, a programmer may be tempted to continue processing after commit. Unless it is required to handle exceptions correctly, the programmer may not use any restart logic. This implies that the program cannot be restarted, and cannot use these simple facilities to handle deadlock without modification.

Job name	Parameter name	Number value	Character value
ABCD1234	Commit rate	500	–
ABCD1234	Logical date	–	01/15/1992
XYZA0001	Logical date	–	01/12/1992
XYZA0001	Commit rate	100000	–
ZZZZ0023	Commit rate	50	–

Figure 16.3 A DB2 job control table example.

Startup parameters

Most batch programs have standard run parameters that are stable but occasionally must be changed. An example would be the commit frequency. A batch transaction program typically has a logical work unit typically corresponding to a single iteration of the main loop.

To COMMIT after each iteration of the loop is a performance intensive operation. Not COMMITting prevents the program from being restartable in the event of an error, and will severely limit concurrent access to the data by other programs. Thus, it is standard practice to define a physical work unit composed of a fixed number of logical work units. This is demonstrated in Figure 16.2.

The number of loop iterations to process per COMMIT is clearly an operational environment design issue. The count can be based on the concurrency requirements of the affected data and the restart requirements for the program. The environmental factors can change, and it is important to design the COMMIT frequency as an adjustable parameter to allow for tuning and changes.

This parameter can be provided by a JCL parameter passed to the program. This is not a very flexible approach, since it is tedious to change production job JCL. A more sophisticated strategy involves using DB2 to store these program startup parameters. (See Figure 16.3.)

There are several program products that offer these services. It is a simple matter to build these in a program. All we have to do is build a job control table. An example job control table is shown in Figure 16.3.

All batch jobs will start by invoking the setup subroutine, which will retrieve the program run parameters. Note that these include a logical run date discussed in relation to the restart table in Figure 16.1. Any program adjustable parameter belongs in this table.

The subroutine can be invoked as follows:

```
CALL 'STARTUP' USING  'ABCD1234',
                       PROBLEM-CODE,
                      'COMMIT RATE',
                       COMMIT-RATE,
                      'OTHER PARM',
                       OTHER-PARM,
                      'LOGICAL DATE',
                       LOGICAL-DATE
```

The first parameter is the name of the program, and the second contains a status code, telling the program to terminate. The following parameter pairs consist of the parameter identifier corresponding to the value in the parameter name column and a program variable to contain the retrieved value.

Note that program ZZZZ0023 also contains a logical date, and is presumably being restarted later.

Design Issues

What do you do if some updates have been applied inappropriately? For instance, suppose a batch transaction update program is run against a tape from last year. Often there is not much that can be done, especially when the problem is not detected quickly.

The facilities that DB2 provides for un-applying activity are simple. A copy of the data can be reloaded from a backup, and optionally some portion of the log activity can be forward applied from that point.

There is no way to back out transactions applied by a specific program. Even with audit traces on, DB2 does not provide means to extract enough information to identify which user caused which update. Only the first update of each work unit is identified in the DB2 audit trace records.

The facilities DB2 provides are:

- The RECOVER utility TOCOPY option. This utility will copy an image copy of a tablespace partition from backup. The image copy source filename to be used can be identified in the SYSIBM.SYSCOPY catalog table. When using an incremental image copy, DB2 will automatically recover to the preceding image copy and sequentially apply all intermediate incremental image copies. All subsequent activity to the tables is lost.

- The RECOVER utility TORBA option will recover to a relative byte address in the DB2 log. This becomes a point in time recovery. The processing is like the RECOVER TOCOPY, where the last preceding log RBA is identified from the DB2 catalog, the appropriate image copy or copies applied, and all committed log activity is applied to the copy. The RBA address can be identified using the DSN1LOGP utility, which is used to produce a summary of checkpoints in a given log, the time that the checkpoint was taken, and the corresponding log address. Even further detail is possible if the user is willing to analyze detailed DSN1LOGP reports.

- DSN1COPY is an invaluable tool for those ugly, unplanned-for disasters. This can be used to do such things as restore a table's data, even though the MODIFY RECOVERY utility has already eliminated the image copy information from the DB2 catalog. DSN1COPY can take as input an image copy that was not created with SHRLEVEL REFERENCE, a backup copy created using some other means, or a tablespace or indexspace, and output to any of the aforementioned data sets.

Most VSAM tools that process at the cluster level (rather than looking at the structure information stored in the data set, which DB2 tampers with), such as the VSAM REPRO command or most data set backup management software, also can be used to restore a physical copy of the data set. DSN1COPY adds the important ability of allowing the user to specify an output data set that differs in DB2 internal data set identifiers. This in turn allows many data problems to be resolved outside the scope of production and returned into production data.

When using these tools in urgent situations, performance can be significantly enhanced by using high numbers of buffers. The RECOVER utility will perform faster in a larger region, and when recovering indexspaces region size will markedly improve sort speed.

RECOVER processing works very well in DB2 if all we have to do is to unapply the last activity that was done, and that was done in a stand-alone fashion. The problems in using these tools are logical issues: Can we unapply some transactions from the middle? What about concurrent processing? What happened in any applications that processed the data after the problem? What about referential integrity? What else is affected? Did any reporting or decision support propagation happen to the corrupted data?

We can still do a little more. If, for example, an update was applied and followed by some other update processing we may be able to identify the data involved.

In Figure 16.4, we have processed some bad updates at 5 a.m., began transaction processing at 9 a.m., and at 3 p.m. discovered a problem. The first thing that normally happens in this situation is to stop any more updates. Next, we research to determine the degree of interdependence between the erroneous batch data and the transaction processing updates. When there is little interdependence, we just want to lose the batch data. If the interdependence is high, we may

Bad batch job | Transaction processing activity | **OOPS! NOW** WHAT DO **WE DO?**

5 a.m. 7 a.m. 9 a.m. 11 a.m. 1 p.m. 3 p.m.

TIME LINE

Problem happens | Problem detected

Figure 16.4 Problems not caught are exacerbated.

have to sift through the transactions activity and "manually" scrub the data clean. Figure 16.5 shows the recovery options.

Technique	Advantages	Disadvantages
Omit COMMIT s from the program	Trivial to program	Expensive to use in time and computer use if the Program aborts
	No design support required	Reduces concurrent access to the data due to locks being maintained
	No operational interaction needed	Program failure can have most significant impact on batch window, due to the time of rollback processing and the cost of reapplying all updates
	Reduces COMMIT processing overhead	
Backup data before batch program and restore to those values if an error occurs	No program changes are necessary	Expensive and slow if large tables are involved
	Simple to manage	Does not allow normal concurrent programs, unless their updates can be unapplied as well
Use DB2 RECOVER to a point in time	Can be done even if not planned for	Complex and slow when much interrelated data is involved
User logging of update activity to be used to unapply updates	Allows complete flexibility	Complex and expensive to program

Figure 16.5 The options for recovering from batch program failures.

Summary

The restart considerations of DB2 applications are a vital part of *application design*. An intelligent design allows an application to automatically restart.

The justification for building this restart capability into the application is the loss of information. Most external restart processing poorly matches application requirements. The result is detrimental to both the application and the overall system.

Review Question

1. How can a batch application apply updates to both DB2 and VSAM? How can it be made restartable?

Answer to Review Question

1. The only way to use system logging mechanisms to coordinate the two database management systems is to write a CICS application that does the processing. This is not entirely absurd, since the overhead of running a batch program under CICS may not be exorbitant. Since CICS and DB2 coordinate recovery, the recovery will be automated with no programmer effort (presuming that CICS restart is in place).

IBM offers a program product called VSAM transparency mode, which traps VSAM calls and converts them to access DB2 tables. This may be an appropriate use of the product. This strategy requires converting the VSAM to DB2 tables.

The application program has the option of logging updates itself. If the program fails, then a restart program can process the log files prior to restart. Consideration should be given to what happens if the log file fails. This option is expensive to implement. Most attempts include application error; for example, this processing should not allow for updates of active data by other applications if this application fails.

The most common strategy in this type of processing is to back up before images of both the VSAM and DB2 data. This allows the user to reinitialize the data and restart the update program from the beginning.

Chapter 17

Operating DB2 Applications

Finishing programming a DB2 application is only the beginning of the application's life. The application has to be run. The run books have to be written. Recovery and restart procedures must be defined. Operational issues are relevant to both operational and development staff.

The operational considerations have two interrelated aspects. An application has to be written to allow it to be operated. This is clearly a design consideration. The operations staff and software should be able to manage the DB2 applications. This is an organizational standards and training issue. Both of the parts have to be integrated to manage a DB2 shop effectively.

Early users are not effective at identifying the operational requirements for DB2 applications. There are new issues and new types of users. This in turn increases the expense and decreases the availability of DB2 applications.

Operational Management

DB2 operations staff attempt to manage the systems issues of DB2 in the most application-independent manner possible. The group must also manage each application that uses DB2.

This generally causes a conflict in DB2 shops. In almost all cases DB2 accounts for only a fraction of overall applications. Operations management is generally more concerned about non-DB2 issues.

Even in shops redesigning applications into DB2, the DB2 issues are often obscured. This can happen because of the burden of the new applications being moved into production. In many cases, knowledge of DB2 issues is not deep.

Managing DB2 Subsystems

DB2 scheduling is the most complicated issue to face. Application requirements are getting more stringent, and available window time is shrinking. Consider the context of all application requirements for DB2.

Should We Use One or More Subsystems?

It is complicated to identify the appropriate number of DB2 subsystems. Most active DB2 sites have at least two subsystems: production and development. Some sites have attempted to put five or six separate subsystems on the same machine. This strategy is often the heritage of CICS, where a rogue transaction can often attack its siblings. DB2 is better at compartmentalizing problems.

Other reasons for having many subsystems are due to naming and migration standards. It often is easier to use a quality assurance subsystem to test production implementation than to test in a development subsystem. The development subsystem can often have conflicting naming conventions.

At the same time, each subsystem is a further burden on the computer. The virtual and real memory requirements are substantial; the maintenance and operation effort increases; the cost in CPU time increases; DASD and tape requirements increase. A CICS region can only connect to a single DB2 at a time; this increases the logistics and often the number of associated regions. DB2 is a very stable product, and can usually defend one user from another.

Managing Batch DB2 Applications

MVS operations have become used to a historic, ungainly means of managing scheduled batch jobs. A successful job completes with a return code of zero. If the job generates an informational message, it returns a code of 4. More severe errors can return higher return codes. This procedure is an artifact of the earliest days of the IBM System 360 architecture, when a protocol of leaving a status code in standard machine registers was established.

The job control language uses the status code to signal job step status to identify if steps were to be skipped. The protocol was too simplistic to manage complex application suites comprising thousands of steps, and another even simpler technique is layered over it. A job that fails can identify itself by simply abnormally terminating — a process that unequivocally notifies the console operator of a problem. Some systems monitoring programs are able to read the console log and identify the offending program.

Over the years, this means of operational batch management has been rudimentarily automated. The first type of product that developed has been *schedulers*, the most common example of which is CA-7 (Computer Associates, Garden City, N.Y.). Schedulers are intended to control standard, regularly scheduled program streams. They collect a database of rules relating to each process.

The scheduler rules recognize the dependency relationships, including ordinal (e.g., do not run job 2 until job 1 successfully completes), temporal (e.g., only run month-end processing on the last Sunday of the month), and resource (e.g., job 3 can only run if four tape drives and a CPU hour are available). This process automates the run books that define the run sequences. The advantages of automated schedulers are the same as the advantages of any other database applications: the explicit definition and control available through automation.

A common facility to add to a scheduler is the rerun manager, such as Zebb (Altai Software, Arlington Tex.). A rerun manager allows adding an additional set of rules relating to restarting a job sequence that is interrupted. The rules identify what clean-up processing should be done, such as deleting intermediate files no longer valid, setting restart parameters, and so forth.

Console automation is the next step in this sequence. This is an aspect of automating operations. The goal is to program the operational requirements of each application. The console automation program can automate many manual tasks if coordinated with appropriate program design and hardware.

The activity that is hardest to automate is *setups*, a category that mostly involves magnetic tape mounts. Programs can reduce their dependency on operators by using DASD instead of tapes. System managed storage is a refinement of this option, whereby rules can be set to automatically migrate files that are staged to DASD onto tape. Another option to reduce operator effort is to purchase hardware assistance in the form of automatically loading cartridge tape drives that are able to load tapes without operator intervention.

A newer development is DB2 restart and recovery software. These products ease the effort of restarting a program after it abnormally terminates. MVS provides checkpoint restart services, but they require program logic to synchronize data with DB2 commit processing.

Most DB2 shops use multiple database management systems. If all the other activity is in IMS, coordinating recovery is trivial since IMS will coordinate synchronization points with DB2. If the processing uses a DBMS that cannot coordinate recovery with DB2, problems can ensue.

For example, consider a shop that uses both DB2 and another DBMS — we'll use Adabas (Software AG, Reston, Va.) as an example. Even if the transaction processing activity completely distinguishes between DB2 transactions and Adabas transactions, the data can meet in the middle. A common example is an extraction program that moves data between the two database management systems.

Often this type of program will need to coordinate recovery checkpoints between the various systems. A common situation is a program addressing one or two DBMSs and several sequential (VSAM or QSAM) files. There are products that simplify the process of coordinating recovery between the various data management systems. The products either replace the standard commit points or else trap them, and then issue the appropriate save commands in tandem. Each of the database management systems is notified to process the appropriate checkpoint. These coordination products can control this process by keeping a status journal.

Note that these products do not truly coordinate recovery! Consider a batch program that updates both DB2 and Adabas files, issuing commits to DB2 and then to Adabas. If

- The commit to DB2 succeeds

- But then the commit in Adabas fails

the files will be uncoordinated. The risk of losing coordination increases if the application is using a nonlogged file structure such as standard files. Unless the application journals all updates, there is a potential of losing coordination. These issues should be considered in the application *design*. Applications that fail in one DBMS and not another may still need operational or application restoration from inconsistent data.

DB2 controls errors a little too well. For example, DB2 errors that result in ABENDs in DB2 (e.g., a division by zero error occurring in processing a SQL statement) only result in returning a SQL error code to the program. Further, under the TSO DSN command processor (the most common means of running batch jobs in DB2), TSO will trap program ABENDs, allowing the program to terminate normally.

This trapping of program ABENDs has two problematic effects. First, since the program terminates normally, DB2 will implicitly COMMIT the last work unit in the program. Rolling back the work unit would better serve most programs. Second, a program designed to signal a problem using an ABEND will not work. The ABEND will be trapped by the DSN command processor and the program will terminate without the identifying ABEND.

Several vendors offer software that emulates the DSN services in running programs, but allows ABEND and condition codes to percolate out. The programmer can get most of this function using the IKJEFT1A entry point in the terminal monitor program.

Summary

Operational considerations tend to be poorly managed in DB2 environments. This is due to the immaturity of its use— the problems are in production applications that were designed before the problems were understood.

Most of the operational issues should be embedded within applications, avoiding operator intervention. Batch programs should be restartable without modification. Transaction processing programs should manage normal problems (such as deadlock) in a reasonable fashion.

Automating operational activity is common at many DB2 shops. Many are heavily involved in various forms of automating operational activity. This does not conflict with the DB2 program error management and design for recovery from problems. The application designer can use facilities the operations management software offers. The designer must not assume that any part of the responsibility has shifted to operations.

A particularly troublesome aspect of DB2 program management is batch programs. The standard mechanism suggested in the manuals is using the DSN command processor. Since this will trap problems, care should be taken to prevent disguising program failure.

Review Questions

1. How can a DB2 environment reduce tape mounts?

2. What is the sequence of events when a COBOL DB2 program running under TSO in batch generates an operation exception?

Answers to Review Questions

1. DB2 itself will use tape mounts only for archival of activity logs. (It also can generate trace records that can fill SMF data sets, causing them to be archived.) Batch programs can use tapes in standard ways. Some DB2 utilities can involve tape mounts; these include RECOVER, REORG, and COPY in order of increasing frequency of use.

It is difficult to reduce the log archival frequency substantially in a normal environment. Running the LOAD or REORG utilities with the LOG YES option can cause substantial logging. This activity can be calculated by a query such as:

```
SELECT TS.NAME, TS.DBNAME, TS.NACTIVE, CP.ICTYPE
 FROM SYSIBM.SYSCOPY CP,
      SYSIBM.SYSTABLESPACE TS
 WHERE   TS.DBNAME = CP.DBNAME/* join criteria */
   AND   TS.NAME  = CP.TSNAME /* join criteria */
   AND   CP.ICTYPE IN ( 'Z', 'X')/* reorg/load
                                       LOG YES */
   AND   CP.ICDATE BETWEEN ? AND ?
                          /* in a given period */
```

Any large numbers should be researched and corrected. ROLLBACK activity in your environment can cause substantial additional logging. The amount of activity can be identified by reviewing the abort counts generated in the DB2 accounting trace. This will not identify the amount of effort involved.

Unintentional ROLLBACK frequency can be reduced by correcting the underlying problems. Intentional ROLLBACK should be a rare event. Programs can (and should) radically reduce the amount of work to be rolled back by committing work units frequently.

If possible, avoid using tapes for sort and temporary storage in the REORG utility. In many cases tapes can be replaced by DASD, either explicitly or by using device-independent secondary storage management software.

2. The program has probably corrupted its instructions. It will ABEND. If any ABEND trap has been set in COBOL (e.g., by an ABEND analysis program), the trap exit will receive control. When it completes, the terminal monitor program ABEND trap will receive control. The trap will clean up the program task and continue processing.

DB2 will be notified by MVS of the (clean) termination of the task and will COMMIT (!) the work unit. If an ERROR block exists in the CLIST it will be executed next. When the CLIST completes, the return code will be 0 and the JCL will not detect the ABEND.

Chapter 18

Performance Planning for DB2 Applications

In the traditional mainframe application environment, capacity planning is an esoteric specialty. Capacity planners are senior systems programmers distanced from the application design issues. Capacity planning is usually considered an activity to perform once a year or once per application.

Several factors in the recent history of data processing and in DB2 applications have conspired to change this situation. The performance tradeoffs of different hardware and software options are changing daily, but are always decreasing. The costs of low-end options are decreasing exponentially, and the high end (to which DB2 belongs) is decreasing in cost linearly.

Meanwhile, the cost of developing and maintaining applications is increasing. This makes downsizing and other alternative options more appealing.

In this environment, capacity planning has to change from a linear review of application requirements to a modeling effort. Capacity has to be looked at far more as a cost/benefit tradeoff throughout the application development cycle.

There are problems with this approach. Capacity planners should be senior systems programmers. The number of senior DB2 systems programmers who understand capacity planning issues is minute. Capacity planning groups in the traditional sense are not equipped by nature, structure, or staffing to interact regularly with application developers.

This leaves us with DB2 applications that may shock the system when implemented. Applications of this sort can take a minute to perform a transaction planned to take a second. Clearly the paradigm has to shift.

Programmers as Capacity Planners

The most rational way to address this issue seems to be to enable applications developers to do rudimentary capacity planning. This will allow the identification of basic tradeoffs based on interacting more with users than was traditional. The basic capacity plans will enable the evaluation of the developed application: is it performing to plan?

The result will be carefully thought out internal planning, which will feed the external plan. The cost of this process is not high, and the reward in developing the performers' sophistication in the use of DB2 is high.

Capacity Planning of Large DB2 Applications

Large DB2 applications require special consideration in many ways. The major reason is that capacity planning techniques tend to be based on finding similar existing applications and presuming that the applications will have a similar load. DB2 throws a wrench into that strategy because of the complexity of characterizing changes in the data access effort of complex DB2 applications.

As a counter example, a typical IMS application gets locked into a few specific access methods that have comparatively constant access rates. Thus, a gross approximation of the cost of an IMS transaction might be calculated simply. (This discussion deliberately ignores network issues.) Figure 18.1 shows a simple calculation of the cost of a transaction, which is typical for IMS and useful for the most basic DB2 transaction.

The gross calculation makes it clear that we can plan for subsecond response time for the process. Similar reasoning would lead to predictions of the number of transactions the system could support and the amount of overhead the application would add to the computer.

Why does this reasoning not work for DB2? The problem of logistics is enormous. DB2 applications are more complex than the IMS ones. A typical DB2 application accesses more than 100 data objects, whereas a typical IMS application accesses one-tenth as many objects. The IMS data structures are more complex, but the DB2 access to the few data structures it has available is less predictable. IMS access methods are inherent to the data structure selected by the designer. DB2 access path selection is dependent on the values and degree of organization of the data.

This leaves us guessing the access path selection of an order of magnitude more objects than before. We use cruder and less accurate models of application performance than earlier systems. The effort required to develop these models is higher than before. A sure route to losing credibility is to provide predictions more slowly and less accurately. It is time to review our options.

A traditional method of predicting application performance is to find a similar application and assume that the new

10 I/O requests per typical transaction
60 percent average buffer miss rate for I/O
30 millisecond to process I/O request
100 milliseconds to provide the needed 50 milliseconds. of CPU time

So the transaction uses:

6 I/Os (60% of the 10 logical I/Os)
x 30 milliseconds per I/O
—--
180 milliseconds for I/O

Adding the CPU overhead we get:

180 milliseconds I/O
+100 milliseconds CPU
—-
280 milliseconds per transaction

Figure 18.1 Calculating a static path cost.

application will have comparable performance characteristics. DB2 complicates this strategy by devaluing the previous experience needed to make these kinds of predictions accurate.

Just to muddy the waters further, let us add two major new themes to the picture. The first problem is systems integration projects, at a scope larger than we are accustomed to. These are hard to predict for all the normal reasons. Their scope becomes frightening, and the effort required for interviewing and modeling to build a capacity plan is enormous. Projects this large are very dangerous; a capacity planning error can result in disaster.

The second reason is that we have new types of applications. Ad-hoc applications with sporadic unplanned demands are hard to manage. These types of application are not by nature easily controllable. The demand on resources cannot be easily planned, unless we either restrict the users or configure systems to support the worst-case demand for service.

Use of DB2 is an effect of these application differences; the cause is the changes in the style of application that have steadily been going on for the past few years. Design of more complex, and often more flexible, applications taxes the capacity planning capabilities of many shops.

This change in the style of applications and their contents changes the art of prediction of system capacity requirements. The traditional forms of modeling and planning come into play. New issues and new problems force us to develop new strategies to plan for the capacity requirements of different types of application.

Typical Applications

Typical applications are small and medium-sized applications. A typical example is a program that joins two large tables and generates a report. Most of these applications should be capacity planned. The simple approach is the traditional one. To predict the amount of I/O, multiply the number of pages to be referenced by about 25 ms per access. Add any unusual CPU cost, and the prediction should roughly correspond to the program result.

This process is not capacity planning in the traditional sense. The goal here is efficient programs. If the program roughly corresponds to the prediction, presumably it is running efficiently. If not, the reason for the deviation should be researched.

The problem addressed here is that many DB2 applications programs are simply inefficient, without anyone realizing the problem. Most DB2 programmers are poor judges of the performance expectations for their programs. By identifying a performance goal, several important considerations come into view:

- The programmer learns to consider the performance objectives of the application. This can result in programmers becoming more sophisticated users of DB2.

- The application performance expectations become explicit. Knowing which applications are performance sensitive allows management to decide which ones are worth refining. This also predicts the most expensive applications early in the design.

- Problems are identified earlier. This simplifies the programmer's job and allows programmers to evaluate their work in terms of the prediction. A corollary to this point is the tendency of a measured activity to perform to prediction. The very existence of the prediction will often work as a self-fulfilling prophecy if the programmer trusts the estimate.

A fascinating result from this type of activity is the improvement this can bring to application performance. It is a common occurrence for a DB2 batch application to take hours to run, where minutes are justifiable according to this guideline. Exposure to this expectation will direct programmers to evaluate causes (program design, EXPLAIN, etc.) and correct them.

This use of the DB2 tools often makes programmers more willing to use facilities that confused them in the past. Is a correlated subquery appropriate in transaction processing? Often the answer is yes, but many DB2 application programmers have been warned against doing so. This restriction is based on strictures instead of teaching programmers how to evaluate problems associated with this type of DB2 activity.

The prediction will often free the programmers from parochial rules of thumb.

Summary

Performance planning spans a broad spectrum in DB2 applications. In large applications, this means that capacity planning issues are spread to more layers. This means that less experienced planners are responsible for more of the capacity planning process.

In smaller applications, capacity planning in the traditional sense is unrealistic. DB2 applications are created too fast. In many cases, training programmers to understand the performance issues is more useful than traditional performance planning.

Review Question

1. List some potential bottlenecks limiting a new DB2 application's performance. Which of these would be eliminated if the application was a purely reporting application?

Answer to Review Question

1. The most common bottlenecks include:

- Locking problems
- CPU capacity
- I/O speed and contention

None of these limiting factors will be eliminated if the program does not update any data. If no applications update a portion of the data, then locking issues can be ignored.

Chapter 19

Capacity Planning for Large Applications

As noted before, DB2 is part of the change in the function of information systems. The changes in application style are changing the style of application planning. Very large-scale application design can force capacity planning to become involved intrusively and actively in the entire application life cycle. This is a tremendous drain on capacity planning resources and takes much application designer effort, but is very useful in getting predictions of the capacity needs.

This form of capacity planning parallels the application development process. Application development is generally a process of progressive refinement of an application design. Capacity planning progressively refines a model of the performance characteristics. This idea is not new to capacity planners, but the scope and degree of modeling is changing.

This process has some entertaining side effects. The planner begins modeling the behavior of queueing systems with the goals of load balancing and prevention of bottlenecks. The process of refining a model takes consistent hardware specifications as input. Radically changing user requirements can often change the planning from an operational research problem into the more complex prediction of what the system will ultimately do. It would be fascinating to see a study of which path is the better.

New Technology

It is a truism that the first applications built in any new technology are terrible. They misunderstand the goals of the technology, poorly use the facilities, and have too much freedom. There is no base on which to build, and the start-up effort in the technology can often override the business rationale to build these applications. Often, pilot projects in a new technology have little purpose beyond "practice."

It should be a further truism that modeling the behavior of these systems will be poorly done. Capacity planning is always most accurate when dealing with systems like existing ones.

Further, consider the main types of new technologies. Image and voice processing can be brutal to a DB2 system under current architecture. A typical image contains 50,000 bytes, which doesn't naturally fit into DB2. The size of the object makes buffer pool management difficult, especially since most of these systems have inconsistent operation schedules. Much worse is the manner in which a few of these objects can monopolize and serialize a DB2 log.

Distributed issues also complicate the picture. Again we see sporadic use, high throughput requirements, and multiple objectives to concurrently balance.

MVS is constantly getting closer to being capable of running at 100 percent of capacity. A major goal of capacity planners is to maintain this equilibrium. At the same time, DB2 adds a new twist: the ability to absorb any available resources.

DB2 was designed to use any excess CPU, I/O, or memory capacity effectively. For example, we can run long decision support queries in batch at a low priority during the day shift with minimal impact on more urgent activity. Doing so helps keep an unkempt system looking well run. The problem of capacity management arises: If we add more horsepower that is quickly absorbed, are we discovering latent demand or simply exercising the hardware?

For example, many existing DSSs are intelligently utilized simply because of system limitations. Adding more iron can change a well-used, well-constrained system into an uncontrolled mess, wasting human and computer effort. This issue is strategic, and requires a policy decision. The policy determined should be publicized and adhered to by all users of computer resources.

Object-Oriented Systems

"Object oriented" is a hot theme in the press and, to some extent, in the real world. Object-oriented databases are means of storing data together with the standard processing the data undergoes. These databases are very hierarchical in nature and valuable for storing certain types of information (such as image data, or bill of materials data) that is processed in standard ways.

Conversely, the most appealing data to store in an object database are those data that we are not interested in manipulating in many different ways. The standard processing reduces the value of the orthogonal search capabilities of the relational structure. Object databases seem to have little relationship with DB2.

Object-oriented design, and object-oriented languages, are means of packaging data and function (called, in object terms, *behavior*) in order to create reusable and modular systems. This is an outgrowth of both software engineering issues, such as module cohesiveness, and the cost and complexity of large system implementation.

The major sales point is that packaging may allow easier system maintenance. Object-oriented techniques are often understood to allow system development without rigorous understanding of other system components. This is an overselling of the process, but many aspects of "OO" are here to stay.

This type of system is very burdensome to a capacity planner. The core pieces of the system (objects) tend to be easy to model. The distribution of the design of peripheral components complicates the planning process in two ways:

- The distribution of the design aspects implies that many systems seem out of control. The independence of the objects, and the number of inheritors of aspects of the objects with profoundly different performance characteristics, means that the number of designers to be interviewed increases dramatically.

- The object-oriented data hiding paradigm (encapsulation) allows for deferred decision making in the design process. How can you model a system that is composed of many pieces, most of which are distorted mirrors of each other, when their size can constantly change?

The short-term solution is to model each package independently. The unit of *object* is more fundamental to these systems then the module. A successful object-oriented project will use a "Chinese menu" selection from the object list: 2 from column A, 3 from column B. This combination of data and behavior should be very natural to a capacity planner and should coincide with the normal manner of modeling an application. Knowing the performance characteristics of the objects provides insight into the performance of the entire system.

Insight is not the same as understanding. Objects react differently to various stimuli. An application is a Markov walk, where each action is dependent on its context and history. This means that early estimates of object systems are crude and inaccurate. This implies that any large object-oriented system needs to undergo more iterations of capacity planning reviews than more traditional systems. This may be considered a simple outgrowth of the higher productivity of this type of development paradigm.

In the longer term, as the complexity of these objects increases, capacity planning becomes a risky profession. Either the object performance characteristics get inventoried as a component of the object behavior, or performance planning becomes totally unreliable. Tools have to develop in the application design side of the fence to help in predicting capacity requirements.

Luckily for capacity planners, most applications currently in DB2 that profess to be based on object-oriented design techniques only pay lip service to the concepts. These can be planned the same way as any other application. Capacity planning for true object-oriented systems is currently mostly done using traditional methods:

- Despite the "OO" label, we are dealing with large-scale development, for the most part using traditional incremental design and development strategies. This allows standard incremental capacity planning approaches during the external phases of design. This is traditional "top-down" capacity planning. When the objects themselves grow in granularity and evolve in various mutated and inherited forms, incremental capacity planning becomes cumbersome.

- At this point object manipulation becomes the key activity. The object systems allow a large degree of decentralized development. Then capacity planners often look at these systems as applications undergoing continuous development — the gross performance parameters are in place, and development takes on many characteristics of maintenance. Fine tuning of capacity issues here is done through modeling the designs and by exercising the completed components. This is traditional *bottom-up* capacity planning.

Offloading DB2 activity is a tempting thought. Non-370 or 390 architecture mainframe machines (Tandem, Teradata) are capable of executing many queries at lower cost than DB2 with better scalable growth. Lower-end platforms (RS/6000 with Sybase, Sun with Ingres, etc.) can run the same queries at tremendously lower cost at the risk of lower growth ceilings. The ceiling to the growth is rising so fast that it is a rare shop that will threaten it. The problems in offloading are always contextual. Missing application software on the platform, interfacing topics, inconsistent security features, training overhead, and other issues not directly relating to the specific application are the problem.

Capacity Planning a Cooperative Processing Application

In the smaller sense, a coprocessing application is easy to plan for. The mainframe component is usually a simple application. The application from a mainframe usually consists of a composition of the system software building blocks: dynamic and static SQL calls to DB2, interface management calls to the telecommunications manager or VTAM, and authority checks. From this aspect, coprocessing seems the same as small DB2 applications.

Problems arise from two factors. First, almost all cooperative processing applications tend to incorporate some sort of decision support capabilities. If the application contains simple transaction processing as well, we can capacity plan the application as a hybrid. Plan the transaction processing through a cost model, and plan the decision support by bucketing the activities by cost into categories and estimating the number of queries of each category.

Second, coprocessing applications require complex network planning. Often this consists of several networks, such as an

SNA network interfacing through gateways to several distinct local area networks.

This type of planning can be done through modeling appropriate scenarios of usage. Common wisdom admits that users often do not have a clear understanding of network volume, and the tendency is to build at least twice the expected network capacity, and on the LAN side to use the highest capacity network available at reasonable cost that fits the corporate architecture.

This excess capacity may be justifiable by the nature of coprocessing applications. The major rationale for the coprocessing features is the ability for the user to customize the product. Custom configuration is more important to user convenience than the better front ends or the graphical capabilities. The specialized applications tend to mutate their capacity requirements, which makes demand for this type of application very unstable.

A common phenomenon is a cooperative processing application using two to four times as much capacity as planned. This develops for several reasons:

- It is hard to develop coprocessing applications. Once they are completed, they can be used flexibly for more purposes than planned for.

- In many cases, use of these applications is discretionary. The flashy front ends of these applications can sell their use faster than traditional applications. The most common use of these applications is for data analysis. Good applications of this type can be used for more than original planners intended.

Summary

Large DB2 applications tend to be more complex to capacity plan than others, because more design is distributed into more programmers' hands. Complex applications require some form of incremental modeling.

DB2 applications have different issues to deal with than traditional programs. There tend to be more interfaces with other applications and other systems.

Object-oriented design requires specialization of the capacity planners to match the new development strategy. Client-server applications require modeling of several machines, networks, and their interaction.

Review Questions

1. What are appropriate points to analyze the performance of a new high-volume transaction processing application?

Answer to Review Question

1. The appropriate points to analyze the performance of any application depend on the shop's development methodology. The new high-volume transaction processing application will probably have some very concrete management checkpoints.

Typical phases of a development project include:

- Requirements gathering
- External design
- Logical database design
- Physical database design
- Application internal design
- Coding
- Unit testing
- Integration testing
- Quality assurance
- Implementation

Each of these phases can have very explicit performance reviews:

- **Requirements gathering**: This is a major capacity analysis point. The goal here is to roughly determine the platform size needed and develop a cost/ benefit tradeoff for nonstrategic application components. The result of this process should be a template containing a partially generic application profile and listing shop performance limitations.

- **External design**: Planning here consists of formalizing the performance issues. The application schedule should be identified, interfaces and interaction with other systems quantified, and components named. The performance characteristics of the components should be roughly quantified. Summing these quantities can produce early predictions of bottlenecks and deviations from the previous phase.

- **Logical database design**: This is the major DB2 performance design planning stage. The database aspects of the application can be quantified. Summing these quantities can produce early predictions of bottlenecks and deviations from the previous phase.

- **Physical database design**: This is generally a reaction to the problems identified in logical database design.

- **Application internal design**: This phase involves stepwise refinement of earlier identified data.

- **Coding**: This phase involves stepwise refinement of earlier identified data.

- **Unit testing**: This phase involves stepwise refinement of earlier identified data. Programmers can warn of performance deviations, and system statistics (e.g., SMF data) can be used for some model refinement.

- **Integration testing**: This phase will identify the accuracy of the evolved model. The performance characteristics should be clear at this point.

- **Quality assurance**: The model can be further evaluated. The accuracy of the model should be reviewed at this point. The modeling practice errors can be determined at this point.

- **Implementation**: Capacity planning at this point becomes reactive to change requests.

Chapter 20

High-Throughput DB2 Applications

What Is a High-Throughput Application?

There are many definitions of applications that strain the limits of technology. There are three types of high-throughput applications

- Those that approach the theoretical limits of the capability of modern systems
- Those that put inordinate strain on our current platform.
- Those that attempt to do more than other applications we use

The common factor in each of these cases is that we are dealing with an unknown; in each we may overload the system.

The capabilities of hardware have been getting better, and MVS has become the most efficient vehicle for running a balanced workload at near peak capacity ever. At the same time there is a basic rule of dealing with a system: some load (below peak capacity) allows fastest use of the component. (See Figure 20.1.)

Rate of Requests for Service

Each software component and hardware component used to assemble an application has a peak capacity. When building any application, there are dozens of things that can "hit the wall" and limit the overall system performance. These become bottlenecks limiting our system's capability to grow.

Of course these are moving targets; IBM has clear motivation to allow maximal growth in its systems. The wall created by these bottlenecks affects the most glamorous uses of IBM products and IBM's most important customers. Any identifiable bottleneck should be a moving target, and we can expect each release of software and hardware to improve the most odious problems.

System Bottlenecks

We should look at the limiting factors for a DB2 application. This can provide insight into the thresholds of our capabilities to support more avaricious systems. The major performance strategy IBM has used has been the idea of balanced systems: designing hardware made up of components, each of which can run at full capacity on a correctly configured system.

CPU load

DB2 applications are unique in requiring massive amounts of CPU time. Previous IBM software (with some exceptions

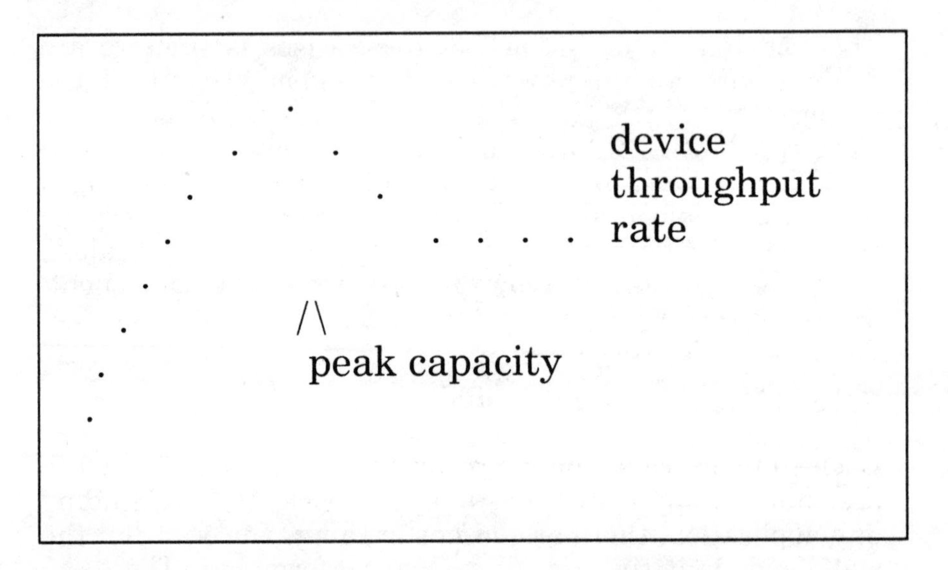

Figure 20.1 Device peak capacity.

such as early releases of IMS/DC and nonoperational software such as Script/GML) would rarely make CPU a limiting factor in performance. In fact, most traditional data processing activity is I/O bound.

DB2 was designed after the CPU cost had become less significant a cost factor in relation to the total price of hardware. It intentionally will use enormous quantities of CPU in efforts to reduce the I/O cost of an application. This activity can be very stable in well-defined transaction processing. On the other hand, ad-hoc reporting and other less restrictive activities can load a CPU complex completely.

There are some rare system bugs, systems configuration errors, or systems tuning requirements that cause tremendous performance drain. With these exceptions, the CPU load imposed by DB2 is completely dependent on application design and implementation. This is a profound issue that distinguishes DB2. DB2 is also capable of absorbing all system capacity in processing a single request, so an erroneous query can consume an entire system.

Most earlier systems with high performance requirements had a small core of applications that demanded most of the resources. These could be well designed by the best programmers, and were generally I/O bound.

An example of this, historically, is an IMS application that had a fraction of a percent of the code (the DL/1 database calls) responsible for most of the work. In many installations this was an easy task. The most skilled computer practitioners, systems and IMS experts, would be responsible for the crafting of this small amount of code. These experts, who became known as database analysts, could control overall system performance of these large systems centrally based on their deep understanding of the system.

This worked for a select few sites, which were characterized by being large central computer users with small numbers of very complex integrated applications. Most shops have had tremendous problems with this approach. Distributed management structures and fast changes in requirements necessitated design of smaller applications, spreading the load and camouflaging the fundamental use patterns.

DB2 grew out of both of these worlds. The lesson we learned from the integrated applications has been the need to control the data design centrally. The cheaper tactical application approach has shown us the need for distribution of database management skills.

Application load

Any application can be a CPU hog. DB2 applications often enter into new areas of technology, where design techniques are unclear and vendor software performs poorly. These performance demands are not just from DB2, but from applications and application building tools. This issue has to be addressed in terms of the systems development life cycle, where the CPU cost of developing a DB2 application can be enormous. It also must be dealt with in running the applications.

Although this is not a DB2 problem per se, applications built in DB2 can often overambitiously use CPU. Be particularly careful in the cases of new technology: image processing, expert systems, and other activities that your shop is not accustomed to managing.

High-throughput applications and a high-throughput application mix

There are many similarities between a large-volume application and a large-scale environment consisting of multiple applications. From the performance management perspective, the major difference is that the individual application is build with a coherent design. The application suite is structured on a design philosophy or architecture.

A large-scale application is built with a single design philosophy. A large shop tends to have its shop philosophy. The large application may look at first hand like it is more tightly designed.

In many cases, large applications are *less* cohesive because internal developers are overwhelmed by the implementation requirements. The implementation has to be partially farmed out to contract programmers less aware of company standards. An application design and development methodology can only partially address this issue.

Aspects of DB2 Processing

Relational processing and transaction processing conflict in several ways. Despite the political tendency to belittle this issue, it comes up frequently in high-transaction processing applications. The major problems are:

- Nonnavigational processing conflicts with the transaction processing requirement for controlled access.
- The relational structure is customized for query processing flexibility. The transaction processing applications are often so customized and constrained that this will never be realistic. Thus there is overhead in a relational system that is based on a political constraint. I am not claiming that relational flexibility does not help low volume transaction processing. In a high-volume processing environment the additional overhead of the relational processing often forces silly looking and awkward customization that hurts flexibility anyway.

Locks as a Performance Bottleneck

Lock contention is a fundamental problem as transaction rates increase. DB2 locks data on a block (page or index leaf subpage) level. Lock contention can be caused by:

- **Logical database design** — for example, consider a table in which a *high record number* is stored to be used whenever a new row is added. This design will force contention between multiple users adding rows.
- **Physical database design** — for example, clustering a table in the order in which data are inserted will force contention between multiple users adding rows.
- **Luck** — multiple users may independently and arbitrarily choose data on the same page, and so there can be contention between multiple users adding rows.

Luck is typically a factor only for small tables with frequent updates. Most other locking factors can be dealt with by proper design.

Log as a Performance Bottleneck

The DB2 log is the most obvious general bottleneck in the system. All update processing is logged, centralizing the writes. Let us review the log processing services. Logging (also frequently called journaling) is the activity of writing updates to secondary storage. (See Figure 20.2.)

- **Work units** guarantee that either an entire transaction will be completed, or all the activity will be rolled back by reversing the activity recorded in the log if a problem occurs before the work unit COMMIT occurs. The latter action is called ROLLBACK, since the updates are undone in inverse order. The process of rolling back is called backward recovery, referring to restoring the data to a previous state. Rollback will undo the activity of only a specific work unit. DB2 supports both one-phase commits and two-phase commits, which allows DB2 the capability to coordinate rollback with other database management facilities.
- **Forward recovery** is a means of rebuilding data to a more recent state by reapplying the changes from the log onto a historical version of the data, such as a backup image copy. Forward recovery will apply the updates from all work units that were successfully committed during the recovery period. This process is also called roll forward, since the updates are applied in sequential order.

Write the log buffer undo/redo records
to each active log copy

Wait until one completes

(If using two phased commit,
apply second phase and wait for
completion.)

Figure 20.2 Log actions processing a COMMIT.

Log activity for each thread (connection to DB2):

- Any DELETE will log the before image of the row.
- Any INSERT will log the after image of the row.
- Any UPDATE will log both the before and after image of the changed columns (if there is an update to a var column, the entire row from the var column to the end is logged).

Some DB2 utilities (LOAD, REORG) will optionally log a mass change. (This is rarely justifiable in practice.)

Figure 20.3 Transaction log activity.

DB2 provides the option during installation of using single or dual logging (maintaining one or two copies of the journal data). We will assume that your system uses dual logging, which is demanded by the limitations of DASD technology. We will also see that dual logging can be used to improve performance. (See Figure 20.3.)

Fast write hardware

Fast write hardware, such as the IBM 3990-3 controller that was designed specifically for DB2 use, can be an enormous improvement on a particular DB2 bottleneck.

Writes in DB2 to tablespaces and indexspaces are staged in the bufferpools (unless the write threshold is exceeded). The log, however, is a sore point for update-intensive applications. The log is limited to the write speed of the DASD, typically at best 16 to 20 ms.

This write delay adds to the time of each transaction since the transaction waits for the log to be written. The write also adds another potential bottleneck.

Fast write hardware can reduce the write delay to 2 to 3 ms. This is done by using battery backed up semiconductor memory. The log is an ideal candidate for this type of writethrough cache because the processing is sequential.

Rollback

Rolling back processing activity is disastrous for log contention. Rollback causes backwards log reads as well as writes to the beginning of the logs. The reads look for the UNDO before images of the update activity. The writes are of TODO records identifying what rollback processing is itself doing.

In many cases the writes and reads all take place within the log buffer. This is less onerous to the system. If the scope of the rollback increases, the rollback will thrash the log between reads and writes.

Multiple concurrent rollbacks and rollbacks of large work units (especially of batch programs) can be serious offenders, causing system delays. This is one of the exceptions in DB2 where an activity of one application can delay another.

Performance Tradeoffs

Whenever we push a technology, we find ourselves in a world of tradeoffs. Understanding them, and balancing them in the application design, are the points where the performance characteristics of the application physical design develop.

Clustering the data where it is most likely to be accessed by multiple applications is ideal for I/O reduction and bufferpool utilization. The conflict here is between DB2 block-level locking and transaction throughput. If we design a high-transaction rate application where some updated data is clustered tightly together, the transactions will experience lock delay or deadlock. We can separate the data, for example by clustering on a more random key, but this will add I/O cost to the application.

Checkpoint frequency and commit frequency is another example of these tradeoffs. The less frequent the checkpoints, the faster updating applications can run. The cost here is in DB2 restart cost. The more frequent the checkpoints, the less work DB2 will have to do when it is being started. The implication is that we cannot build a high-transaction rate application with high availability requirements with an infrequent checkpoint.

Summary

High throughput applications are those which put more stress on a system than we are used to. Planning these types of applications should focus on the limiting factors that can slow processing.

DB2 adds some complications to planning a large applications. The problems we see in planning large applications include

- DB2 throughput capability, since DB2 cannot handle all applications
- DB2 performance characteristics, especially since DB2 can be very CPU bound
- DB2 logging and recovery characteristics, although log issues can be alleviated using specialized hardware

Review Question

1. Why have the IBM DB2 developers been reluctant to add support for the MVS/ESA hiperspace data-in-memory facility?

Answer to Review Question

1. The IBM DB2 developers been so reluctant to add support for the MVS/ESA hiperspace data-in-memory facility for several reasons:

- It is complicated and expensive to change the internal design of DB2.
- There are only rare situations where the hiperspace would improve performance over equally enlarged bufferpools.
- Managing the environment would be much more complicated. Hiperspace data could be in a three-tiered buffering configuration: hiperspace, bufferpool, and virtual

memory. It is fantastically difficult to configure and control these elements correctly.

Chapter 21

Security Management in DB2

Overview of Security Issues

Security is not relevant in a vacuum. It is a combination of business issues and the application of a security plan. In almost all cases, audit will show frequent cases of excessive authority. Most shops have a hierarchical view of access to data. A very simple strategy is summarized in Figure 21.1.

Database security can be considered the application of rules defining the users authority to access or change data. A security strategy will define the authorization required to access or change most data. This can be viewed as a spectrum, where the strategy defines your place on the spectrum and the implementation defines a range of access in the shop. A very controlled environment will have a narrow range, while a less controlled environment will have a very wide spectrum of access. (See Figure 21.2.)

DB2 is a complex product in a complex environment. It is meant to manage sensitive information, and includes rigorous security management. At the same time, these facilities have to be designed into the applications to be effectively used and designed into the environment to be controlled.

DB2 differentiates between three types of security. DB2 manages:

- The systems aspects
- The data themselves (with a variant for views on the data)
- Controlling the program access path, plans, and packages

Outside of DB2, security managers must manage the interfaces between DB2 objects and other security mechanisms.

In an application design there are fundamental choices to be made. The most obvious is: Do we use DB2 security at all? Many applications have successfully embedded security management in the application, or used CICS security management facilities in lieu of the DB2-provided security.

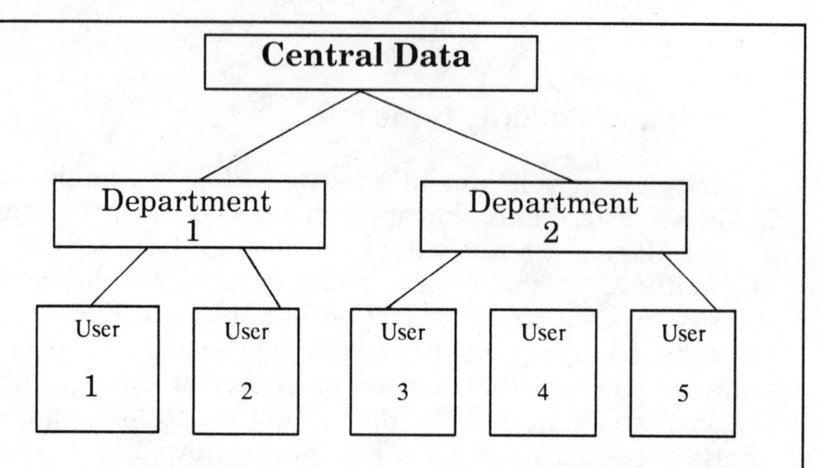

An common example of hierarchical authorization is to allow each user to:

- Do anything with their own data
- Insert but not update or delete their department's data
- Read only data of other users in their department
- Only read unrestricted parts of the central data

Thus User 1 could, for example, insert data in a structure belonging to Department 1 but not even read data belonging to Department 2.

Figure 21.1 A security management strategy.

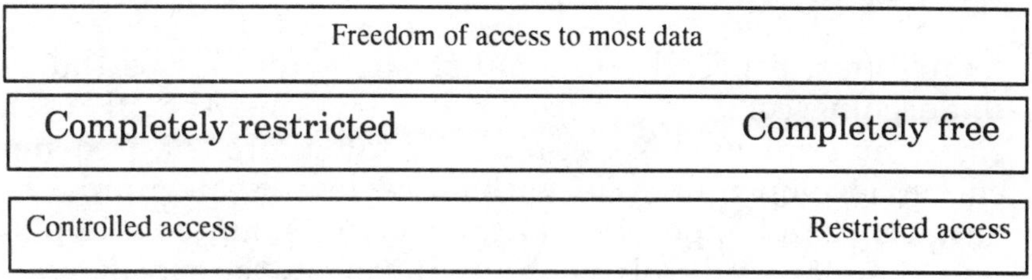

Freedom of access to most data	
Completely restricted	Completely free
Controlled access	Restricted access

Figure 21.2 The spectrum of data control.

This kind of decision may make sense for the company strategy or for a very complex application. In the absence of a strong reason not to, however, most applications use DB2 security.

The security structure imposed and the style of management of the security can have tremendous impact on the ease of using an application, on its performance, and on its viability. I have seen applications that have failed in the users' minds simply because the glamorous security management structure did not correspond to their view of the world.

The security structure in your DB2 environment should fit comfortably in the framework of your security management software. There are simply too many security managers in a shop. Beside DB2 there are security facilities in:

- MVS, such as RACF
- Teleprocessing monitors, such as CICS
- Fourth-generation languages, packages, and applications

There are too many products and too many unintegrated means to the same end.

New DB2 shops have a special battle to fight. Adding another security control facility to a shop that cannot control the existing ones effectively will decrease security quality. Adding a new security structure to a shop that has painfully accepted central control of other security management will reopen old wounds. Most shops need a crisis or warning before accepting the requirement to implement some level of corporate DB2 security management.

DBA Control as a "Stopper"

Sometimes, especially in smaller shops and shops that are undergoing conversions from other systems, the DBA function is not enfranchised. That is to say, there is a free application development cycle, without review or safeguards. This situation can happen when a shop is in a maintenance phase and abandons a development methodology for expediency.

In this situation the security mechanism in DB2 can be used to provide the skeleton of a development methodology. Application developers will not develop their applications before DBA review if they do not have the tables to test with. This is the most basic of development procedures and is painless except for grumbling from the developers.

DB2 Audit Trace

DB2 audit trace is not a complete audit facility. It works using the trace facilities initially built for performance tracing. Even when all traces are started, it will record only the first update processed in a work unit. This was done for performance reasons. If properly used, the audit traces will allow the user to identify the responsible party for DDL and DCL. The audit trace can identify the list of users who accessed or changed data in a time period.

User-Managed Audit Trails

The only way in DB2 to identify each user responsible for a change is to embed logic within the application program to identify the responsible party. DB2 has some convenience features to allow this type of processing. It is a common practice to add identification fields to each application table as shown in Figure 21.3.

```
CREATE TABLE EXAMPLE (
      LAST_CHANGE_D TIMESTAMP NOT NULL,
      LAST_CHANGER  CHAR(8)   NOT NULL,
    /* the rest of the columns */
                      )
```

Figure 21.3 Audit trail columns added to a table.

The intention in Figure 21.3 is to store the time and date of the last change in LAST_CHANGE_D. Also, the rule is to store the identifier of the user who changed the data in the LAST_CHANGER field. This approach requires application developer discipline in coding to a standard. Examples are shown in Figures 21.4 and 21.5.

```
INSERT INTO EXAMPLE VALUES(
     CURRENT TIMESTAMP,
     USER,
     /* the rest of the columns */
```

Figure 21.4 Adding a new row to an audited table.

```
UPDATE EXAMPLE
   SET LAST_CHANGE_D = CURRENT TIMESTAMP,
       LAST_CHANGER  = USER,
        /* the rest of the columns to be updated */
WHERE CURRENT OF CURSOR1
```

Figure 21.5 Updating a row in an audited table.

The user must, of course, be willing to pay for the extra data on every row. DB2 provides a means to set these values. An EDITPROC can be used to set the values on first write and reset them to new values during a change. The overhead of adding an EDITPROC to normal processing makes this an unpleasant option. The option can be justified in some cases, where the application audit importance can justify the expense. The procedure may be valid where an EDITPROC is already required for other reasons such as data compression.

In many shops there is a shop standard that the first two columns in a table must be the *change time stamp* and the responsible party (or even that the first four columns should be the *initial create time stamp, initial creator, last change time stamp,* and *last changer*). A valuable tool for this type of table is a VALIDPROC that will simply verify that the application has developed following the appropriate discipline.

This procedure requires the developer to code appropriate initial values in SQL inserts and updates. The VALIDPROC will verify that the values are correctly set. The power of this technique is that the VALIDPROC can always be used in development for detecting inconsistency, and used in production if auditors require it, or turned off for performance reasons.

A static technique to check developer compliance to the standard of setting the audit columns is to analyze the DB2 catalog table SYSIBM.SYSSTMT. When any application program or package is bound, all of its SQL statements are copied from the appropriate DBRM to this catalog table. The update and insert statements in this table must conform to the shop standard. This can be easily verified with a simple program that parses statements retrieved from SYSIBM.SYSSTMT and verifies that the programs update the audit trail appropriately. This statement analysis requires that the statements update the fields to the SQL *special registers* CURRENT USER and CURRENT TIMESTAMP, rather than using host variables.

This technique will not work in applications using dynamic SQL updates or inserts to the relevant table. The audit program can only verify the existence of the dynamic SQL EXECUTE IMMEDIATE statement, and optionally explore the authorization tables to verify that the users are not authorized to update values dynamically or insert data into the relevant tables. This type of procedure fits best into shops with much DB2 development in process and strictly enforced development standards.

The DB2 transaction log contains before and after images of all updates and seems ideal as a means of preserving an audit trail. In fact, this is not an easy process. Every transaction performing an update will be identified by a transaction identifier. DB2 does not present a direct means to identify the user associated with this transaction identifier. Associating the two requires some sort of identification protocol. An audit trace can be used, but it is difficult to associate audit and log records.

An example protocol would be having each updater first insert his or her name into a identification table — resulting in a log record containing both the user ID and the transaction ID. DB2 audit trails (or some of the other DB2 trace trails or security management facilities or the DB2 sign-on and authorization exits) could then be used with the log information as a means of detecting any user who violates the identification standard. The effort involved in this process makes it an unlikely option for a development shop, leaving users waiting for support from tools vendors or from IBM. An example product of this type is ProAudit (On-Line Software, Inc., Fort Lee, N.J., a subsidiary of Computer Associates, Inc.).

Summary

DB2 security is actually composed of system security issues and application security issues. In application security, each shops adopts a security strategy. In most cases the security is defined in a hierarchical structure.

As applications are defined, the security approach should be defined. The first decision is to select from the security options in the operating system, teleprocessing monitor, or DB2, or to build the security into the application.

Database applications often require audit trails. This issue should be defined together with the security strategy. DB2 provides incomplete audit trail information.

Review Questions

1. How can DB2 be used to restrict inappropriate users from accessing restricted data?

2. How can the users authorized to access DB2 restricted data be identified?

Answers to Review Questions

1. DB2 can be used to restrict inappropriate users from accessing restricted data by not granting the users the authority to access the data. Users can be authorized to process the data directly, or indirectly authorized through plan authorization.

2. The users authorized to access DB2 restricted data can be identified from the DB2 system catalog authorization tables. For example, the relevant table authorizations are in SYSIBM.SYSTABAUTH. This identifies user ability to access data through dynamic SQL and ability to BIND programs that access the data.

Authorization to execute a plan in DB2 allows the user to access data through the program. The programs referencing a table are identified in the catalog table SYSIBM.SYSPLANDEP. The users authorized to execute a program are identified in the catalog table SYSIBM.SYSPLANAUTH.

Chapter 22

DB2 Security Facilities

Security in a database management system usually has two meanings. Security in the pure database sense refers to protection of the data. But database applications do not operate in a vacuum. Controlling access to the entire system will protect the data. A further definition of security is prevention of data loss, a subject discussed under the heading of operational considerations. DB2 provides security through GRANT and REVOKE statements. These come in different flavors.

Tables and Views

There are table privileges, which deal in access to the data. For example,

```
GRANT SELECT ON USER1.TABLE1 TO USER2
```

will authorize user 2 to access the named table. The authority can be withdrawn by

```
REVOKE SELECT ON USER1.TABLE1 FROM USER2
```

and in general all GRANT statements have a converse REVOKE statement. The privileges held are stored in the DB2 catalog in the various "AUTH" tables. The table privileges are stored in SYSIBM.SYSTABAUTH. Revocation of privileges will delete the corresponding rows from the catalog. A special user identifier, PUBLIC, is used to denote that the privilege is granted to all users:

```
GRANT INSERT ON USER1.TABLE1 TO PUBLIC
```

This will allow any DB2 user the right to add rows to USER1.TABLE1.

Table privileges are the meat of the DB2 access control; they can restrict users to certain types of access, for example,

```
GRANT SELECT, INSERT, DELETE, UPDATE
ON USER1.TABLE1 TO USER2
```

```
GRANT INDEX, ALTER ON USER1.TABLE1 TO USER2
```

which together give user 2 the authority equivalent to:

```
GRANT ALL ON USER1.TABLE1 TO USER2
```

DB2 privileges can be passed from user to user:

```
GRANT SELECT ON USER1.TABLE1
TO USER2 WITH GRANT OPTION
```

The privilege authorizes user 2 to further allow others to access USER1.TABLE1. If user 2 in turn specifies the "WITH GRANT OPTION," the next grantee will also be able to authorize users. If a user authority is revoked, DB2 will revoke all of these cascading authorizations.

A user can be authorized multiple times with the same authority, even the exact same authority, which would seemingly simply mess up the DB2 catalog. This can create an awkward situation if a user receives a given privilege in multiple ways. DB2 will resolve the situation by comparing when an authorization was granted.

Table privileges are needed for the various development staff involved in creating programs, and by users of dynamic SQL, such as users of decision support systems.

Plan Security

Plan privileges are a means to control application plans. In order to control development, only certain users are allowed to bind plans by authorizing them:

```
GRANT BIND ON PLAN1 TO USER1
```

or cancelling them:

```
REVOKE BIND ON PLAN1 FROM USER1
```

Even if user 1 is authorized to BIND PLAN1, he or she still needs the authority to do any activity specified in the plan. For example, if the plan includes a statement:

```
EXEC SQL
  SELECT COL1 FROM USER2.VIEW2
    WHERE COL2 = :variable
END-EXEC
```

User 1 needs the authority to access that data in order to bind PLAN1. In general application programs use only static SQL, but if the plan contains dynamic SQL — the PREPARE and EXECUTE IMMEDIATE statements — these statements will be validated against the authority of the user who is executing the program.

The most important plan privilege is the authority to execute the plan. Having authority to execute a bound plan implies authority to execute any of the static SQL statements in the plan; table access privileges are tested for each plan user. In some cases, especially transaction processing applications, the application design opts to grant PUBLIC access to the plan, then uses system security software such as CICS security mechanisms to control access to the plan.

There are several types of authority used to manage DB2. System privileges are used to manage the managers of DB2. Use privileges allow access to storage groups, bufferpools, and tablespaces. Database authority allows for management of databases.

Overview of Security Issues in Application Design

Security is a major design component of any large application. It is a functional requirements issue. User requirements, other departmental requirements, and anyone else's requirements have to be coped with in the early stages of application design. Often security requirements become aspects of the logical database design. Security issues will otherwise come back to haunt you as artificial and awkward layers are artificially grafted onto an existing design.

Smaller applications often frequently follow shop standards; this often consists of repeating what was done to manage security in the last application. This is a typical human trait: whoever identifies a problem implicitly is associated with it.

Problems will always arise in a changing environment. Thus, the first few DB2 applications in a shop are used as guinea pigs. They should be reviewed to see if the shop standards still apply to those applications, to see what problems arise, to see if internal audit will accept the DB2 applications as designed, and so on.

Since DB2 is often associated with new concepts within a company, such as end user data access, these problems can get bundled up into a collective predicament. These things tend to (justly) threaten a developer trapped in this situation. Management evaluates the developer on producing "on time, on budget." In most cases the problem is dealt with by convening a committee to deal with global issues slowly. The developer becomes less productive. This delay and reduced productivity must be counted as part of the price of change.

An obvious solution to security problems is building the security into the application itself. This has the advantage of providing the exact features needed, and total control. Designing security into applications has a delightful aspect: the issues go away — they are part of the structure. That does not imply that one should design applications with internal security facilities. Replacing security management software with application logic is risky for several reasons.

The security management code has to be designed, written and debugged — at a high level of quality if the application or data are important. The possibility of change can complicate the application further. Internal or external audit will often require thorough review of the entire component because of its sensitivity. Application-specific security will not integrate with the general security management software.

Doing anything yourself is a commitment to maintain it forever. Replacing a system function internally requires strong long-term arguments in its favor. Any kind of coding of the security into the application is reasonable in only two situations:

- The application is so all-encompassing that it takes over the environment. These types of so-called *solution* applications can dictate corporate policy simply because of size.

- A combination approach where standard security facilities provide a 90 percent solution, and the application security management solves some problems that the security management packages cannot solve directly. This can work, and is best implemented using standard programming interfaces to the security management package, rather than building redundancy of function inside the application.

An awkward situation in implementing security arises when software is ported from a different environment. In this situation (which is equivalent to the problems in preparing an application for implementation in production that was designed ignoring or misunderstanding security issues), security management has to be overlaid onto the existing structure, and a price has to be paid in security, flexibility, and function.

User access to individual tables and views through dynamic SQL presents a complex problem in applications of which several versions are maintained. A typical project will involve dozens of tables, and each has to be named correctly in the application. The appropriate DB2 GRANT and REVOKE authorization statements have to be built.

DB2 provides the SYNONYM label; for example,

```
CREATE SYNONYM MYTABLE FOR TSOUSER.HISTABLE
```

will cause a reference to "MYTABLE" to refer to a table called "HISTABLE" created by user "TSOUSER." This seems like a convenience, but becomes impractical because of a quirk in the statement design. A SYNONYM will apply only to the user who created it. To use SYNONYMs on an application, every user has to create the appropriate SYNONYMs for any table needed. This makes a SYNONYM useful as a means of borrowing a table from a neighbor, but annoying if used for managing an application's security.

Conveniently, a feature DB2 version 2.2 added for simplifying access to distributed databases, the ALIAS, can be used for this purpose. The statement

```
CREATE ALIAS MYTABLE FOR TSOUSER.HISTABLE
```

will cause a reference to "MYTABLE" to refer to a table actually called "HISTABLE" created by user "TSOUSER." The ALIAS will be accessible to the user who created it, and to anyone else who uses the appropriate *authid* qualifier.

Problems in Providing Row-Level Security

Row-level security seems to be the ideal security mechanism. In many cases this can work. Views in DB2 were explicitly designed to provide this service. It is important to note that for most applications, view-managed row-level security is the rare exception. The reasons the mechanism is not used may be useful in understanding potential issues at your site.

The most common reason to ignore DB2 view-managed security is misunderstanding of the view mechanism and facilities on the part of the security designer. For example, secondary authids have been available in DB2 for several years, but many designers do not understand the control they provide. Views can depend on secondary authids in this fashion:

```
CREATE VIEW EXAMPLE AS
SELECT COL1, COL2
 FROM  TABLE
 WHERE COL3 = 'value'
   AND COL4 = CURRENT SQLID
```

CURRENT SQLID is an SQL scalar function returning the currently set secondary authid. This allows COL4 to function as an "owner" column, preventing access to others. Similar delays in using packages to control security effectively can happen until the programmers are acclimated to their use.

The second most common reason for partial use of DB2 security mechanisms is structural mismatch between the DB2 mechanisms and the preceding security mechanisms. Security software has a tradition of being a jumble of vaguely interconnected components, where system security (e.g., RACF, CA-Top Secret, CA-ACF2), transaction processing security (IMS/DC or CICS security and TSO password control), and other component security (application managed security, vendor package security, etc.) all uneasily coexist: each software package developer has been forced to assume that its security facilities might be the only ones available. Each package alternatively may supplement several of the others.

Another common problem in using views is the difficulty in controlling their proliferation. This is a very legitimate issue. In many cases when row-level security is used, the number of views used per application can grow rapidly. Given the large number of existing views, it becomes hard to find the correct one. As other applications are implemented, one is tempted to create a new view. This creates a flat security structure that is impossible to manage. Clarifying the security requirements into a reasonable hierarchical structure is vital for the long-term control of applications.

Another common reason for not using view security is the fear that DB2 security is in a state of flux. CA-ACF/2 and

CA-Top Secret (both from Computer Associates, Garden City, N.Y.) already provide security facilities that bypass DB2 security management. This type of facility completely overlaps DB2 security management. Presumably RACF will follow suit.

Usually VIEWs can be enough to manage fine granularity security. For example, if TABLE contains a view, one can

```
CREATE VIEW PROGVIEW AS
SELECT COLUMN1, COLUMN2
 FROM  TABLE1
 WHERE DATA_OWNER = user
```

where the DATA_OWNER column is populated with the AUTHID of the user authorized to access the data. If the data are departmental, the program can use a secondary authid (EXEC SQL SET CURRENT SQLID='mydept' in the program) to make the view more global in scope:

```
CREATE VIEW PROGVIEW AS
SELECT COLUMN1, COLUMN2
 FROM  TABLE
 WHERE DATA_OWNER = current user
```

This scheme can be used in static SQL in programs where there are only small numbers of types of users. Implement it either by using conditionals based on the user ID or by using user ID associated plan package collections, issuing the appropriate SET CURRENT PACKAGESET command to retrieve the appropriate views. The latter approach simplifies program and security management.

The available information for this kind of security management is shown in Figure 22.1.

Data source	Type of data
DB2 current user	The SQL chosen secondary ID, defaults to primary
DB2 user	The SQL primary authid
RACF	Data retrieved from a security manager
Program generated	Defined in program design
TP monitor	Data from teleprocessing monitor security mechanism

Figure 22.1 Sources of security information.

These considerations mainly apply to static SQL. Static SQL only authorizes users to the privileges of the current SQLID. Dynamic SQL authorizes users to the union of all privileges of all allowed IDs.

Joins to a "Security Table"

A common security requirement is row-level security. Sometimes this cannot be naturally implemented through special register functions such as CURRENT USER. In this case, a common practice is to join all user-accessible data to a security table. (See Figure 22.2; this table is typically defined by the database administrator, even though a system table such as SYSIBM.SYSTABAUTH could artificially be used to the same end by GRANTing appropriate authorization to dummy IDs. This is not normally done, because catalog tables cannot be indexed and because of lock problems.) In practice, this strategy only works for small amounts of data.

Large tables tend to be associated with very complex queries. Adding an extra table to each query or, more typically, doubling the number of tables joined (since each table refer-

Data_owner	Column 1	Column 2
'accounting'	34.23	'some data'
'management'	22.45	'more data'

Figure 22.2 Tagging data with authorization fields.

enced has an associated security lookup) makes query optimization haphazard. This makes the join approach reasonable for occasional use for small amounts of data but an impediment otherwise.

A security table is flexible, cheap to implement, and clean. It is the obvious choice if performance is not an issue. For example, it can work well as a simple means for managing extraordinary ad-hoc searches against operational data. If the window to run the queries is big enough, the simplicity of the technique here can make up for the performance problems.

Denormalizing: Row Security Flags

Relational applications often use join security — security information is stored in a separate security table. User access to other table data is through a join of the requested table to the security table. This is especially prevalent in decision support systems. An example security table is shown in Figure 22.3. An example of a data table is shown in Figure 22.4.

```
CREATE TABLE SECURITY (
USER_NAME      CHAR(8),
USER_AUTH      SMALLINT);
```

Figure 22.3 Example of a security table.

```
CREATE TABLE SALARY (
AUTH_LEVEL  SMALLINT,
EMPLOYEE    DEC(8),
SALARY       DEC(6,2));
```

Figure 22.4 Example of a data table.

The data are accessed through the VSALARY VIEW:

```
CREATE VIEW VSALARY AS
SELECT EMPLOYEE, SALARY
FROM SALARY, SECURITY
WHERE AUTH_LEVEL = USER_AUTH /* only if allowed*/
 AND USER_NAME   = CURRENT USER/* for this user  */
```

so when the user is authorized to access VSALARY, he or she can access only those that match the USER_AUTH entered for the user by the security administrator. This process works, but requires every access to refer to twice as many tables: each table is joined to the security table. This becomes very expensive in performance, and confuses the DB2 optimizer into generating poor access paths.

Many applications using this strategy are forced to react to the performance consequences. The standard solution to slow join processing is to denormalize the data. Why not embed the security data into the data itself?

This strategy will work in many instances. In fact, the common type of application in which this becomes an issue, decision and planning systems, tends to have such minimal amounts of updating that denormalization is a reasonable action. Be careful not to distort the data structure before analyzing the application consequences.

Denormalization is a compromise between corporate and application goals; it is unrealistic to compromise until the themes have been established. Make sure that the security requirements have been fully identified before denormalizing.

In most cases security operates as a direct hierarchy. In this context, it is tempting to create set/superset authority, such as a single security token denoting security level. For instance, a new column could be added to each table. An example of this token is:

```
     SECURITY_TOKEN (CHAR(1))
```

containing encoded values, such as shown in Figure 22.5.

0: The user is allowed access to everything

1: The user is authorized to access all nonsecured data

2: The user is authorized to access all planning data

3: The user is authorized to access only historical data

Figure 22.5 Example of security token codes.

and the arrangement becomes the view strategy discussed above. This can work in some instances. In many environments, there are simply too many parallel or departmental boundaries for this approach to be effective. Often designs of this type evolve into a collection of security flags (usually between three and five) that allow more detailed management of the security procedures. This works well, but is much less flexible.

Secondary ID Structuring

It is a delight to work in applications where the secondary ID structure matches the application requirements. In this situation, security design is automatic. The hard work has been done, and it is only necessary to assemble the pieces.

Secondary authids are preferred in almost any application. The standard DB2 primary ID support is burdensome to administer, damaging to performance, and has no redeeming qualities. One can, of course, achieve just as poor an environment with secondary authids by illogically grouping the users. It is difficult to do worse with secondary authids than with primary ones.

In order to work nicely, security IDs must correlate with the way the business works. It is not coincidence, or an artifact of capricious design, that the standard source of secondary IDs is the security manager group rather than internal DB2 design.

Most security managers have implemented groups slowly, and they have evolved through the process of "group-think." Much effort has gone into mimicking what the company does. The more mature the groupings are, the better (unless there has been a recent radical company reorganization). The groups are the product of much analysis and can save a lot of development time.

The security manager groups also have a huge advantage: these corporate meta-data can be shared across environments. This is the only reasonable place to manage resources, such as DB2 applications, which have a irrepressible tendency to cross the traditional run-time environment borders.

As application security requirements are analyzed, see if the existing security groupings match. If so, some effort has been saved. If not, perhaps additional secondary authids may have to be added.

Functional ID Grouping

A common approach is to organize collections of users in terms of the activities they perform. This is often called functional definition of security. Secondary authids are defined based on activity. Users are authorized to the appropriate authids only when the facilities are needed. This strategy has some clear advantages: Each user gets those secured facilities he or she has need of. The security features are used to best advantage. Audit becomes much simpler. As fine a granularity of control can be imposed as needed.

In practice, it is often a complicated means of managing security. The problems arise as each minor change in staff responsibility causes an authorization crisis. Users may not be provided the appropriate permission to perform their duties.

Thus functional grouping can work well under very stable conditions where the need to change is limited and control is important. An example of this is large-scale transaction processing where each operator has a very defined role.

Functional grouping can also work in a well-managed environment with clear definition of responsibilities and a responsive management of security. In that kind of environment, which accepts the overhead in exchange for well-controlled facilities and has a high regard for security, functional security is ideal. An example would be decision support activity dealing with sensitive data, where each "exceptional" request must be authorized.

Departmental ID Groupings

Most businesses are not willing to simply turn user security off and on often. The overhead of doing so is high. Unless the process is scrupulously managed, the user may be left with excess authority that should only have existed temporarily.

This leads to a simplified version of the functional grouping strategy. Most businesses are organized in hierarchies in which each level of the hierarchy has similar functional requirements.

This structure can be used to manage security. Each user exists in a very defined role in terms of the great majority of the activity. A security template can be built that authorizes users to standard activities. This structure can coincide with departmental structure in the company, and this organization structure is often called *departmental security grouping*.

The departmental grouping can be very effective. A new employee or transfer can immediately be given access to all normal secured components. Exceptional authorization requirements can be dealt with on a case-by-case basis.

This convenience makes this structure the most common for any site requiring flexibility. The template provides convenience, and the exceptional authority provides functional authorization for the exceptional cases. As an example, this is a common security structure for IS developers who would be hampered by more restrictive control.

Security within the Program

A program can manage secondary authids in two ways. The IDs can be hard coded into the program. For example, an accounting program can simply

```
EXEC SQL SET CURRENT SQLID='ACCOUNT'
```

which is a strategy that works well for many applications and eases their administration considerably. The other option is to set the value based on external input. For instance, an application security may be managed under CICS security, and the appropriate secondary authid can be passed to the application from a CICS table.

The easiest strategy to manage is the hard-coded option. Variants can allow a surprising level of security management. For example, the following can be coded:

```
EXEC SQL
SET CURRENT SQLID='CAPODTC';
END-EXEC.
IF SQLCODE = 0 THEN
EXEC SQL
   SET CURRENT SQLID='CAPO'
END-EXEC
.     IF SQLCODE = 0 THEN
EXEC SQL
SET CURRENT SQLID='HITMAN'
END-EXEC
ELSE
EXEC SQL
SET CURRENT SQLID='PEON'
END-EXEC.
```

This code fragment will set the user to the highest level of permission authorized in a four-level hierarchy. The overhead of this type of processing is not high; all processing is in memory and RACF is not called repeatedly, but it may be inappropriate for fast transaction processing.

The DB2 exits can be used to implement special security mechanisms. VALIDPROC can be used to only restrict the user or plan that references data. EDITPROC can be used to encrypt and decrypt data.

The performance implications of this processing may be severe. These exits should be used only for requirements that cannot be managed any other way. In particular, EDITPROC should be avoided unless the processing impact is judged reasonable.

Departmental ID Translation

DB2 version 2 release 1 added the secondary ID facility. Until then, security planners had problems managing DB2 security as groups. The DSN3@AUTH and DSN3@SGN exits did exist previous to DB2 version 2.1.

Some shops attempted to secure DB2 objects in groups by using these DSN3@ exits to map user TSO IDs into logical groups. This typically is based on naming conventions for TSO user IDs. If the first three characters of the TSO ID corresponds to a department name, an exit can easily translate user IDs to group IDs. An example of the translation table is shown in Figure 22.6.

An exit can translate the TSO ID to the group ID by simple truncation. The first three characters of the ID are used as a group.

TSO ID	Department	Group ID
PRGTOMMY	Programming	PRG
PRGJENNY	Programming	PRG
ACTNORM	Accounting	ACT
ACTTINA	Accounting	ACT
DATBILL	Data entry	DAT
DATTOM	Data entry	DAT
DATSUSAN	Data entry	DAT

Figure 22.6 Translating TSO to Group IDs.

Summary

DB2 security has to be managed as an architectural issue. Applications that do not consider security as part of the design can create tremendous problems. DB2 provides a rich set of capabilities for managing application security. VIEWs can be created to restrict access to columns or confine data access to data value ranges. ALIASes provide a simplification of table name management. It is vital to consider the security philosophy of the company in deciding to manage security as a functional or departmental organization. This can be used with DB2 authid switching to effect a clean security structure.

Review Question

1. Are there benefits in using the DB2 group identifier mechanism over simple ID translation?

Answer to Review Question

1. There are benefits in using the DB2 group identifier mechanism over simple ID translation. The group ID mechanism is more flexible. It allows multiple alternate group identifiers, under programmatic control.

Moreover, the use of an authorization identifier translation exit is a nuisance to program and maintain. Authorization changes generally require bringing DB2 down.

The translation strategy is typically only reasonable when the following conditions are satisfied:

- There is a standard prefix to user IDs identifying the group.
- There is only a single group authorization needed for a each user.

Chapter 23

24-Hour DB2 Applications

The Reason for Having 24-Hour Applications

A new phenomenon in information services is the common need for 24-hour-a-day application availability. Global business needs are demanding computing environments that provide round-the-clock services. Information service departments are generally not comfortable with the problems this kind of system create.

The early 1980s saw the first of these systems. They were usually cumbersome, but often provided their users with tremendous competitive advantage. The glamour of these systems and the inability of IMS to provide 24-hour service was a driving force in IBM's design of the DB2 database management system.

Twenty-four-hour systems include a wide range of capabilities. We must understand the range of requirements implied in this type of system. The more limited versions of 24-hour applications are available for 24 hours a day, but not available every day.

The so-called 24/6 (for 24 hours a day, 6 days a week) applications allow standard maintenance chores to be performed during an off-prime hours shift. These services can be provided much more easily than 24/7 operations, which do not allow a regular weekly outage. The ultimate variation is the 24/365 operation, where there are no scheduled outages at all (which are rarely developed because of their cost).

Within the application types mentioned above, there are variants, defined by the restrictions imposed on their processing activities. An inquiry-only time period allows some database maintenance by preventing update activity. A domain restriction only allows processing of certain data values, such as data from within your time zone. Most environments allow a few seconds stoppage of the applications for maintenance activity as long as the end user's processing is suspended rather than aborted.

Be careful to differentiate between 24-hour applications, which are designed to provide extended scheduled availability, and high-availability applications, which are designed to limit unscheduled outages.

The major technical problem that round-the-clock applications raise is the complication in management of standard database maintenance operations, in particular reorganization of file structures. Other problems include standard maintenance of application programs, and hardware and software designed presuming scheduled outages.

DB2 does provide several key facilities that reduce scheduled outages. These include the capability to change database structure while applications are active. Also relevant is the ability to take backup copies of files while applications are updating the files' data. DB2 also can continue processing after some forms of I/O failure, reducing the likelihood of unscheduled outages.

These facilities, in themselves, are not enough to easily accommodate building round-the-clock applications. There are still major design considerations required to provide this type of service. Most applications of this type incur tremendous additional costs over more typical data processing applications. These costs include more complex design, programming, and testing; more complex operational support of the systems; and much higher processing cost to execute the applications.

Technical Considerations in Building 24-Hour Applications

DB2 has two major limiting factors in supporting round-the-clock applications. The major obstacle to 24/7 applications is the physical data structure. The DB2 file structure design assumed frequent data reorganization based on update frequency. Poorly organized files can cause tremendous performance degradation, but reorganizing them requires stopping the application. The other obstacle is the time it takes for DB2 to recover from failure. This is technically a separate *serviceability* rather than a *scheduled availability* issue, but it constrains the DB2 application designer in many ways in developing nonstop applications.

DB2 is very well designed to support 24-hour-a-day, 6.5 day-a-week applications. In this case, we have allowed a batch window that allows us to reorganize files appropriately and recycle DB2. Often a 24-hour requirement allows a periodic scheduled maintenance application outage. Even allowing monthly or national holiday scheduled maintenance may provide enough window opportunity to allow us to construct normal applications.

Thus, 24-hour applications split into two groups. There are applications that can be supported under normal DB2 services and design conventions. There are also rare applications that require manipulation, tricks, and extra effort to support. Remember that these applications tend to be operational systems central to the IS mission.

The goal of any technical design is to support the business requirements. A prime objective in designing a 24-hour DB2 application is to use standard facilities. Standard facilities work. They are more stable, there is more support for them, and they are much cheaper in the long term.

Much of the following discussion related to "tricks of the trade." It is obvious that these are often strategies chosen out of desperation. Use them judiciously, and only if you must. Changing a logical design will usually impair an application's flexibility. Even physical design choices will limit the application's future. DB2 is adding features that ease support of this type of application.

This implies that a designer should be constantly trying to produce the cleanest possible design, given the constraints of the assignment. A well-designed application often gets faster as DB2 develops to better support it. Application change requirements tend not to have great impact. An application forced to perform unnatural services usually will not gain much from external improvement; maintenance will reduce the application to a slower, more limiting beast.

My point is simply: do your design well and — if possible — do not be clever. A good design can often rise above the limitations of the environment; a poor design becomes a limitation. Database design is the most stable component of most companies' infrastructure. Sometimes the technical issues force the designer to distort design; much too often the design is done without research, rhyme, or justification.

High-Availability Issues

High availability refers to the amount of unplanned downtime in an application. Twenty-four-hour applications are often high-availability applications as well. There is a broad overlap in the design considerations between the two areas.

Recovery time from failure is an availability issue. It *strongly* relates to backup strategy. For example, backups done using the COPY utility SHRLEVEL CHANGE option require extra processing in a recovery situation and slow the return to availability. Not bringing DB2 down periodically increases the effort (and time) required to start up.

A most common technique in designing high-availability applications is the shadow database processing. This involves a periodic switch of the tables used by the applications (and sometimes the DB2 subsystem as well). This process obviates many of the 24-hour application considerations.

A high-availability consideration that can complicate 24-hour applications is the requirement for resilient application. Some applications are built that can recover from a range of software or hardware failures. The designs for this type of processing can include built-in redundancy in the software and files, both of which will affect 24-hour design.

Clearly the architect of the application has to consider both the scheduled and unscheduled availability requirements in planning applications.

Summary

Modern global businesses and changing requirements are creating the demand for 24-hour applications. DB2 is capable of cheaply allowing for 24-hour-a-day, 6-day-a-week applications.

DB2 allows for changes of table structures while applications are active. It does not have to be stopped regularly for maintenance.

DB2 tables need to be regularly reorganized. In most cases, not reorganizing tables and indices frequently will degrade performance significantly.

Review Questions

1. Who should make the decision to implement a 24-hour-a-day application?

2. How should a decision to implement a 24-hour-a-day application be made?

Answers to Review Questions

1. The users footing the bill are the only ones qualified to make a decision to implement a 24-hour-a-day application. Information services (IS) are relevant to this process because of the enormous potential cost of the IS services involved.

The IS cost of implementing a 24-hour-a-day application are directly proportionate to the degree that the organization is prepared for this eventuality. A second 24-hour-a-day application is cheaper than the first. This is because operational planning, systems management, and other investments have been made.

2. The decision to implement a 24-hour-a-day application should be made by executive staff. Because of the much higher cost of the first 24-hour-a-day application, the decision to implement this type of application tends to be done for one of two reasons:

- The company implements a strategic decision to implement 24-hour applications. This allows the cost of the organizational changes to support 24-hour applications to be absorbed centrally.

- An individual application is so vital that it must be implemented as a 24-hour applications. The paramount importance of this application can make the cost of the organizational changes to support 24-hour applications acceptable.

Chapter 24

24-Hour Application Design Considerations

Designing longer scheduled availability applications is a systems architecture issue. A shop should never consider a 24-hour application in isolation. A decision that is this expensive must be made in terms of how the application fits in with complete application support. Review the application requirements considering the degree to which the application must interact with other (probably non-24-hour) applications, and in particular in terms of the goals for application data and their availability. The limited facilities supporting these efforts force us to make many compromises in the design of these applications that may turn out to backfire in the end.

Systems Management Issues

DB2 is a limiting factor in planning a systems environment that can support round-the-clock applications. The most limiting factor is that the more processing a DB2 subsystem has performed, the longer it takes to restart DB2. The DB2 startup time can grow to hours if the system is continuously operating with infrequent checkpoints. If the recoverability is a serious concern, consideration must be given to managing it. This delay is influenced by:

1. The amount of log activity that DB2 underwent during the previous run.

2. The number of data sets open when DB2 terminated.

3. The DB2 setup log checkpoint frequency parameter (LOGLOAD).

4. The amount of effort required to coordinate recovery with other systems (IMS, CICS).

5. How your shop handles recovery processing. Are plans clearly defined and practiced? Are there enough operators and tape drives? This may seem a silly question, but in a partitioned system (PR/SM, etc.) or a semiautomated shift, the facilities may not be available.

In general, the only systems programmer-adjustable parameter is the checkpoint frequency. Increasing the number of checkpoints each hour will decrease the maximum amount of effort DB2 requires to return to a previous checkpoint to validate work unit consistency.

This may not be enough to provide a reasonable recovery delay when DB2 goes down. Another option is to find a time-window to periodically bring DB2 down (even once a month). This is a good idea, but may be in conflict with our application scheduled availability goals.

The only option DB2 provides to accommodate us is to work on points **1** and **2** above. We can reduce the amount of log activity in DB2 in many ways. Logging is dependent on the work being done, and the structure of the underlying data. Sometimes simple fixes, such as moving VARCHAR columns to the end of a row, can significantly change logging. Utility logging is frowned on, but many shops do not specify LOG NO for small LOAD and REORG utility jobs. A table that undergoes mass deletes should be segmented, which reduces logging.

We can try to reduce the number of opened data sets by combining appropriate ones into segmented tablespaces, and not doing unnecessary partitioning. Even changing CLOSE NO to CLOSE YES for appropriate tablespaces and indexes can help. Both categories may be reduced by destructive techniques such as denormalization. DB2 provides several ways to defer restarting objects, which provides a well-controlled shop with a means to recover DB2 partially. There is always the problematic option of doing some of the work out of the scope of DB2.

DB2 uses its standard I/O and buffering mechanisms for recovery. We can always increase the priority of DB2 as it is recovering. Since DB2 can effectively use a huge bufferpool in this process, it is possible to significantly reduce the work DB2 performs by starting DB2 with an enormous buffer size, letting it recover and restart, then stopping it and starting it normally. Since your users are not being serviced this can be an effective use of system memory.

In a DB2 environment with IMS or CICS, the transaction processing system is responsible for coordinating the recovery. This means that any action reducing the duration of each associated IMS or CICS recovery will help get DB2 back as well.

DB2 does not handle ROLLBACK processing efficiently. This is true in the case of standard processing. Even if ROLLBACK seems to be a convenient means to a programming goal, it should be avoided. The ROLLBACK requires rereading the log to the beginning of the work unit. Recovery processing is delayed by this process as well, proportionally to the duration of the work unit and the amount of work processed.

There is still a basic problem here. The amount of logging and number of open tablespaces are a system wide quantity, and not wholly dependent on the application design. This provides the only other out: We can always implement the round-the-clock application in a separate DB2 subsystem.

This application isolation is a painful choice — it reduces our ability to integrate applications, and is very expensive. It is an option that should be taken only if the application requirements force our hand.

DB2 Physical Design Considerations

DB2 application data physical design is generally the most limiting factor in designing 24-hour applications. Data set management is always required, even when the programs can run forever. There is a very small set of physical design facilities within the DB2 product set. Most design issues DB2 increased scheduled availability applications concerns itself with partitioning considerations for tablespaces, and free space allocation considerations.

Partitioning and clustering considerations are very important. Many tables have hot spots where a disproportionate amount of update activity takes place. Introducing a more random clustering order by using a less intuitive choice of clustering index can often dramatically reduce the frequency of page splits.

The converse technique of isolating frequently updated data into special tablespace partitions may work in certain situations. This will increase the likelihood of finding available space on pages (since delete processing often happens in the same neighborhood as insert processing). This allows for very generous allocation of extra space where appropriate. Analyze the concurrency and locking implications of funneling all updates to a single partition before opting to use this technique.

Unstable length rows can cause very rapid data set disorganization. There are many methods of stabilizing the length of variable-length columns or bucketing them in another table to reduce the impact of row indirection. Consider, for example, using CHAR fields instead of VARCHAR; or replacing a LONG VARCHAR that can grow or shrink with a table that can manage the data as a list and rebuild the column,

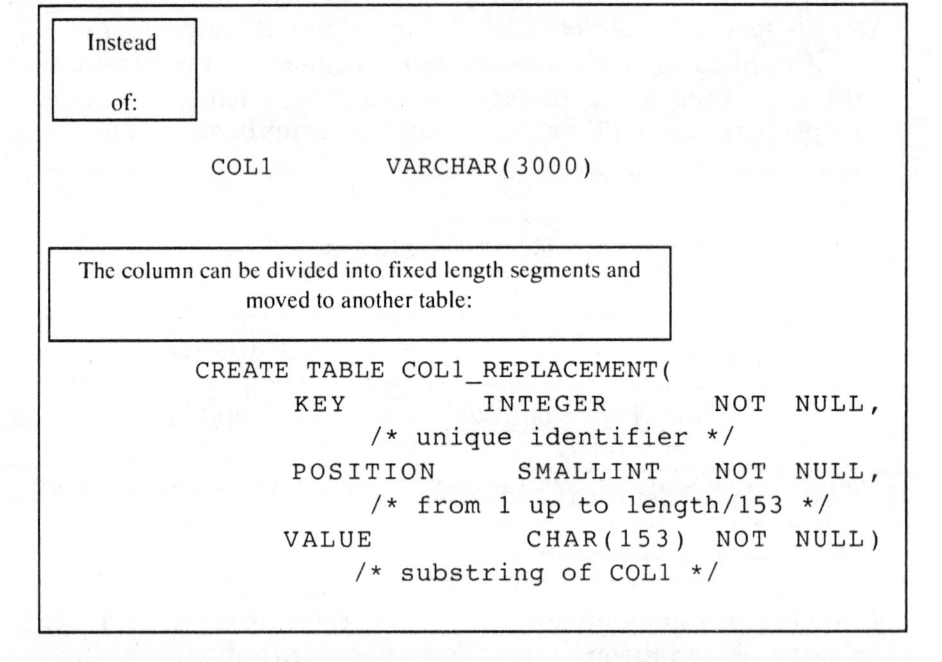
Instead of:

```
COL1        VARCHAR(3000)
```

The column can be divided into fixed length segments and moved to another table:

```
CREATE TABLE COL1_REPLACEMENT(
        KEY          INTEGER       NOT  NULL,
             /* unique identifier */
        POSITION     SMALLINT      NOT  NULL,
             /* from 1 up to length/153 */
        VALUE           CHAR(153)  NOT  NULL)
             /* substring of COL1 */
```

Figure 24.1 Breaking up a long VARCHAR column.

where needed, through a join. (See Figure 24.1.) This can be a nuisance, but can also save a lot of data structure distortion. Note that the VALUE field length is determined by reviewing the data length and change characteristics of COL1, and the rows per page blocking factor.

Another technique that is sometimes used to force columns that change length out of order is to define the table without the unstable columns, load it, and ALTER the table to add the problem columns. This, with judicious use of PCTFREE and FREEPAGE, can sometimes limit the structure distortion caused by the volatility of the columns. This technique is justifiably rarely used, since the structure forces an extra read to get the added column, and a REORG will change the table structure to the standard "no row is on more than one page."

In this discussion, partitioning can mean either partitioning in the DB2 definition — a tablespace split into multiple data sets based on cluster index key ranges — or application-managed collections of tablespaces, tables, and indices that emulate this process. Although this is ungainly it can eliminate some nuisance restrictions that DB2 imposes, such as some utilities bringing the entire partitioned tablespace off-line,

This discussion has focused on data set structure. This is usually the limiting factor in building long-availability windows. Recoverability may be another issue. There are several design options for abandoning DB2 data recoverability. This does not require ignoring application data recoverability. The application can allow recovery via duplicated data sets (such as can be automatically managed by some models of the IBM 3990 controller), or the application can manage its journaling itself. This type of design is outside the scope of this analysis.

Domain Restrictions

In many cases when users require 24-hour application availability, there are large quantities of data that will not be accessed or will be read only during certain time periods. An example would be a global application with locally relevant data. When the Tokyo office closes, its data can be brought off-line, though the application is still running.

The intent of domain restriction is obviously to identify any data value range or rule about the data that would make them available for reorganization. If one is identified, then consider using the rule for partitioning the data.

Domain restrictions can often be very helpful in reducing the effort in creating a 24-hour application. Be very careful, though, in being "clever" in defining domain restrictions. Often, an application that does not immediately make use of some data will later establish a requirement to use it. Domain restriction often produces applications that are very resistant to this type of change.

Bucketing and Application-Managed Data Availability

A common practice in designing high-availability applications is to take over aspects of the database management from the database management system. This is a case of just saying, "if the DBMS won't do it, I'll have to do it myself." This option gives the designer tremendous power, but please remember that you are using a DBMS for a reason. It is very rare (and painful) when a relational DBMS is required to function as a file handler. Use of DB2 as a file management system is common — and in most cases unwarranted. These design techniques tend to box you into a corner. As DB2 adds features, your choice may seem less and less justified.

Perhaps the most common technique of self-managed file structures is the bucket. This is a technique in which the application preserves the read-only stability of a table by logging unapplied updates in a secondary table. The bucket data are still available for searching; the primary table can be used for behind the scenes reorganization. The technique works well, but puts an additional burden on the application programmer. Since this is another technique that concentrates updates into a small space, very serious modeling of the potential for lockout has to be considered.

This leaves us with an easier question: How do we manage the bucket? The answer often is: A bucket worked for us before, let's use another one. Thus, application logic replaces every access to a table with a three-way choice. This process is shown in Figure 24.2.

Note that reads have to be done in the buckets first (in case the bucket changed, but the primary table did not). DELETE processing has to be done using flags. Instead of issuing a DELETE against the primary table, INSERT a copy of the

Replace:

```
EXEC SQL SELECT something FROM table
           WHERE condition
```

With a three way conditional:

```
IF time-for-bucket-1 THEN
       EXEC SQL SELECT something FROM bucket-1
                 WHERE condition /* new data? */
ELSE
     EXEC SQL SELECT something FROM bucket-2
               WHERE condition  /* new data? */
FI
IF SQLCODE = not-found THEN
     EXEC SQL SELECT something FROM table
                WHERE condition  /* old data */

FI
```

And replace update processing:

```
EXEC SQL UPDATE table SET something=:anotherthing
          WHERE condition
```

with:

```
IF time-for-bucket-1 THEN
     EXEC SQL UPDATE bucket-1 SET something=?
               WHERE condition
     IF SQLCODE = not-found THEN
                  EXEC SQL INSERT INTO bucket-1
                      VALUES (?, ?, ?)
     FI
ELSE
     EXEC SQL UPDATE bucket-2 SET something=?
                WHERE condition
     IF SQLCODE = not-found THEN
          EXEC SQL INSERT INTO bucket-2
                         VALUES (?, ?, ?)
     FI
FI
```

Figure 24.2 Bucket processing.

row into the bucket, with a deleted flag set to true. Reads are first done from the bucket (in case the bucket changed, but the primary table didn't) and have to check for the aforementioned deleted flag. Like the example, all update processing including DELETE, UPDATE, and INSERT requires checking the active bucket table first. If the row exists, it is updated. If it is not there, a copy is inserted.

This process thus becomes an additional onus to application development. It requires trusting your programmers to follow defined protocols that normally are managed under the covers. The advantages to the DBA are obvious — the table is divided into three files, of which two are read only and only the third is volatile. Management of this logical file consists of programmatically applying the inactive bucket and the active bucket (at a point in time) to a copy of the primary table, and reorganizing it.

The window is reduced by this process to the time it takes to perform the DB2 stop tablespace/indexspace, perform the VSAM renames, and copy the new active bucket (since the point in time of the copy). This generally can be done in seconds.

Summary

A major consideration in 24-application design is management of the DB2 system itself. DB2 recovery considerations may complicate 24-hour application design.

Designing a 24-hour application requires more detailed understanding of the processing patterns of the data than do other applications. Often a 24-hour application has segments of data processed in logical categories. This knowledge can turn a complex 24-hour application into several simpler applications where domain restriction of the data makes processing simple.

When data must be accessible at all times, shadow tables are a viable but expensive option. Updates are bucketed into several spill files and two copies of the data are kept. One copy of the data can be reorganized, while the other copy is still available for processing.

Review Question

1. Are there different recovery considerations for a DB2 application using shadow spill tables than for other DB2 applications?

Answer to Review Question

1. There are no special recovery considerations differentiating a DB2 application using shadow spill tables from other DB2 applications. The updates should be processed in a single work unit. The only difference is the increased amount of log data needed for recovery.

In many cases, 24-hour applications do have urgency of recoverability. This issue does not relate to the spill tables, but rather to user requirements.

Chapter 25

DB2 Utilities

DB2 must be able to recover data in the event of a system problem. Updating, adding, or deleting data will distort the files DB2 uses to store the data. The DB2 utilities COPY and REORG assist in these two goals. DB2 utilities are a major limiting factor in the design of DB2 applications. The purpose of the COPY utility is to allow recovery of the data. The REORG utility corrects structure distortion caused by updates.

DB2 COPY Utility Considerations

The DB2 COPY utility creates backup image (i.e., exact duplicate) copies of tablespace data sets. The COPY utility has two major relevant varieties, incremental (backup data pages that have changed since the last backup) and full (back up the entire object.)

There is also a MERGECOPY utility that can be used to create a new more recent full copy. The copy is built by merging an older full copy with later incremental copies to reduce the time in recovering a tablespace.

The COPY utility has two concurrency modes, allowing either read-only access (SHRLEVEL REFERENCE) or update processing as well (SHRLEVEL CHANGE). DB2 is capable of creating a copy of a tablespace that is changing because the changes are logged. Note that the utility will exclusively lock a tablespace partition that has the LOCKSIZE TABLE or TABLESPACE.

The COPY utility window can be compressed by:

- Running concurrent COPY utility jobs, with each processing part of a multiple data set or multiple partition tablespace. This technique can reduce the elapsed time significantly if the data sets are on different volumes, paths, and so forth. Note that multiple data set partitioned tablespaces can be copied concurrently only with the extra overhead of SHRLEVEL CHANGE. The number of concurrent jobs is most limited by available tape drives.

- COPY utility speed ups such as effective blocking and buffering of output data sets, and raising the job dispatching priority.

- There are independent vendor products that replace the COPY utility. The first such product is BMC Software (Sugerland, Tex.) COPY+, and other vendors' products of this ilk have been announced. This product will reduce the elapsed and CPU time for many backup activities, but does not support SHRLEVEL CHANGE.

Of course, COPY utility requirements can be eliminated by abandoning DB2 recovery. There are a variety of options for this type of design decision, such as allowing recovery via duplicated data sets. These can be automatically managed by the IBM 3990 controller, or through application managed journaling, or else an application can opt to abandon recoverability. This type of design should not be approached lightly, and is outside the scope of this analysis.

DB2 REORG Utility Considerations

The REORG utility forces a tablespace partition off-line during approximately a third of its processing. The REORG time for large, disorganized tablespaces can be substantial. The utility forcing the data off-line is clearly a problem in designing extended availability applications.

As data are updated in DB2, the data structure gets distorted. When initially loaded into a table, there is a fixed definable percentage of space available for row insertion or growth in length of variable fields. When inserting a row where the page it belongs in (to retain clustering order) does not have the required space to fit it, the row is placed in the next available page that it will fit. If a row is updated to a larger size than would fit in the available space in its current page, the row is replaced with an indirection pointer to the next available page it would fit in, and the row is inserted there.

Whenever a row is deleted, free space is left in pages. It is an unfortunate stochastic characteristic of many applications that this free space is not in the same pages as is needed to insert rows in clustering order. This processing results in less efficient operation of the applications. If the table is processed in clustering order, the indirection required by rows out of clustering order increases I/O cost and delay, since the deterministic buffering and read ahead become less successful and processing slows. Indirection adds an additional read to any index-based read. Sparsely populated pages waste bufferpool by reducing the amount of data in the pool which reduces the buffer efficiency in reducing the need for I/O services.

The REORG utility consists of four relevant phases. UNLOAD reads the data by scanning the clustering index and retrieving the pointed-to rows, then unloads the data to a sequential data set in clustering order. RELOAD loads the data back into the tablespace. RELOAD will also output a sequential data set of index key values and page/row record identifiers for each index on the table(s). There is a SORT for each of these index data sets. BUILD loads the index from the sorted data sets. At this point the data and index are correct.

Generally, most of the effort and time are spent in the UNLOAD phase. If there are numerous or large indices, the SORT and BUILD time become significant. If the tables use EDITPROC processing, for example for compression processing, the UNLOAD and RELOAD phases increase substantially.

- The REORG window can be compressed by running concurrent REORG utility jobs each processing part of a multiple-partition tablespace. This technique can reduce the elapsed time significantly if the data sets are on different volumes, paths, etc.

- The REORG utility can be sped up by using effective blocking and buffering of intermediate data sets. An efficient sort utility which is optimally set up, uses the correct sort technique, has a large enough region size, and uses the right number of well-placed data sets will help. Raising the job dispatching priority can help.

- REORG is very bufferpool dependent. A larger bufferpool and less contention in a bufferpool can have substantial impact.
- There are independent vendor products that replace the REORG utility. The first such product is BMC Software (Sugerland, Tex.) REORG+, and other vendors' products of this ilk have been announced. This will reduce the elapsed and CPU time for most standard REORGs, but can increase the REORG time for some tables with variable-length columns.

A REORG utility can be replaced by a LOAD utility, if the appropriate data is available to be loaded into the table. This technique can sometimes naturally fit into an application design that has the raw data available. The LOAD time for a tablespace is generally much less than the REORG because it eliminates the unloading and sorting of data.

A variant technique is to copy a tablespace (for example, by using the DB2 DSN1COPY utility with the XLAT option) to a temporary tablespace. There it can be reorganized using standard methods, and the reformatted data sets can be made available to DB2 This can be done by:

- DSN1COPYing with XLAT a full image copy of the data to new data sets
- Issuing the DB2 command

```
-STOP DATABASE(a database) SPACENAM(a tablespace)
```

- Using VSAM to delete the existing tablespace underlying data sets
- Using VSAM to rename the reformatted data set copies to the names of the deleted ones
- Issuing the DB2 command

```
-START DATABASE(a database) SPACENAM(a tablespace)
```

This technique thus consists of repeatedly tricking DB2 to manage the data sets as you would prefer. This type of processing allows the application to run (in read-only restricted mode unless additional processing to capture transactions processed in the REORG window is done) while the reorganization takes place. Indices can be reorganized in the same process.

Of course, REORG utility requirements can be eliminated or made infrequent by ignoring the performance impact of unstructured data sets. There are a variety of design decisions that can reduce the rate at which a data set becomes disorganized. Increasing the amount of expansion space available, using the PCTFREE and FREEPAGE parameters is an obvious consideration.

Quiesce Points

An application with interdependent tables starts with a specific point of consistency. As concurrent applications update multiple tables, we create a network of indirect relationships. Referential integrity sets are a special case. Here there is a collection of specific relationships between the data structures. DB2 provides a utility to synchronize referential integrity sets, by stopping their activity collectively.

This process can enormously simplify the effort and time needed to recover from failure. The process of stopping DB2 tablespaces is, of course, contrary to our desire to keep the applications running. How can we achieve quiesce points in a nonstop application?

DB2 does not help us here. Our only option is to quiesce the set of tables no longer updated, either because we are using a shadow database and switching to a different set of tables, or else because we have a partitioning scheme that isolates some data as temporarily not updated.

Indices

Indices cause enormous problems in management. In particular, clustering indices are required (by definition) to be in clustering order. Even if we manage to reorganize each partition of an always available tablespace, we still have no way to restructure the indices without bringing the tablespace offline. A nonclustering index is generally not in as bad shape as a clustering index, because the B-tree structure of DB2 keeps the number of levels fairly stable. The logic in managing clustering indices is different, especially the DB2 optimizer assumptions about index order and prefetch hit rate.

DB2 manages index insertions fairly poorly, often creating large gaps of available space. Row at a time insertion often causes excessive secondary data set extent allocations as DB2 searches forward for free space. This less dense index structure performs poorly.

Many of DB2's access assumptions are based on index buffering. Wasted space with sparsely populated pages does not make effective use of the bufferpool. Physical page order that does not match index key order has a severe negative impact on the effectiveness (the "hit ratio") of prefetch processing.

Indices, in particular partitioning indices, thus can become the limiting factor in database design. It is sometimes possible to construct a partitioning strategy (see the discussion under table design strategy in Chapter 5), which allows for undercover index reorganization.

The only other technique available is to intentionally design duplicated access paths, which force use of different indices. The application would then conditionally choose the appropriate path. The logistics of reorganizing an index partition while an application is actively updating are messy.

```
CREATE UNIQUE INDEX WEEKDAYINDEX
    ON TABLE1(
                    KEY)
CLUSTER...
```

Figure 25.1 A unique index preventing duplicates.

```
CREATE UNIQUE INDEX WEEKENDINDEX
   ON TABLE1(
               PREFIX,
               KEY)
   CLUSTER....
```

Figure 25.2 An index prefix field.

Creating duplicated access paths and forcing DB2 to select one or the other is even harder. DB2 has an overwhelming tendency to use the clustering index, even in DB2 version 2.2 where it has more path options. The options the designer has is to add prefix field, i.e., if the clustering index looks like Figure 25.1 we can "enhance" the new index with the prefix column, which of course has to be a column in the indexed table. Usually this requires adding a new single-valued column to the table. An example is shown in Figure 25.2.

At this point, selecting an index is as easy as changing your where clauses, so the weekday logic branch looks like Figure 25.3.In some cases DB2 will opt for the WEEKDAY index even on the weekend path. DB2 is actually doing a reasonable thing — avoiding an index whose leading key field never changes. This can be solved by updating the FIRSTKEYCARD field for the index in the DB2 catalog in SYSIBM.SYSINDEXES (normally set by the RUNSTATS utility) to a high number, increasing the value from 1. DB2 allows this kind of catalog update.

This artificial key field looks ugly, but the other option to perform the same task is uglier. Without the additional selection criteria we have to convince DB2 to choose a specific path by updating the RUNSTATS statistics in the DB2 catalog. The relevant SYSIBM.SYSINDEXES columns are CLUSTERED, CLUSTERRATIO, FIRSTKEYCARD, FULLKEYCARD, NLEAF, and NLEVELS.

Another option is to eliminate the index completely. This process is sometimes called *self-managed indices*. The developer uses DB2 tables to simulate index processing, including coordinating the values in the "index" with the values in the table. This procedure is rarely used, except as a performance enhancement for sparsely populated indices.

Coordinated Processing Concerns

Many applications exist in mixed environments, such as CICS/DB2/VSAM applications. Planning these types of applications implies working with the union of the limitations of each of these systems. A CICS region is difficult to manage over a 24-hour application if any change is required. VSAM reorganization requirements tend to force CICS outages. DB2 outage concerns have been discussed in detail above.

Each of these processes can be managed separately. For example, the application can switch to a shadow VSAM database during VSAM reorganization. The logistics tend to become more complex as each additional subsystem is added to the picture. To the extent possible, limit the number of systems the application has to coordinate with.

```
        EXEC SQL
          . . . .
          WHERE KEY = :something

and the weekend branch becomes:

        EXEC SQL
          . . . .
          WHERE PREFIX = 'X'
                    /* prefix ALWAYS equals X! */
            AND KEY    = :something
```

Figure 25.3 Directing DB2 to an alternate path.

Distributed Processing Issues

Distributed processing is not in itself a hindrance to a long-availability window for applications. DB2 (and SAA) distributed processing calls for each node to manage its own data. It does complicate matters in several ways. By tying together multiple computers and applications, we combine the limitations of the systems. Obvious example include the availability of machines in different time zones, or referential integrity constraints between two applications.

In designing a limited scheduled outage distributed application, also consider:

- The location constraints of each node in the system (e.g., if communications alternatives are not available).
- The network capabilities and available capacity throughout the schedule.
- The coordination requirements of each designed planned reduced availability window. For example, if one site has no operator available during a scheduled outage, it may limit the ability to create a synchronized point of consistency.

Application Change Considerations

Application programs undergo maintenance. Consideration should be given to strategies for managing the software changes in defining an application.

If there are standard scheduled outages for the application, it is convenient to organize software maintenance to revolve around these outages. This has the advantage of simplicity, but can be frustrating if a required fix is completed the day after the monthly scheduled maintenance.

There are several software packages that allow some forms of "on the fly" updates. For example, a CICS load module can be replaced with a new version. If this type of option is considered, it requires design effort to implement. This type of change will take effect only when no CICS converses are active.

DB2 can be a limiting factor in using this type of facility. Application changes generally require a BIND, but a BIND will limit the availability of the application. DB2 requires a plan name to be identified in the RCT (the DB2-CICS coordination Resource Control Table). The plan name will thus remain static until the CICS-DB2 attach is brought down or stopped. If the application is precompiled and relinked (but not rebound), the existing plan table time stamp will not match the new code time stamp, and DB2 will refuse to process the application calls.

This problem can be partially solved in a variety of ways. The application structure can be made very modular, allowing parts to be changed with minimal impact on the whole. Modules accessing DB2 can be separated from the whole. As long as a module is not recompiled, it will not change time stamp, so a COBOL application can be broken into separate externally callable modules. The modules can be relinked into a new program, which can then access DB2. Of course, this method will not allow changing the DB2 data access modules.

Another option is to make dummy entries into the RCT and use those names for the new application programs, or use the plan name conversion module to point to the correct plan. These techniques are complicated to manage, and unrealistic if the application uses dedicated threads. The capability of dynamic plan name switching that DB2 offers in release 2.1 and above is another possible option.

Dynamic plan name switching is intended to free a collection of CICS transactions which perform a general function (i.e., an application) from the need to use a common plan. An application that provides a menu, then selects a transaction to process needs this facility in order to disassociate the transaction identifier from the plan name. The facility provides deferred binding (in the sense of connection, not related to a DB2 plan) between an application and its plans.

PACKAGESETs, combined with a versioning mechanism in systems management or within the application, can be the easiest strategy. If the application explicitly identifies the appropriate PACKAGESET using the SET CURRENT SQL statement, the program has complete control. A clean approach is to store the package name in a CICS table.

Various schemes can be worked out to dynamically redirect applications to different plans. This can be combined with a menuing front-end application that uses CICS table-driven logic to select an appropriate transaction identifier. This combination allows modifications to both application logic and data structures.

A final option to consider is using dynamic SQL. This can allow some additional flexibility by designing a generic data handling routine, which is the only module associated with a plan. This allows using standard techniques for changing the CICS transactions, and leaving the DB2 alone. The negatives in this technique are the cost of this process to the code structure and cohesiveness, and the overhead in processing dynamic SQL.

It is obvious from these facts that it is much easier to manage application maintenance on a system that has a 30-second daily or weekly CICS recycle window than on a system that is always up. The short recycle allows changes; otherwise the application must be designed to support the changes and the type of changes to be done must be guessed at application design.

A method many shops use to compress scheduled unavailability is auto-operator software, which automates the responses to system prompts. This, in conjunction with automated tape mounts (or backups to DASD), can guarantee constant (near minimal) batch windows.

Database Structure Changes

If a change brings with it required data structure changes, it can cause enormous problems. Either the change involves redefinition of a field, with the implied unload/drop/create/grant/bind/load window, or it involves the addition of entirely new data structures.

Redefining a field thus normally requires substantial downtime. The only other option typically available is to ignore the changed field entirely. This can be done through application logic changes by simply ignoring a column defined as NULLable or NOT NULL WITH DEFAULT or putting dummy values into a NOT NULL column.

DB2 supports dynamic addition of columns to a table via the ALTER command (at some short locking expense). The entire table can also be replaced with another, redesigned one. The problem is, of course, the data. There is no effective way to manage rapidly changing data that cannot be temporarily stopped.

The best option I have seen is to build an intermediate change application that uses and maintains both the corrected and the obsolete table structure. This intermediate application would continue processing until both table structures are synchronized. At this point the intermediate application can be replaced with a final version.

DB2 can accommodate building an entirely new table structure much more easily if the application uses dynamic SQL. Contention for catalog and DBD locks can be alleviated by using multiple databases. Simply create an extra few before the application is installed, and add the new tables to an empty one.

Tuning

DB2 does not allow updating a table while it is building an index for the table. Most new large indices are built using the LOAD utility, rather than using the CREATE INDEX statement directly. This is not a problem in most cases of long-availability windows.

It is a reasonable demand that any production round-the-clock application should be tested and tuned. The facilities for tuning an application with a minimal window are limited, and their cost is high. Furthermore, this kind of application tends to have much of the design considerations built in at the application level, with little externalized.

There are those unfortunate situations in which some tuning must be done. There is no good way to do it.

Summary

Minimizing the required scheduled outages for an application requires understanding the application availability requirements and the cost/benefit tradeoffs for the application. In particular, there is a substantial difference between full and qualified availability. For example, having a window where no updates are being processed will allow much undercover management of data. There is an exponential cost increase as more of the scheduled unavailability window is removed.

Logical partitioning of the data is the most powerful design technique. There is a substantive difference between requiring availability of all data and requiring only a logical subdivision of the data. Having data that can be logically partitioned into data that are used in a specific region or time can simplify the design considerably.

A DB2 application designer has some tools provided by the database manager and some provided by the operating system. The most powerful tool is a deep understanding of the application requirements in order to use the correct tools for the job.

Review Question

1. What are the advantages and disadvantages of updating DB2 catalog statistics?

Answer to Review Question

1. The advantages of updating DB2 catalog statistics are in the expedient influence of access paths. This is useful in an emergency and in simulating some data changes.

A common and useful use of updating DB2 catalog statistics is in simulating production statistics in a development environment. Note that DB2 used CPU speed in determining access paths and so may choose different paths in different computers.

The disadvantages of updating DB2 catalog statistics are the effort, sloppiness, and inconsistency it engenders. Updating production catalog statistics is a particular nuisance, since the updater can be forced to repeatedly change values until the access paths become the preferred ones.

This process of updating production DB2 catalog statistics can become impossible to sustain as different applications with conflicting access path requirements are implemented. Some users are forced into this process as a temporary expedient until the next version of DB2 adds new optimization options.

Chapter 26

24-Hour Application Design Issues

Round-the-clock applications should be based on a different philosophy of application design than that of traditional large-scale applications. Understanding the history of this approach will provide insight into our goals.

A traditional high scheduled availability application was the logical extreme of the traditional database application design. This is shown in Figure 26.1.

Historically, transaction processing was artificially grafted onto batch processing. Initially transaction processing functioned as intelligent data entry for these applications (in fact, this is still a major use of these systems). The transaction processing typically was very restricted: often only 9 a.m. through 5 p.m. Monday through Friday. This allowed for an enormous batch processing window.

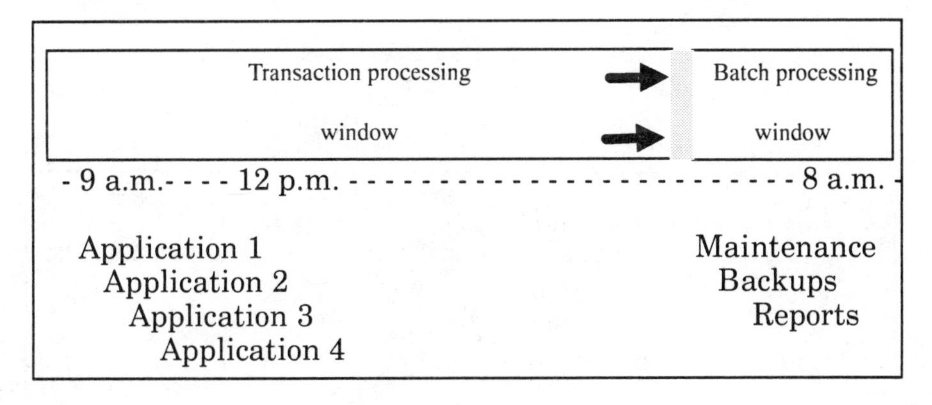

Figure 26.1 The shrinking batch window.

The batch processing window allowed for such application control activity as:

- Reconciliation, correcting data errors, consolidation of data, and other resolution of data failures and applying data fed from other applications

- Report programs, which traditionally have problems working with transaction processing because of data inconsistency, locking, and resource competition.

- Backup processing of the data

- File maintenance processing, such as correcting files in extents or sorting files into order for ease of access

The nightly and weekend shutdown had a major external benefit: shutting down data entry and transaction processing allowed a mutual synchronization between different applications. The business could function as a whole. Data could be shared between applications when the transaction processing was closed down. The problem was that both reporting and transaction systems need the same information, as shown in Figure 26.2.

Over the course of time, the requirements for the transaction processing window grew larger. Early efforts emphasized attempting to shrink the batch window. When that effort reached practical limits, mirrored systems evolved.

	Transaction	DSS
Core data (relatively)	X	X
History data, appended regularly	X	X
Codes and calculations	X	X

Figure 26.2 TP and reporting overlap.

The various technical solutions in the traditional methods have become an enormous burden. The collection of limitations imposed by the required cleverness of each of the problem solutions brings to mind the old maxim: the cause of problems is solutions. The result was rigid and expensive systems.

Modern round-the-clock applications have more complex requirements. Also, they have the need for more flexibility. Application architecture goals have changed. These design approaches are very similar to the changes in developing a standard application approach for large DB2 applications.

The fundamental change is to remove the requirement for a batch window completely. That means that there are changes in managing technical resources. There are even more fundamental changes in the business components of a transaction processing system. Without the reconciliations, the transaction processing system manages only raw data.

At the same time, there are much more dynamic data reporting needs to be managed. Rather than post-hoc creation of a decision support system fed from the transaction processing data, it seems more rational to fulfil both requirements together. (See Figure 26.3.)

A transaction processing system that functions as a look-up and data updating facility is a vital component of an application. It is no longer the entire application. What historically was a fixed reporting requirement has grown into an effervescent combination of both fixed and ad-hoc reporting, where even the fixed report requirements change quickly. The data

TRANSACTION DETAIL DATA

REPORTING SUMMARY DATA

REPORTING SUMMARY

Figure 26.3 The cascade of data through systems.

NONHISTORY-AWARE TABLE STRUCTURE

account #, bill #, amount, date, status, ...

HISTORY-AWARE TABLE STRUCTURE

account #, bill #, **adjustment #**, amount, date, status, ...

Figure 26.4 Active data vs. complete data.

have to quickly flow from operational to reporting applications. (See Figure 26.4.)

This architecture seems more robust than the previous. The problem is what to do with corrections and intersystem interfaces. The major detail data in many transaction processing applications are some form of history data, typically consisting of a single central table. An example is billing history in a billing system.

We can structure this table to allow update transactions in a form that preserves the previous data history. If all transactions processing the data are made aware of history of updates, corrections become feasible in a nonbatched form.

Adding the adjustment number allows for changes to a bill while maintaining the entire sequence of changes to the bill. This will seem trite to many, but in fact an enormous proportion of applications update all records in place. This often forces the updates to be deferred until batch update processing, a step we are attempting to eliminate.

Dealing with interfaces between systems is much more complex. In fact, this is the design area resulting in the most compromises. The past comes to haunt us here. (This should be the major rationale for good system design: not having the one system damage others.) An application interface may be, for example, a tape carried between disparate computers weekly. This seems not to allow constant currency of the data.

This problem has three potential solutions:

- Accept the limitations of the cyclical data transfer.
- Temporarily use the data transfer cycle, but build the application in a bimodal form that can work with either periodic or continuous data transfer. Then wait for the other application to mature.
- Change the offending data source to transfer data continuously.

The merits of each of these approaches depend on the context. My approach is to attempt the most aggressive option of changing the data source — I would rather pay now than later. If this approach is unfeasible, an application design that will use a batch update procedure that is later removed may work. Be very careful with this type of project, since later maintenance to the application may change a clean but unused interface into a mess. If all else fails, the batch interfaces of two generations ago can be a workable option.

Can a Batch Application Coexist with Transaction Processing?

The conflict between types of system is a fundamental impediment to nonstop application development. Often, it is feasible, but the locking and performance issues have to be dealt with a complex set of problems. This subject is discussed rigorously in Chapter 20. We will review the topic as it pertains to this topic of allowing 24-hour applications.

The basic issue is lockout. We will consider the most basic forms of applications: transaction processing applications doing few reads with short durations, and batch applications that generate reports or processing to apply updates.

Batch reporting applications are disastrous to transaction processing. They tend to lock data in large quantities, often needing repeatable read or even escalating the granularity of the lock. These applications would be preferably run elsewhere, on decision support copies of the data. It is possible to run this type of application amid transaction processing. Consider a low-priority reporting application run with low-volume TP, with both not needing immediate response.

Batch apply programs that read a list of updates and apply them to a database can coexist well with TP. The batch applications can look to the database as if the processing were standard TP. In fact, the batch programs are called transaction apply programs. The work units should be kept small to minimize lock duration.

The question about the batch apply program is more subtle: Are the data meaningful between the start of the apply program and its completion? This is really a business analysis question, but we should note that the process can often be designed to make the data valid during processing.

Reducing REORG (or LOAD) Impact

When a tablespace is being reorganized or loaded, the data are not available. The impact can be significantly reduced by simply doing the process off-line. This technique requires:

- Not updating the data in the tablespace or partition for the duration or
- Using some means to capture and reapply the updates done during this duration.

The data can be loaded or reorganized in another DB2 subsystem on the same or a different computer. The reorganized data will differ by the DB2 internal identifiers. DB2 stores a database ID number, a page set ID number, and a logical table-within-tablespace ID number called, respectively, the DBID, PSID, and OBID. These can be corrected to the appropriate values through the DSN1COPY "XLAT" (translate identifiers) option.

The process typically involves keeping a parallel set of tablespace and table definitions for each table to be refreshed. To reorganize, copy the data from the source table (which is read only). Either use DSN1COPY or else use the image copy utility with a share level of reference, and then use DSN1COPY to copy from the copy utility output. The DB2

```
-STOP DATABASE(dbname) SPACENAM(tablespace part)
```

command may be required to force DB2 to flush from the bufferpool all deferred updates. If stopped, the data set should be immediately restarted. The normal REORG is performed against the new table. In order to load the data, the data are simply loaded into the new table. Both processes continue in the same way.

DSN1COPY is used to copy the output to new data sets with the original internal identifiers. These data sets contains the appropriate data and are to replace the current tablespace partition data set and all matching indexspace data sets. This can be done by:

- Issuing the DB2

```
-STOP DATABASE(dbname) SPACENAME(list of
dataspaces)
```

  command. This will cause DB2 to close the data sets.

- Using the AMS "ALTER RENAME" statement to rename or delete the original data sets. Then rename the newly formatted data sets to match the original data set names.

- Issuing the DB2

```
-START DATABASE(dbname) SPACENAME(list of
spacenames)
```

  command. This will cause DB2 to reopen the newly refreshed data sets.

This entire process takes the time for the LOAD or REORG, when the data cannot be updated. But it will only take applications off-line for a fraction of a second, the time taken to rename the data sets. Independent vendor replacements for the LOAD and REORG utilities can be used for this procedure.

Multiple Partitions

If there are multiple nonclustered indices (and most secondary indices are never clustered), partition REORG time becomes close to tablespace REORG time. The only user option here is to remove the secondary indices. In some unusual cases a translate table can be used as a user-maintained index if maintenance of the translate table would not be unreasonable.

Free space

Free space in the data will help reduce the reorganization frequency. DB2 allows allocating free pages or a percentage free of each page. The free space is allocated when the data are loaded using the LOAD utility and when the data are reorganized using REORG. The more natural approach is a free percentage of each page.

The problem with PCTFREE is that if only a small percentage of data is updated, overall performance of frequently accessed tables suffers because of the reduced amount of data per page. Bufferpool hit rates decrease proportionately with the percentage that free space increases, and I/O rates tend to increase exponentially if the bufferpool is not resized proportionally.

This can be a justification for use of free pages. These will not be read into the bufferpool unless:

- There is a sequential prefetch. Most 24-hour requirements do not make use of sequential prefetch.
- Data grow onto those pages.

Note that if the data have clear *hot spots*, partitioning based on hot spot key ranges can allow for tremendously large allocations of free space for the hot spots and more conservative allocation for the rest.

Index reorganization issues are more complex. If data tend to be inserted in index order, or synonyms are added to specific areas or other hot spots occur, the index structure will be quickly distorted. Free space generally will not significantly help. This issue generally has to be addressed at the physical database design level.

Preformatted Data

Also known as saturated files, this technique involves preallocating all data with a "dummy entry" flag of some sort. Insertions then involve marking the data as active; deletions, marking the data as inactive. The data never needs to be reorganized, since physical page order never changes.

This technique precludes use of *alternate indexes*. The interrelationship between the cluster order and the secondary key order cannot be known at preformatting time.

Fixed-Length Rows

Variable-length rows cause grief to the designer of a system attempting to minimize the frequency of reorganization. When indexed, variable-length columns are padded to the maximum length of the row. This can cause a low blocking factor in the index. If variable-length columns can be updated and grow in length (which is the norm for this type of data), the growth can force *row indirection*.

DB2 will attempt to get the necessary space from the page on which the data existed before the update. If not enough room is available, DB2 will insert the updated row according to standard INSERT processing rules and place an indirection pointer in the old position of the data. The net result is that any indexed read of the data requires an additional read. The price is always only one read.

If the already indirected data grows again, DB2 will update the original page indirection pointer to point directly to the final page on which the data resides. The extra cost here is in the update. The net effect is to slow processing, requiring reorganization to stabilize the data access time.

A design can allow data to be added only to the end of the tablespace. Data added to the end of a tablespace have a much smaller effect on the tablespace organization than random data insertion. The problems with this approach are:

- If all insertion is on the same page, insertion will be serialized. Each data inserter will wait for the previous one to complete. This makes this technique useful only for low-volume transaction applications.

- Insertion in sorted order seems appealing from the tablespace organization perspective. Typically the insertion is in index order as well — that is the normal way to enforce this order. But sorted insertion into an index will quickly distort its structure, repeatedly causing page splits. This will normally disqualify this procedure.

Snapshot Data

Switching tables to allow for reorganization is appealing, but has a fundamental problem. How can we propagate the data from the first table to the second? It is simple if there is a read-only period but is complicated otherwise.

Sometimes it is easy to identify changed data. A standard of keeping a *last changed* TIMESTAMP is a convenience here. A partial solution is to log changes. Since DB2 does that anyway, several vendors are developing software that can extract the changes from the log. The designer also can consider logging updates to a snapshot table that will speed getting the updated values. This works at the expense of tremendous overhead at the time of the update and nuisance in programming.

Do We Have to REORG?

If reorganizations are the limiting factor, the application can simply decide not to reorganize. Some have tried simply ignoring the issue, but the overhead of worse case I/O processing can be tremendous. This becomes reasonable in certain situations. A small or minimally updated table is a reasonable candidate for this technique. The table order becomes unimportant if a table is accessed through scans, with no need for indexing.

Application availability is dependent on the union of all requirements. Rare is the complete application that needs only these specific table types. Index use is the rule of DB2 access. Indices lose order quickly and index-related access performance degrades as data are inserted.

An obvious answer to this problem is not to do inserts at all! We can load tables with all possible values of the unique clustering index. A flag is added to denote whether the data are meaningful. Thus, to add a row we simply update the appropriate row and set the flag to "on." To delete a row, set the flag to "off." The table cannot contain any VAR columns which can grow in length and disorganize the table, but these can be expanded to maximum length.

There are potential problems with this technique. In general the performance is consistent, but bad — physical database design for performance is relegated to a low priority. Often it is unreasonable to generate all permutations of the data values because of the size of the data spaces required. A common answer to this problem is to use a synthetic key (a generated key with a smaller range of values) as the value for the clustering index. This technique works especially well in history tables.

A more fundamental problem is that secondary indices rarely work in this procedure. The same problem we have with the clustering index losing order can happen to the secondary indices. It is unusual to find multiple indices that we can effectively saturate. Usually these tables are designed with a single index.

Given a table with only a single index, often on an unnatural key, it is hard to access the data. The obvious answer is to create translate tables that match natural access values to the stored key. Of course these tables will have the same disorganization problems as the original table (although the narrowness of the rows may reduce the problem), and the access will be made more awkward by the additional joins required. This procedure also precludes use of DB2 referential integrity, which typically requires a secondary index on the foreign key for performance reasons.

The philosophic problem is that the burden of managing the data ourselves is too harsh. DB2 is not only not a help, but an impediment over simple file processing.

Summary

The design of 24-hour applications is different from those of traditional applications in that they lack an off-shift. This lack tempts us to design these applications with access to all their raw data, eliminating the concept of active data.

The data for reporting purposes should be extracted on a periodic basis. A batch program can do this without contention simply by frequently committing.

The major problem in an application without an off-shift is the need to reorganize the data. REORG can be performed against a shadow copy of the data. The reorganization frequency can be reduced by designing a more stable database structure that gets less disorganized.

Review Question

1. Why do alternate indices conflict with a saturated table, with all data values already filled in?

Answer to Review Question

1. Alternate indices conflict with a saturated table primarily in the number of permutations of relationship between the table cluster order and the alternate ordering. Thus, a table with a unique clustering index containing 200,000 entries and an alternate index with 100,000 entries can have up to:

```
100,000 * 200,000  =  20,000,000,000
```

entries. It would be unrealistic to create an alternate index of this size.

Chapter 27

DB2 Referential Integrity

Referential integrity is a simple concept: a foreign key is made to require the existence of a primary key. A NULL foreign key is considered by DB2 to be the only exception. The row containing the primary key is termed the *parent,* the row containing the foreign key is termed the *child* or *dependent* row. Deleting the parent updating the value of the primary key will orphan the child row. Rules are defined to manage this situation.

- **DELETE RESTRICT** — this prevents a parent from being deleted. In order to delete a row all of its children must be eliminated. The application must either delete or change the foreign key of each of the children to NULL or change them to refer to another parent (in both these cases, the row is no longer a relevant parent).
- **DELETE SET NULL** — if a parent is deleted, DB2 will identify all children and set their foreign key to NULL.
- **DELETE CASCADE** — if a parent is deleted, DB2 will identify all children and delete them. This can create awkward situations since the children may in turn have delete cascade rules, creating enormous percolated deletions.

Delete restrict is used for almost all production data. The set null option can be used to defer processing of the child rows, but most processing concentrates on work units. Cascade delete is dangerous if not carefully managed, leaving the delete restrict and the write-your-own referential relationship error management options the easiest to implement.

DB2 or Application-Based Referential Integrity?

In the great majority of cases there is no significant difference in performance between application and DB2-managed referential integrity. In these cases, DB2-based referential integrity should always be used since it is more accurate than user programs. DB2 RI does not get replicated in multiple programs, and by reducing application size makes for better applications.

There are occasions where it may not be best to use DB2 referential integrity. There may be redundant checking, as in the example in Figure 27.1, where the DB2 CPU processing increases. (The redundant checking should be against data in memory.)

```
INSERT ITEM_HEADER
INSERT ITEM_DETAIL1
INSERT ITEM_DETAIL2
INSERT ITEM_DETAIL3
INSERT ITEM_DETAIL4
INSERT ITEM_DETAIL5
INSERT ITEM_DETAIL6
INSERT ITEM_DETAIL7
INSERT ITEM_DETAIL8
INSERT ITEM_DETAIL9
INSERT ITEM_DETAIL10
```

A common situation is adding a header record and then detail records. In a DB2 RI relationship, each item detail record will cause a logical read of the item header. Even though this may only result in a single physical read and subsequent references to the bufferpool page, this requires significant work.

Figure 27.1 DB2 RI depends on data insert order.

Converting Application-Managed Integrity to DB2 RI

It seems like a worthwhile effort to convert user-managed referential integrity to DB2-managed. There are two noteworthy problems in doing so. First, order is significant in DB2. Many user-managed applications add dependent rows before the parent is added. This will clearly fail in DB2 RI. An entertaining way to identify this type of problem is by simply adding DB2 referential integrity to the existing application and then analyzing errors in a test environment (but be careful of exception conditions).

The other problem is based on the fact that errors often occur in user-managed referential integrity. If a conversion is planned, thoroughly review the data and weed out problems. In some cases (especially in older applications) the referential integrity failures are a hidden business rule, relating to exceptions to the RI structure.

Loading Data

Data can be loaded into referential integrity structures in several ways. The referential integrity can be checked either during the data addition or after completion. The performance difference is substantial.

If referential integrity is checked when the data are loaded, data must be added in appropriate referential order. In some cases of weird referential integrity cycles, the checking has to be deferred because the data are indirectly referring to themselves. The options in loading data are

- The DB2 LOAD utility with deferred referential integrity checking. The data are loaded and table is marked with the *check pending* flag. The CHECK DATA option of the CHECK utility can then verify integrity and reset the flag. This is the most common means of loading data. The CHECK DATA mass referential integrity checking is cheaper than the record-by-record checking done in the LOAD utility.

- The DB2 LOAD utility checking referential integrity. This is appropriate for smaller tables.

- A mass insert program. This tends to be the worst option in performance, and generally distorts the files by causing page splitting and row indirection, requiring REORG.
- Kludges. There are frequently situations in which data are known "absolutely, for sure" to be free of referential integrity inconsistency. Data can be loaded without referential integrity checking. The LOAD utility can be used without referential integrity checking. The check pending flag can be reset using the DB2 START command or the REPAIR utility. Data also can be loaded using DSN1COPY, a program that ignores referential checking. These options have a very poor track record in practice because of procedural errors.

Partial Recovery and Referential Integrity

Referential integrity complicates any incomplete recovery. The complication may be simply due to recovery issues that would otherwise be missed. The multiple tablespaces involved in referential relationships can be made inconsistent if only one is restored to a point in time.

Recovering all tablespaces to an arbitrary point in time is not typically viable. While one table is dormant, another in the referential integrity set may be in the process of being updated. It would take much research and luck to identify a point of consistency among all involved applications.

DB2 provides a REPORT utility to identify the tablespaces linked through referential integrity. The QUIESCE utility can be used to establish a point of consistency between the tablespace set members. QUIESCE does this by simulating stopping each of the identified tablespaces, and restarting when all have stopped. Users wait until the quiesce completes.

Quiesce points are identified in the DB2 catalog (SYSIBM.SYSCOPY). These quiesce points can be used for point-in-time recovery, with the knowledge that the data will be consistent.

Summary

DB2 supports referential integrity relationships between parent and dependent row. The supported options are: **DE-**

LETE RESTRICT to prevent a parent from being deleted, **DELETE SET NULL** where the dependent rows are reset to null when the parent is deleted, and **DELETE CASCADE**, which deletes all dependents when a parent is deleted.

Applications have historically managed their own RI. The disadvantage to this approach is that the logic is often distributed between many programs, often with inconsistencies.

There is rarely a performance advantage to user-program managed RI. Application simplicity dictates using DB2 RI in most situations.

Review Question

1. A bill-of-materials application is being built where each parent row has about twenty dependent rows, each of which have about fifty dependent rows. The application is fairly high volume (20 transactions a second/10 hours a day). About five top level parents are deleted every second, with minimal changes to the dependent rows. Is delete cascade referential integrity a reasonable option for this program?

Answer to Review Question

1. The bill-of-materials application is likely a reasonable candidate for DB2 delete cascade RI. The risk of mass deletes is that application transaction volume might cause lock contention that could limit performance.

The most common solution to this sort of problem is to flag the parent records as deleted, and process the deletions during the off-shift cycle. DB2 or user deletion of the 1001 rows in these bills-of-materials should be approximately the same overhead for those brave enough to attempt the deletion during transaction processing.

Chapter 28

DB2 in Production

DB2 has won the battle for the hearts and minds of MVS developers. The competitors selling IDMS and Datacom/DB have sold their product to Computer Associates to be left fallow. Only Adabas is aggressively competing for new sales. DB2 is the clear strategic database option for the future. Meanwhile, most users only use DB2 for a fraction of their production activity.

Using DB2 in production is a tremendous challenge to the production environment. This challenge is a battle to maintain control of production. The refinement of control and the centralization of the computing resource are the justifications for using large mainframes. Most shops have spent over a decade refining the process of managing the computer. Typically, this control structure only developed from problems forcing management's hand.

This is the battle that DB2 is fighting in the less mature shops: Will the production environment evolution reiterate all the mistakes of the 1980s? The current practice of scaling down production staff will exacerbate the management of production DB2. The existing departmental structures are simply unable to manage an additional complex resource, let alone attempt to study and plan for effective management of the DB2 issues.

This issue becomes worse from a career standpoint. The staff managing older systems can feel threatened as their systems lose priority and glamour. DB2 projects are growing and more visible. This combination can often cause those apprehensive of the changes to ignore or even sabotage DB2 efforts. So political battles become a major theme of the maturation of DB2 in many organizations.

Usually DB2 use is hard to justify tactically before it fully penetrates a shop. It is usually cheaper to build systems in the existing technology for a variety of reasons. From the data perspective, DB2 often does not contain a critical mass of data; it requires extra effort to ship data back and forth between systems. Management does not have the experience to plan DB2 projects well.

From a development life cycle viewpoint, early projects simply add an enormous overhead to the process. Training in the new systems, the cost of mistakes in misapplying or misunderstanding the technology, and general shake-out of problems are all artificially added to the early projects' cost. Besides, the first application built in any new technology are usually poorly designed.

There are, though, some very strong benefits that can be derived from using DB2. These benefits are particularly evident in shops that are mainly using flat files (QSAM, BDAM, VSAM, etc.). The immaturity of database issues in these shops allows the DB2 migration to also provide the benefits of general database issues: data independence and data sharing, consistent system-controlled security, improved backup and recovery, better locking, and so on. Users of nonrelational database management systems tend to have only incremental improvements, mainly in the improved capabilities to manage complex data and ad-hoc queries.

System Responsibilities

DB2 is designed for large-scale IBM shops. The users are expected to have the support facilities of large-scale shops. Woe to the user who does not follow the management structure! DB2 itself expects a fine granularity of systems management, the computer is designed for careful management, and all support tools are designed for this management structure.

The standard MVS shop has an information services structure in the hierarchical format shown in Figure 28.1. Even if the number of staff in the systems group is smaller, the number of titles is very large. This division is supported by the tools in each area. This fine degree of specialization can be a shock to users migrating to MVS.

MVS users who do not have a systems management structure that approximates this are generally forced into re-

IS manager

Development manager

New development manager

Group 1 . . .

Maintenance manager

Group 1 . . .

System integration or large-scale project

Group 1 . . .

Data administration

Data administration Group

Development DBA

Quality assurance

Systems manager

MVS systems programming

Telecommunications manager

CICS systems programming

IMS systems programming

DB2 systems programming

Capacity planning

Production control

Operations manager

Production DBA

Scheduling and planning

Security administration

Figure 28.1 A typical DP or IS organization.

peated firefighting. The complexity of the MVS environment requires deep understanding of the technical problems.

The only justification for the expense of an MVS environment is the capability of large-scale processing at a high rate of reliability. Running a very skimpy systems group usually decreases the system's reliability.

Issues in Managing Production DB2 Applications

Defining responsibilities is a painful process. It is a slow battle to control systems. Each step tends to be accomplished only after a crisis. Systems management is a fixed overhead, which is not appealing to users paying the bills.

Even in a fully organized shop, the responsibilities are often unclear. Often there are several groups which overlap in dealing with problems. Allowing unclear accountability is a management failure. Under pressure, problems are bound to develop.

The ultimate goal of a systems management group is to keep users satisfied. The willingness of the users to accept the occasional crisis and system unavailability will determine the degree of systems control.

Controlling DB2 has several aspects. There is the issue of day-in/day-out control of the DB2 environment. This includes monitoring and tuning, routine management of applications, and standard changes such as security administration. Controlling DB2 is ultimately a design issue. Applications have to be designed to be manageable.

It is the responsibility of the production group to enable developers to produce applications that can be managed. Standards for batch program retry, for security management, for performance, and for scheduling need to be set.

This process is not a one-time activity in DB2. Consider how CICS develops in most shops. Use starts in a haphazard way. Central strict management is enforced only after problems occur. Once that central administration is in place, the shop can develop more sophisticated applications. The CICS administration function can remain stable.

Users of DB2 are victims of the Chinese curse "may you live in interesting times." We are living in exciting times in the hardware, software, network, and database world. With the interesting new toys come interesting new problems. CICS administration had a very stable systems environment in the 1980s. No one will promise that stability to DB2 users.

The administration of DB2 cannot expect a stable environment. The planning should be divided between stable applications and unstable ones. This has nothing to do with technology. A DB2-to-DB2 distributed object-oriented application may be stable. A simple DB2 batch application may be volatile. Stable applications are administered on an exception basis, while unstable ones must be monitored.

Planning for the new technologies is not part of the traditional administration job. DB2 administrators tend to be required to analyze new technology. The analysis may be proactive, trying to identify tools to use. It may be defensive, to warn of problems in using new tools.

All DB2 users have to deal with coexistence. DB2 is almost never the only database manager. There tend to be flat files, VSAM, and usually other database manager data to coordinate. Administration becomes very complicated as various recovery scenarios coordinating between them are considered. It is a rare shop that is fully prepared for the problems when they occur. It is a smart shop that practices recovery situations.

In most shops DB2 is a growth industry and other database management systems are less active. This can create tremendous political conflict. Each shop has to deal with these issues in its own terms.

Software Life Cycle Changes

DB2 is part of a changing applications world. The scale of applications is increasing as the goals become more ambitious. For example, integrated applications designed to support disparate groups of users require enormous amounts of support. These issues may not be directly caused by DB2, but they have to be managed in every DB2 shop.

DB2 issues are pervading the entire application life cycle. The earliest design decisions cause many performance problems. Application function limitations can be caused by simple tuning choices. This is why we hear more about DB2 in DB2 applications than other environment issues. The DB2 aspect is constantly in view.

The basic problem of modern applications is to isolate the rules from the process. Knowing the business rules allows designing effective applications. Knowing the application management rules allows designing an effective production environment.

Production is becoming a more intelligent environment, but in a weird way. Rules often are not captured in design, but are guessed at later in the life cycle based on application behavior. This works to the detriment of all concerned.

The DBA

The DBA issues in design are long-range and large-scope issues. Is the application maintainable? Will this application work with another one? These are difficult issues based on tradeoffs and guessing what new development projects will be requested.

The DBA issues in production are controlling the environment to ensure that applications will run. The database issues are the least stable, and the production DBA is responsible for stabilizing them.

Database administration can be either an easy or a very hard job. The problem with any service industry is fluctuating demand for service. Anyone associated with data processing understands these issues — it is a service to the company. DBA is a service industry to a service industry. If information service demands are cyclical, DBA work demands are doubly so.

Unless there are many DBAs, the workload fluctuation makes balancing the DBA schedule impossible. For each application developed, specific DBA tasks have to be done at specific points. Until the components are ready, there is no need for DBA intervention. Whenever a project activity requiring a DBA is reached, the entire project waits for the DBA to finish.

This puts the DBA in an awkward position. The DBA group can act as a barrier to bad practices, but at the expense of project delay. The DBA group can allow freer development, but at the expense of not helping application quality. In either case the DBA can be considered a nuisance. A DBA group cannot function effectively without strong political support.

The DBA and New Technology

In most companies DBAs are at the forefront of the use of new technology. These issues — networks, PCs, workstations, LANs, interfaces and gateways, client-server and distributed applications, image processing, decision support — are all complex. These new technologies put incredible strain on the DBA for several reasons:

- It is hard to understand new technology. There is a learning curve. DBAs should have expertise in the systems immediately if they want to contribute.
- New technology often does not work well. It often has strange environmental issues that are unique to each shop. These problems are hard to predict and impossible to plan for correctly.
- Existing procedures tend to fail miserably when tested against these new paradigms. The fallback position for an overworked DBA is minimal involvement in projects, waiting for project checkpoints before getting involved. New technology means supporting the applications throughout the life cycle.
- New technology always develops as function first, then operational management capability. This means that the new technology makes the DBA the victim who has to specify operational management issues or else nix projects for operational reasons.

IBM Is Getting Better

Everyone using IBM software and hardware over the past decade has noticed two things:

1. IBM has had to become better at providing service and function to customers.

2. IBM has become much better at providing services and function.

I remember my early exasperation with IBM as a regressive force. In the 1970s IBM competed because of its client base and software inventory against inadequate competition from Univac, Burroughs, Honeywell, and CDC mainframes. The IBM behemoth simply rolled over the competition.

The changing world of data processing has caught up with IBM. The mainframe competitors collapsed. The new competition has been on two fronts. Plug-compatible mainframes have aggressively tightened the IBM cost/performance and product release cycle. The real competition, though, has come from the bottom.

DEC, Tandem, and Teradata have all grown small computers into powerful mainframes. Workstations, LANs, and servers are tempting users to decentralize. The new platforms become more appealing in nontraditional applications.

IBM has successfully and aggressively addressed these threats. It has overcome the "not invented here" syndrome. The number of IBM business partners is exploding. It is working with many new technological features. The most important change is that it is taking a progressive rather than a regressive stance.

The IBM of the 1970s fought change since it would destabilize its customers. The current IBM goal is leading change from the point of view of the large and well-managed shop. Distributed database development in IBM is behind the market only in its not releasing partially controllable database management systems. Other products can do more than DB2 or the OS/2 Extended Edition Database Manager, but there are (many) risks and technical sophistication required to use them. IBM is actually pushing areas of the technology.

We can see some of the new attitude in DB2 version 2.3. This release can be criticized for relative lack of innovation, having less new function than the previous ones. It still provides some very interesting features.

The DB2 version 2.3 sample libraries include a basic catalog management facility. This program does not intend to compete with the catalog management products from independent vendors. BMC, Platinum, Candle, and On-Line Software have sophisticated products that provide many functions. DB2 version 2.3 provides basic services, and can be considered a starter set of functions justifying the more sophisticated independent vendor products.

The release also provides for BIND of PACKAGESETs which allows ease of management, more sophisticated design, and performance improvements for complex applications. The sample libraries include a sample EDITPROC to do data compression.

The release also provides a new access method, hybrid joins, which fine-tunes list prefetch. Some utilities work faster. DB2 is becoming easier to manage.

Repository Manager/MVS and AD/Cycle

The repository is by now the Holy Grail of application development. The goals are noble: complete justification of centralized processing. The product is ambitious: a model of a business in which our applications fit. There is nothing there but smoke and mirrors.

In the long term, repository is the pivot on which IBM will sink or swim. In the short term, it is a pain in the neck. Not only do we not have the function expected, but users and vendors are chilled from attempting to compete with it.

Systemview

Without a repository, we need some means to manage our system. Smaller DB2 users need a systems management integration facility. Larger DB2 users may opt for using the repository, but will still need an active way for programs to interact. Repository is a passive facility.

Systemview is developing into an architecture for systems management and operation product interaction. There will be some IBM central control facilities included as well. This will help DB2 users in the next year or so.

Summary

DB2 is currently one of the few database management products that allow fully managed support of a production environment. It is evolving to support a diverse range of production programs. DB2 can support complex enterprise-wide applications.

DB2 users are mostly using DB2 in production in two ways: There are decision support applications that are often managed like development environments and there are operational applications that are managed like traditional applications.

Applications are now comfortably in production in most DB2 shops. The applications are not managed in new ways. The next round of development is going to be the test. Has your shop learned from the first applications developed? Is there a new DB2 application management strategy? Will the DB2 applications work better in the long term than previous software? Only time (and planning) will tell.

Review Question

1. How can DB2 compete against database management systems running on much cheaper massive multiprocessing machines?

Answer to Review Question

1. DB2 can compete against database management systems running on massive multiprocessing machines because of several factors.

- Traditional database applications typically grow in processing requirements by less than one-third each year. The power of the new technology is not necessary for most applications.

- The development of the hardware, especially control and data transfer issues, is still in its infancy. Most users will hesitate in using these products until they stabilize.

- The enormous complexity of developing algorithms to efficiently exploit the hardware will push use of these machines further into the future.

- DB2 runs on IBM mainframes that already run an enormous inventory of required applications. It will take many years until the new machines can compete against the application base in both customer developed and vendor packages available in DB2.

Ultimately, this results in DB2 being the de-facto standard for data processing applications. Newer and cheaper technology will compete well in certain circumstances.

- For new types of applications, such as image processing, for which there is little existing software inventory, the coexistence issues are insignificant.
- Technology oriented consumers, such as engineering design laboratories, tend to be interested in exploring the newer techniques.
- Price sensitive consumers are willing to accept the problems in the new technology for the sake of expediency. In many cases there are applications that cannot be reasonably developed in DB2, but make sense in the new machines.

The result is that DB2 will have a decade to reign over data processing applications.

Chapter 29

Dynamic SQL Applications

Static SQL, where the data structure, selection criteria, and the processing of the data to be returned are identifiable before the application is run, fulfills the needs of most applications. Certain applications have data requirements that are not easily met with predetermined static SQL. An example is a reporting application doing data selection based on input selection criteria, where the comparison operators are not known beforehand. Many distributed DB2 applications use dynamic SQL as well.

Dynamic SQL offers an alternative, allowing the statements to be built as text strings in the application and executed. Any operation that can be done in static SQL also can be done in dynamic SQL. For example, a program can input a condition, such as is shown in Figure 29.1.

```
 CALL GET_WHERE_CLAUSE(STRING);
        /* get the selection information */
 STATEMENT =
    'DELETE FROM TEMP WHERE ' || STRING;
        /* format the string for processing */
EXEC SQL
    EXECUTE IMMEDIATE :STATEMENT;
 IF SQLCODE = 0 THEN
    EXEC SQL COMMIT;
 IF SQLCODE <> 0 THEN
    CALL ERROR_PROCESSING;
```

Figure 29.1 Dynamic processing of a SQL command.

Now the data have been deleted. This code sample includes both dynamic SQL — the EXECUTE IMMEDIATE statement, as well as the static SQL COMMIT statement.

The more common (and more complicated) situation in dynamic SQL is data selection processing: SELECT statements. The problem in selecting data is that the number of columns or the data types of the retrieved columns are often not identifiable beforehand. DB2 supports this kind of processing using the SQL Data Area (SQLDA). This is a memory data structure consisting of a header and an array of slots. Each slot contains information about each returned column: data type, length, and so on. The structure can be allocated dynamically based on the number of columns that are being selected. Selection processing in dynamic SQL is shown in Figure 29.2.

```
EXEC SQL INCLUDE SQLCA;
EXEC SQL INCLUDE SQLDA;
EXEC SQL DECLARE STTMNT STATEMENT;
EXEC SQL DECLARE DYNCURS
   CURSOR FOR STTMNT;
CALL GET_STATEMENT(STATEMENT);
EXEC SQL PREPARE STTMNT
  FROM :STATEMENT;
IF SQLCODE = 0 THEN
  EXEC SQL DESCRIBE STTMNT
          INTO SQLDA;
IF SQLCODE = 0 THEN
     EXEC SQL OPEN DYNCURS;
IF SQLCODE = 0 THEN
     DO;
     CALL SETUP_SQLDA;
         /* adjust pointers etc. */
     EXEC SQL FETCH DYNCURS
         USING DESCRIPTOR SQLDA;
     END;
```

Figure 29.2 Multiple row SELECT in dynamic SQL.

Problems in Dynamic SQL

The advantages of dynamic SQL in flexibility and power are enormous. However, there are many problems with dynamic SQL. The fundamental problem is that there is a lot of additional DB2 catalog activity inherent in a dynamic SQL request. The statement components are validated against the catalog, and authorization is checked against the catalog. The locks are held for the duration of the work unit (assuming the traditional DEALLOCATE(COMMIT) in the application bind). The significant change of catalog locks into latches may not be enough of an improvement for high-volume users. (See Figure 29.3.)

The concurrency level of any database application with a relatively small amount of data stored is low. Lockout is bound to happen if catalog update activity is occurring. This means that dynamic SQL reporting activity will conflict with any DDL or DCL. (This applies whether the DCL and DDL are dynamic or static, although it is rare to have this activity in static modules.) Plan binding can conflict, although the DB2 version 2.3 package mechanism may be a means of

Issue	Dynamic SQL	Static SQL
Bind	Each statement as run	Once beforehand
Security checks	Each statement as run	Each statement as run, or when the program starts
Flexibility	Complete	Only can deal with predefined problems
Performance	CPU, I/O overhead, but can give more access info to optimizer (data values)	Best typically
Catalog contention	DML, DDL, and DCL	Only ifBIND VALIDATE(RUN) used or when DCL or DDL is embedded in a program

Figure 29.3 The tradeoffs in use of Dynamic SQL.

reducing bind duration. RUNSTATS, if it is updating the actual catalog (DB2 version 2.3 does not require it to do so), or any user application updating the catalog also directly conflicts with any other catalog access.

The implications of this resource contention are broad. Dynamic SQL applications should only be built after a long-term projection of the DB2 subsystem usage.

Programming Complication

It obviously takes more effort to build a dynamic SQL application than to build a static SQL application *if the application could easily be built in static SQL.* The real-life tradeoffs are less intuitive. Many dynamic applications must be done in dynamic SQL, while some applications can either be built in fewer dynamic statements or else built using more static statements. The application requirements tend to dictate the selection.

Some environments cannot directly use SQLDAs, since the languages lacks pointer facilities. An example in COBOL (as opposed to COBOL II, a language that includes pointers). This means that COBOL shops can use varying list parameterized dynamic SQL only by calling an external routine in another language to match up the pointers. This type of application often seems unappealing.

Another environmental issue is staff capabilities. Some developers have an abhorrence for pointer and dynamic list processing as their programming product shows. On the other hand, as many technically flashy applications are written in dynamic SQL as truly poor ones. Many flashy applications do not seem to meet requirements. Be careful if application programmers are having too much fun writing an application that they describe as getting more and more general purpose.

Potentially Poor Statement Design

A less obvious reason is the cause of most of the problems in dynamic SQL applications. Except for some programmer tools, and certain specific application techniques, almost all dynamic SQL is generated by programs. The effort required to build a statement generator that will always build reasonable SQL code is considerable. In almost all cases we end up with SQL generators that can build the intelligent choice of statement only in some circumstances.

SQL generating applications that are not targeted to a very restricted data environment tend to be capable of producing terrible SQL. The extent to which the application use produces bad SQL, and the severity of problem that this creates are very hard to determine before the application is developed.

Summary

Dynamic SQL can allow for some programs that simply cannot be built using static SQL. It allows for complete flexibility at the price of more effort in processing and some DB2 system catalog contention.

Dynamic SQL can improve the performance of some access paths by providing actual WHERE clause values instead of host variable place holders. Most dynamic SQL is produced by programs such as fourth-generation languages.

Review Questions

1. When should dynamic SQL be used?

2. Should dynamic SQL be used in transaction processing?

Answers to Review Questions

1. Glibly, use dynamic SQL whenever you have to. Typically, applications use dynamic SQL where parameters are not known when the program BIND is done. DB2 cannot parameterize table names or add additional WHERE clauses to a bound statement. This fact forces very flexible programs to use dynamic SQL.

Dynamic SQL is also used in some rare cases for performance reasons. DB2 cannot optimize a parameterized statement based on the parameter values in static SQL. The static SQL plan is completely general purpose, and the value is not known at BIND time. Dynamic SQL in some cases can make use of more qualification information. Dynamic SQL will therefore have an advantage over static SQL for certain statements.

2. There is no inherent reason to never use dynamic SQL in a production transaction processing environment. Dynamic SQL can cause catalog contention and has complex performance implications. It is often complex to design applications where catalog contention is a consideration. There are no easy means of controlling performance issues.

Many shops are unwilling to expend the design and operational analysis overhead to manage a system which can have these sorts of problems. This commonly causes shops to avoid these techniques. More mature DB2 shops and aggressive shops do use dynamic SQL in production. CICS QMF provides an example of the use of, and problems with, dynamic SQL in transaction processing.

Chapter 30

Transaction Processing and Dynamic SQL

Dynamic SQL adds some extra overhead to the data access process: mini-bind, authorization checking, and the increased risk of lock delay. This delay tends to be inconsequential in an environment of low transaction rates and long delays expected as the computer processes complex ad-hoc or batch reporting. In transaction processing that generally deals with processing more requests that access less data, each of these problems can be a stopper.

Dynamic SQL can be considered as an option for transaction processing. There are cases in which the increased information passed to the optimizer can markedly improve transaction performance. The overhead has to be factored into the application design. An aspect of this is runaway transactions. The designer of dynamic SQL transaction processing should be careful of both environment (locking) and performance issues.

It is much easier to design a transaction process that uses a very constrained dynamic SQL statement than a transaction building SQL statements that have unclear performance characteristics. This is primarily a problem of the transaction processing monitors CICS and IMS, which are not designed to manage long transactions among shorter ones.

Authorization Requirements

Dynamic SQL inherently requires more authorization support than static SQL. Static SQL is normally bound in production with the VALIDATE(BIND) option, allowing the overhead of authority checking to be done at BIND time.

The dynamic SQL application data requirements or authorization requirements are not known to DB2 at BIND time.

Every time a SQL PREPARE or EXECUTE IMMEDIATE is performed, DB2 must reanalyze the authorization of the user.

The impact of this deferred authority checking is that the user must be explicitly authorized to access the data. In the case of static SQL, authority to execute the PLAN is enough. Only the owner of the plan needs the authority to access the data, and even that can be avoided using **BINDAGENT** authority.

This means that we must explicitly GRANT the authority to access the data to each user. This becomes burdensome for two reasons. First, the administration overhead of managing a large number of GRANT and REVOKE statements is onerous. The number of objects involved makes this complicated. Second, the data may be at risk. The application can limit the types of actions the user can take against the data, but is this application the only means the user has to access the data? Access to QMF, SPUFI, and many other generic dynamic SQL tools could allow the user to access inappropriate data or to modify data without regard to constraints built into the application.

The nuisance of authorization management can be reduced somewhat by using secondary authorization identifiers, which are called for short secondary authids. Secondary authids are used to allow DB2 to use the hierarchical grouping mechanisms in your MVS security manager.

Thus, groups in RACF (IBM) or profiles in CA-Top Secret (CA) authorized to a user's identifier can be used to manage the security on a group basis.

If the appropriate mechanisms are installed, the user will receive the UNION of all authority granted to the user specifically, and to any security groups the user is enrolled in. This allows the security management to be done at a group level. If everyone in a department is in a department security group, everyone can be authorized at once by authorizing the group.

DB2 does this feat by getting a list of IDs from an exit at connection time to DB2, which DB2 retrieves from the security manager. When checking permission for a DB2 activity, DB2 will check to determine that the CURRENT SQLID is authorized to perform the action. If it is authorized, there are no problems. If the activity is not authorized, DB2 will search the secondary authorization identifier list, testing each entry until finding appropriate authority. The request will be denied if the proper permission has not been granted. This process can be expensive in system resources, proportionately to the number of alternative IDs and the number of authorization failures.

Design Strategies

Dynamic SQL should be considered in terms of the problems it can cause:

- DB2 catalog and directory (DBD) locking
- Potential *runaway* queries
- More complex programming

and in terms of the benefits. Dynamic SQL can do processing which static cannot. Sometimes there are performance benefits to us of dynamic SQL.

The designer of a dynamic SQL application is building a code generator. All traditional software engineering issues relating to this type of processing should be used. Most dynamic SQL applications have a skeleton that looks like the example in Figure 30.1.

```
MAIN_LOOP:
     CALL GATHER_REQUIREMENTS;
     CALL ANALYZE_REQUIREMENTS;
     CALL GENERATE_SQL;
     CALL PROCESS_SQL;
END MAIN_LOOP;
```

Figure 30.1 The generic program skeleton.

Maintaining the clear distinction between these phases is important if the application can grow. The tasks are different and should be isolated.

Static SQL Alternatives to Dynamic SQL

Permutations of static alternatives

In some cases where dynamic SQL is used, especially in program-generated statements, it turns out that there are only a few standard paths that could provide the same function. We can use this technique to escape the overhead of dynamic SQL.

Static for common paths, dynamic for exceptions

In many cases, an 80/20 rule applies. Even though the process cannot be converted wholly to static SQL, the most common alternatives can be processed statically. This can give us the best of both worlds, where most of the processing is done in static SQL without adding any constraints to the application.

Plan size issues

There is a significant overhead to having multiple static statements for each database access. The plan size can grow exponentially. The designer has to balance data access overhead with the potential EDM pool thrashing that could require extra reads and competition for bufferpool space.

Dynamic Applications

DB2 provides the options of embedding data definition or data control directly in our program.

We can for example:

```
EXEC SQL CREATE UNIQUE INDEX MYINDEX ON
MYTABLE(COLUMN1)
```

or

```
EXEC SQL GRANT EXECUTE ON PLAN KANGAROO TO JOEY
```

These types of statements act in many ways like dynamic SQL, only more so. They require catalog access; in fact, they involve updating the catalog. In the case of the DDL, we are also updating the directory. All problems inherent in using dynamic SQL should be considered in this circumstance.

This type of processing is fairly unusual; it is typically done only if there is some sort of in-house tool development. These tools may be building a DDL execution facility for a CASE tool, or implementing a security management system. If this type of processing is expected against an active DB2 system, attempt to build in facilities to optionally stage the processing. The staging is to a batch queue where the processing can be allowed when there is less load on the system. Note the fascinating security issue that embedded DDL or DCL implies, mixing both the binding user and running user authority.

We also have the option of executing DDL or DCL using the EXECUTE IMMEDIATE statement against statements that we build. This type of processing is far more common, because of the flexibility it provides.

The Benefits of Dynamic SQL

We have seen that there are problems in using dynamic SQL, but in many cases the benefits outweigh them. In most environments there is a line that can be drawn. Operational applications with consistent performance requirements are built on the more stable static SQL, while all other applications use the flexibility inherent to dynamic SQL.

The primary advantage of dynamic SQL is the ability to define requirements at run time. This allows on the fly report building, as well as DB2 support tools and self-customizing applications.

A dynamic SQL application will immediately take advantage of a new index. A static SQL program will not change its path selection until it is rebound.

In some cases dynamic SQL will perform much better than the static equivalent. Dynamic SQL has a relatively constant fixed overhead, but in some cases more information can be passed to the DB2 optimizer using dynamic SQL.

The standard example is shown in Figure 30.2, where LAST_NAME is indexed. This is static SQL. If we set the field **value** to 'ZAPP%', DB2 would not be able to do an index search — the optimizer will search an index only if there is no preceding wild card. In static SQL, the optimizer doesn't know what **value** equals, and must choose a worst case path. This query will require some sort of scan, either index or table, which may be slow. If we had coded the query in dynamic SQL, as shown in Figure 30.3, the optimizer would

```
EXEC SQL DECLARE ACURSOR CURSOR FOR
      SELECT FIRST_NAME, LAST_NAME
            FROM ADDRESS
            WHERE LAST_NAME LIKE :value
```

Figure 30.2 Data values in static SQL.

```
      CALL GETVALUE;
         /*value is set to 'ZAPP%'*/
      TEXT =
     'SELECT FIRST_NAME, LAST_NAME'
 ||    ' FROM ADDRESS WHERE '
 ||    '  LAST_NAME LIKE '
 ||       VALUE;
```

Figure 30.3 The dynamic SQL alternative.

have seen the value containing the antecedent literal characters and would have chosen the more efficient index search.

Another significant benefit of dynamic SQL is in minimizing plan size. Dynamic SQL creates, in effect, generic applications that do not have access paths specified; the lack of identified paths reduces the run-time overhead (EDM pool contention). This can be used for a variety of purposes. Very complex applications with low throughput requirements may be built using dynamic SQL, but verify carefully that catalog contention won't be a problem anywhere these are run. Some applications are built using dynamic SQL to handle exception conditions for the reason of reducing the size of monolithic plans; the preferred technique in this situation is generally separate plan packages, though.

Dynamic SQL has the interesting characteristic of not needing to be rebound to take advantage of data structure, indexing, or RUNSTATS information changes. This can be helpful in several ways.

In an environment of constant change, dynamic SQL becomes a powerful ally. Tables are frequently dropped and rebuilt in a development environment, often for changes irrelevant to our application. Dynamic SQL can access those tables with equanimity, while static access will result in the requirement to rebind.

This function can work in production as well, in an unsettled environment. If user authority is established through use of views, but the view definition changes frequently, dynamic SQL can be used to immediately use the changes.

Forced Dynamic SQL In 4GL and Similar Systems

Many flexible systems cannot easily accommodate static SQL. This problem is a major rationale for bimodal tools that build dynamic SQL in development and static in production. Most of the common 4GL tools will allow development using dynamic SQL with the inherent speed of testing and lack of need to rebind constantly, and allow optional conversion to static SQL in production for speed and security purposes.

Statement Building — "Cursor Pools"

Dynamic SQL, for all its flexibility, cannot create new cursors that were not defined in the program at precompile time. Each cursor has to be explicitly, statically declared, and the SQL open, fetch, and close statements must be precoded. Large applications using dynamic SQL often require a variable number of cursors, where the number is not known until the program is in use. If you do not have an example application at hand, consider any 4GL you have that can reference an arbitrary number of tables.

This process can be managed by use of pools of cursors. A module containing a list of cursor declarations combined with their corresponding processing. An example of this processing is shown in Figure 30.4.

This procedure allows the main program to simply set up the SQLDA, choose the cursor from an available cursor queue (which it has to maintain), and deal with the cursors as a logical entity rather than a physical one.

There is still the danger of running out of cursors, depending on usage and the number allocated. Each cursor carries a cost in program size, especially EDM pool use. This tradeoff can best be dealt with by parameterizing the number of cursors allocated, and generating the cursor pool module in a macro, allowing the installation to define a size to meet its requirements.

Dynamic SQL and Work Units

Like everything else in DB2 except cursors with hold and locks in programs bound with the RELEASE(DEALLOCATE) parameter, everything in dynamic SQL goes away at the end

```
CURSOR_POOL: PROC(CURSOR_NUMBER, ACTION, SQL, SQLDA);
 DCL CURSOR_NUMBER FIXED BINARY,
      /* instance number in pool      */
     ACTION         CHAR(4),
      /* PREP,DESC,OPEN,FETC, or CLOS */
     SQL            CHAR(*),
      /* SELECT statement to be PREPed*/
     SQLDA          POINTER;
      /*  SQL descriptor area */
 SELECT (CURSOR_NUMBER);
    WHEN (1):
       EXEC SQL DECLARE CUR1 CURSOR;
            IF ACTION='PREP' THEN
            EXEC SQL PREPARE CUR1 FROM :SQL;
       ELSE IF ACTION='DESC' THEN
            EXEC SQL DESCRIBE CUR1 INTO :SQLDA;
       ELSE IF ACTION='OPEN' THEN EXEC SQL OPEN CUR1;
       ELSE IF ACTION='FETC' THEN
             EXEC SQL FETCH CUR1 USING :SQLDA
       ELSE IF ACTION='CLOS' THEN EXEC SQL CLOSE CUR1;
    WHEN (2):
       EXEC SQL DECLARE CUR2 CURSOR;
            IF ACTION='PREP' THEN
         EXEC SQL PREPARE CUR2 FROM :SQL;
       ELSE IF ACTION='DESC' THEN
         EXEC SQL DESCRIBE CUR2 INTO :SQLDA;
       ELSE IF ACTION='OPEN' THEN EXEC SQL OPEN CUR2;
       ELSE IF ACTION='FETC' THEN
            EXEC SQL FETCH CUR2 USING :SQLDA
       ELSE IF ACTION='CLOS' THEN EXEC SQL CLOSE CUR2;
    WHEN (3):

    etc......

  END; /* select */

  IF SQLCODE ^= 0 THEN CALL ERROR;

END CURSOR_POOL;
```

Figure 30.4 A pool of SQL cursors.

of a work unit. This often creates a design dilemma: it is a tremendous bother in both programming effort and computer resources to commit and reprepare the statements to reestablish position. On the other hand, not committing when using dynamic SQL, which locks portions of the catalog, is often an act of bad citizenship.

SQL/DS provides a feature to solve this problem: extended dynamic SQL. This allows an application to commit or roll back but maintain the dynamic SQL already prepared. The fact that this feature is not available in DB2 defines these environments in many ways. IBM is looking to DB2 as a transaction processing and complex query environment. SQL/DS, on the other hand, is mostly positioned in the small query arena, and 4GL and interpretive language support is a high priority in that context.

Dynamic SQL in Transaction Processing

Transaction processing applications can certainly use dynamic SQL. The obvious example is QMF under CICS. Many server applications operating as front ends for cooperative processing have all the design sensibilities as a transaction processing monitor, and most use dynamic SQL exclusively. The design considerations for using dynamic SQL in transaction processing are fairly straightforward: Can we accept the extra overhead, and is there a problem of catalog contention.

Control: RLF, EXPLAIN, and the Like

Dynamic SQL does not make for a static environment. Queries have much more latitude than in static SQL, and the performance implications are significant. Using large amounts of dynamic SQL requires careful planning to manage your system.

Control is the key here; the versatility allows any number of activities which may in fact be very beneficial to the users. These applications have to be reined in within the context of the goals of the users. Rarely will even a very useful application be expected to impede the use of mainstream operational applications.

At the same time, it is very hard to define the control goals. Typically the resolution of the control requirement is to guarantee a constant amount of system resources to an application. Thus, the application users are constrained by MVS to a fixed limit of resources for various time periods. This simplifies capacity planning, since it defines a "quota" for the amount of resources required. The MVS tuning to provide this is not trivial, especially in light of the changing aspect of how the resources are employed.

Even more complex is the managing of the internal environment of a decision support system or similar dynamic SQL application. We take it for granted that some queries here can require incredible amounts of resources to process.

Managing a System with Heavy Dynamic SQL Processing

Heavy use of dynamic SQL complicates management of DB2. Pervasive locking should be expected, planning for system requirements becomes guesswork, and performance becomes unpredictable. Different issues arise depending on the type of environment: Developers have different expectations and requirements than end users.

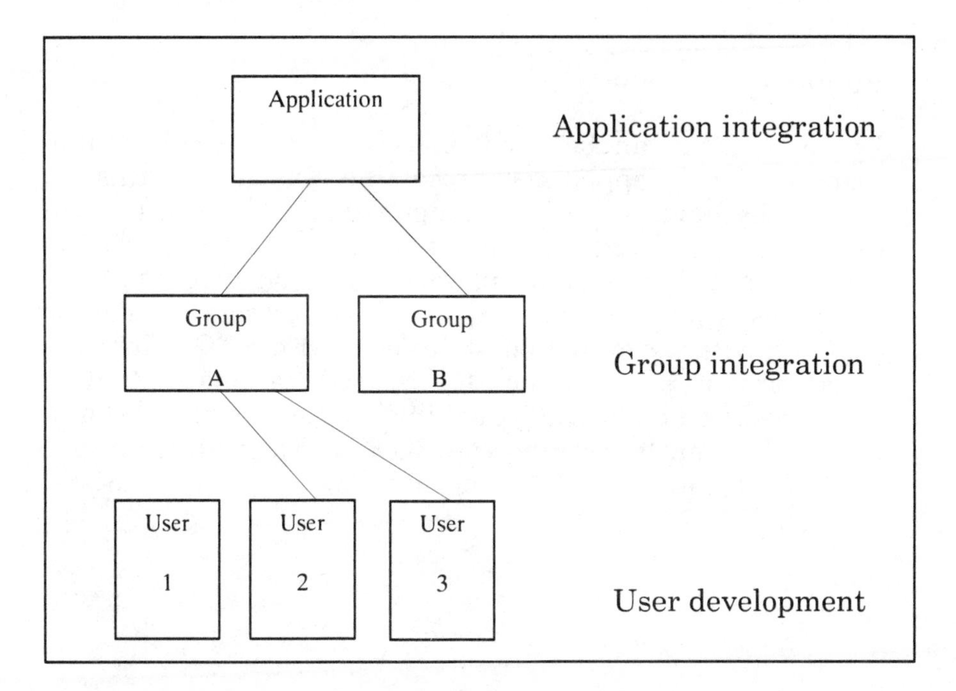

Figure 30.5 Database mirrors management format.

Development environments are the most complex to manage. A common strategy of "I'm not bothering" is often justified in terms of the limited payback, but these decisions should be made explicitly.

Developers tend to have the worst catalog contention, due to frequent DDL and DCL activity. This, in turn, can delay DML — which the environment should help use.

Contention can be reduced significantly by using more databases, since it reduces the DBD locks on the DB2 directory. Ideally these databases should be allocated in logical groupings based on DDL requirements. A typical application of this divide and conquer strategy is shown in Figure 30.5.

Some DML contention can be prevented by not using the *repeatable read* isolation option of BIND whenever possible. In some cases, such as environments involving frequent complex and slow DB2 catalog queries it is worthwhile to only provide the cursor stability isolation level plans for QMF, or to replicated the catalog data to a read only shadow copy. Most vendor catalog manager tools provide this option. Expect this issue to come up if your environment is using the DB2 catalog as a data dictionary.

Summary

Dynamic SQL can be used effectively in several circumstances in heavy application processing. Examples of this can be seen in fourth-generation language applications. Fourth-generation languages use pools of preallocated cursors to allow them to process multiple SELECTs concurrently.

In cases where dynamic SQL seems necessary, it may be replaced with permuted possibilities in static SQL. In cases where production dynamic SQL is used, catalog contention can be reduced by logically dividing users into multiple databases. Frequently running the RUNSTATS utility can give the DB2 optimizer the best information.

Review Question

1. What is the impact of BIND processing on dynamic SQL processing?

Answer to Review Question

1. The impact of BIND processing on dynamic SQL processing is primarily in locking contention. There is also contention for standard DB2 system resources, including bufferpool and EDM pool.

A special case of this is if the SQL is processing DB2 catalog data; another is if DDL or DCL is being issued in the dynamic SQL.

Chapter 31

Distributed Applications

Distributed applications involve processing on multiple computers. They are very viable from a technical point of view. Moving more processing power closer to the user results in more powerful applications, more easily customized, that are better integrated with the user's activity. Often these applications can trade much of the expensive central mainframe processing activity for local processing on smaller and cheaper machines. In doing so, the application design will eliminate costly and slow network traffic.

Also, distributed applications have high associated risks. There are tremendous organizational risks in downsizing. Downsizing is a decentralization strategy. Decentralization in a uncontrolled manner is the most risky thing a MIS organization can do. The shop will lose the consistency that MIS could potentially offer. Controlling decentralization is a very complex task, and one that IS is notorious for failing at.

Distributed Applications in DB2

DB2 is the flagship product in the IBM attempt to facilitate distributed databases. The IBM strategy is to provide such a high level of functionality that large corporations would not risk the missing capabilities in generic alternatives. This would guarantee the software base, which, in turn, would assure IBM control of the majority of the market.

Most users are not prepared for any distributed capabilities at all. A small percentage of shops are currently interested in distributed processing for some peripheral applications. A tiny fraction of users are prepared to use distributed processing in a way that would affect their businesses. Combining the IBM priority with the user interest provides a picture of what will happen with distributed capabilities in DB2.

IBM has to deliver a rock-solid product, and users are generally in no hurry to use it. But the longer it takes to provide the capabilities, the more risk IBM assumes. Other vendors may reach distributed capabilities in the interim, which would raise the stakes of the functional high ground IBM is seeking. Further, there is a constant nibbling of the advanced technology vendors into IBMs base.

We still have to consider distributed applications as a new concept. There are very few high-profile distributed applications in DB2. The implication is that those who prefer not to build applications on the forefront use distributed capabilities for low-profile applications, such as data transfer for decision support, or for peripheral components of mainstream applications, where a distributed capability failure will not imperil the main activities of the application.

In fact, the major hazard is the VTAM links. If your shop has a stable VTAM network that can comfortably absorb the additional load your application will build, you are in clover. By eliminating the network risk, we have returned the distributed application architecture to a database and application design issue.

If the VTAM load tolerance is questionable, your design team requires network expertise. VTAM is a fairly complex system, and far afield from where database expertise is normally needed. Relational database issues are very straightforward; in most cases the network issues can be directly dealt with by network experts. Using existing SNA and VTAM expertise is vital. This process will allow the network planner to understand the issues, make recommendations before the design goes too far down the garden path, and give the network planner the understanding to tune and balance the network requirements.

Capacity planning for networks is an expensive and long-term process. Using expertise (which doesn't mean that a DBA involved in a distributed DB2 application design should not understand what VTAM *pacing* is) is the key to reasonable utilization of the platforms.

Should Networking Design the DB or DB Design the Network?

As data distribution comes into being, the fields of network design and database design overlap. Distributed applications use both, and the functions tend to overlap. At some point a choice seems required: Do we have the network designers design the physical database, or does the physical database design include network design?

Clearly, a field merging the two will develop as distributed database becomes a staple. There is much to be said for both sides of the argument. Network design is a complex technical subject, combining understanding of engineering and operational research issues.

Relational database design tends to have a simple and small set of physical design options — often giving the impression that relational database design can be learned in days. The same cannot be said for network design. This leads some to conclude that networking could most easily take over much of the database design. A background in network design can lead to better balanced utilization of fewer resources.

In fact, this structure can work well in some environments. A meticulously planned application with scrupulous capacity planning can benefit from precise "design to load" of the data component. Database analysts are notorious for gross errors in this regard, and often overestimate capacity needs.

This scenario of a well-crafted system configuration requires deep understanding of application requirements. Unfortunately, the meticulously planned application is the rare exception. In most cases, application needs are only crudely estimated. In fact, the reason DBAs tend to overestimate database requirements is that this is a behavior learned in other application planning.

Most businesses tend to react mildly to excess capacity and forcibly to functional inadequacies of systems. The functional aspect provides for qualitative improvements, while the capacity issue can offer only quantitative improvements. This theme has been a major justification for DBA services. The DBAs know where their bread is buttered and emphasize the function and serviceability aspect.

That issue will decide the question for most businesses. It is possible to train network designers well in DB2 design, but that is not the issue. The information services world divides into systems and applications sides of the fence; network design lives on one side, and database design lives on the other. The typical database designer will be better prepared to gather application requirements than the typical network designer.

At the same time, network designers' lives will get more interesting. Issues are getting more complicated, and network options are constantly changing. The database designer is getting further distanced from systems issues. It will benefit all parties if the network designer works with the database designer in checking for reasonableness of logical designs, working with the database designer to produce rough physical designs and take over from there.

Distributed and Optionally Distributable Applications

The basic question in building any distributed application is the degree of site independence. In some applications loss of connection to another site is completely transparent; in others it completely disables the application. The choice is partially that of the developers, reflecting their application design philosophy. In part the decision on site independence is a reflection of the required system functions and environment.

The philosophical issue of a desire to allow sites to function in a network breakdown is normally a function of corporate style. A company that maintains independent local offices will tend to enable their activity even if the connection is lost.

A company that strongly centralizes activity will tend to have too little data available to allow a branch to function on its own. It takes a mature and well-disciplined shop to allow for centralized data design and distributed data, but those will win in the distributed world.

In an application design, the decision of degree of site independence should be the first one made in application design. In many cases this is in fact a IS strategy imposed from above. Expect a higher overall cost to allow site independence, unless the cost of managing redundant data is offset by the ability to locally customize the systems.

What Do You Do If You Lose Contact?

The major problems in distributed databases are due to the tremendous risk in creating an application on several components. Each part has a risk of failure. There can be a high risk that the application will not be available.

The networking component is the most complex part of this puzzle. A simple SNA network involves hundreds of computers at dozens of sites. Given these circumstances, the typical network is extraordinarily reliable. However, it is still possible to lose contact with the other parts of the application.

The question becomes: Are we willing to make the networking completely redundant? In most cases this is not justifiable. In that case the only available option is to build networking-independent applications.

Building distributed database applications that do not need the distributed capabilities seems contradictory. That is not the case; it is part of the process. The problem is that there is no natural strategy to manage this, because the tools to support application independence are not yet available.

The cost of building utilities to reconcile the systems data when the link is reestablished is extraordinarily expensive. The track record of application shops in succeeding in keeping the data reconciled has been terrible. The cost of building an application that can

- Run with access to another database
- Run without access to the other database
- Reconcile the two

approaches triple the cost of building a straightforward application. The issues should clearly be resolved in the database management system.

This problem (and not the problem in optimizing a distributed join) is the primary reason for the IBM reluctance to release distributed database capabilities. Figure 31.1 shows the basic database application distribution strategies.

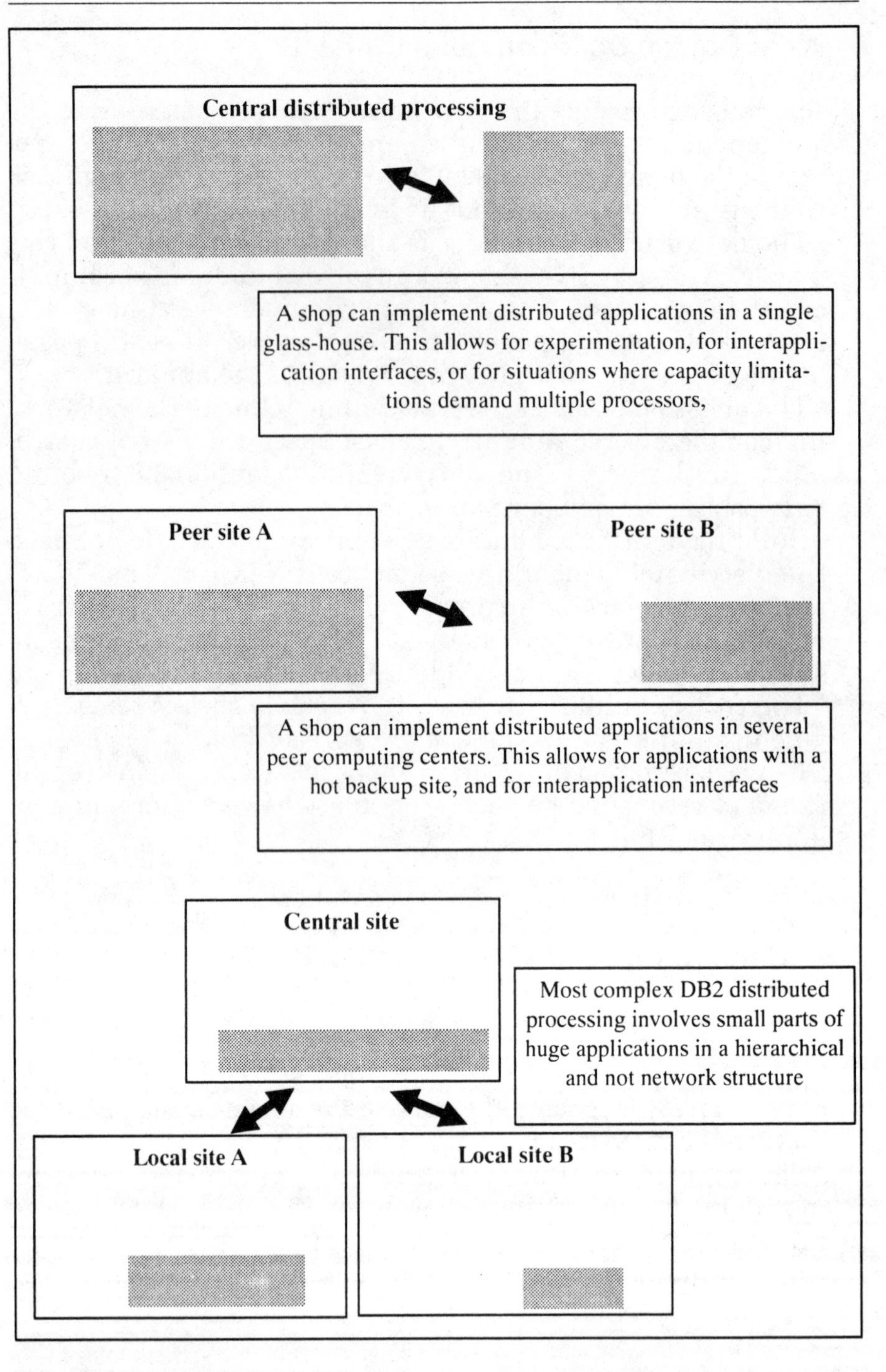

Figure 31.1 Forms of distributed applications.

Network Design

Network design is not an application-specific issue. A mature network's requirements are far more complex than those of a single application. A network built for a single application will tend to grow to support a variety of tasks anyway. From here on I will discuss networks in isolation, expecting the reader to frame the comments in a particular context.

Database Design Issues

Distributed databases come in three forms: there can be a centralized database that is implemented in a distributed manner, there can be a hierarchical structure resulting from the growth of central and departmental application interfaces, or there can be a network evolving from arbitrary interconnection between systems. Most real systems grow into a mixture of all three.

A critical design distinction can be made between a stable distributed load and an unclear one. This is not the standard distinction between DSS and operational systems that we see in a single DB2. The issue in distributed data is the likelihood of drawing a heavy load on the network. Often both operational system and DSS needs will be met by small amounts of data drawn through the network.

Summary

DB2 distributed processing is at an awkward stage. The facilities are too immature to be used for mainstream applications. Tools are not available to support developing distributed applications. The need is there in the shops, but few applications are being built.

DB2 distributed processing is appropriate for occasional processing, especially an occasional query. As the integration with other platforms grows, it will become even more complex.

Review Question

1. What is the difference between downsizing and distributed processing? In what ways are they the same?

Answer to Review Question

1. Downsizing attempts to redeploy existing application function on cheaper low-end platforms. Distributed processing allows for integrated processing activities on multiple computers linked on a network.

In many ways they are the same. Whenever a central processing function is downsized onto multiple communicating computers it is being converted to a distributed application.

Distributed applications using distributed database or client-server processing cannot be considered downsized applications. The functions added by the different architecture tend to allow the applications to do things which were not feasible centrally.

The most significant connection between the two is the ability to "de-consolidate" information services. Both of these strategies can easily come into intense conflict with central operations.

Chapter 32

Downsizing

Downsizing Scenarios

Why would anyone downsize applications? There are high expenses involved: buying new hardware, training staff, putting together all the pieces needed to manage the systems (operational procedures and such). The reasons range from tactical considerations of cost or deployment to strategic attempts to build new styles of applications.

Tactical: Cost Control

Tactical application downsizing reasoning is generally based on the cost of computing. If a low-end PC is fully utilized, the cost of processing is only about 1 percent of the cost of the same application processed on a mainframe. Even if there is additional cost in providing these nontraditional data processing services and the equipment is only partially used, it can often be much cheaper to use applications on PCs.

Often existing staff is building PC applications in infocenter departments. The knowledge base is there, and often the competing hardware and networks are in place already.

A common downsizing scenario is the loaded mainframe. Mainframe growth is a step process. Most companies will delay deploying a new mainframe computer as long as possible. This issue is illustrated in Figure 32.1.

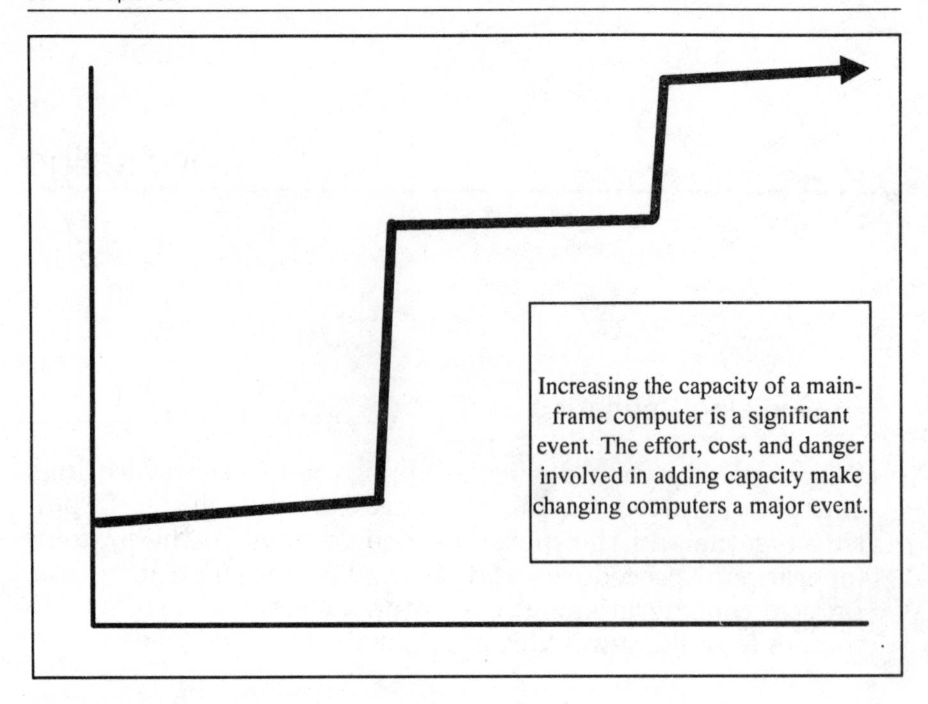

Figure 32.1 The stepwise growth of mainframe use.

As a mainframe approaches each step, it gets saturated with work, especially at peak times. This tempts developers to use the low-cost off-loading alternative: mainframe throughput is poor, and no one wants to be the straw that broke the mainframe's back, and is considered responsible for a multi-million-dollar upgrade.

The ideal option for a downsized application is a low-risk one: the need of an application that does not involve high availability requirements and where data lost will not disrupt the enterprise. This type of requirement should not compete with the mainframe's strengths of high availability and support.

This chapter will assume use of a MS-DOS-based PC platform for small applications and UNIX-based computers for any larger applications unless explicitly noted. This is because these operating systems define the market — they provide the cheapest computing power. IBM high-end mainframes are a very branded product and offer some of the highest cost computing power. (In making comparisons we must be careful not to overstate the difference in performance — many articles compare the cost of operating, managing, and buying a loaded IBM mainframe to the purchase price of a stripped PC.)

Strategic Design for a New Generation of Applications and the Limitations of Technology

The normal problems in downsizing are not in day-to-day processing. It is amazing how small a platform a typical day's transactions can run on. Smaller platforms tend to get awkward when the pressure increases. It is not uncommon to find that month-end processing can take an order of magnitude longer on a smaller platform.

The wonderful thing about mainframes is the many iterations of improvements that have been completed. The mainframe is a refined beast. Granted, the improvements have been incremental, but each one has worked off another rough edges of the problem areas in the machine.

Not so with most downsizing platforms. Each vendor will provide benchmarks showing amazing performance in a very specific task. Often the task defined becomes a definition of the characteristics of the hardware. The hardware is customized to execute a TPC-C benchmark (which is a simple update transaction) or some other very restricted workload. It becomes important to identify the range of workloads that the platform can perform.

Remember that hardware is normally not the limiting factor unless we choose a platform without enough growth potential. More common problems result from software restrictions.

As platforms shrink, expectations from software decrease as well. Often this is perfectly reasonable. A database server running on a local area network on a separate processor need not worry about being a well-behaved process in a multi-programming environment. Issues such as *locality of reference* and *working set size* do not have to be dealt with if the operating environment doesn't support virtual storage.

But system and application software function decreases in some downsizing environments. This includes less sophisticated collections of functions in software packages, or even not having any software to perform the service. Often the level of sophistication in systems management is not what a mainframe programmer would expect, even when there is support for easy development of new applications.

Architecture for Existing Systems and Redeploying Existing Applications

There are many facilities available to simply run an application developed on a mainframe on another platform. An example is simply excising a COBOL — DB2 — CICS application from MVS. The same application can be run on a personal computer using MS-DOS, Micro-Focus COBOL with CICS emulation, and XDB emulation of DB2 data management.

This type of system can provide a high degree of function. A high-end PC can support a medium-sized transaction processing application. This environment also can support large-scale development activities. It will not, though, be a good facility to manage large sorts and other heavy data throughput application needs.

The essential problem with this type of system is not the data transfer rate limits or the overshadowing threat of the lack of scalability. The issue is sensibilities of scale. This type of application straddles the mainframe and PC worlds and suffers the problems of both intensely. Mainframes offer highly scalable and tunable applications backed by enough power to manage enterprise-wide processing. The mainframe additional cost is high processing cost and conservative, expensive application development. PCs offer cheap processing and clever application development tools at the price of many limits on application processing and the lack of more complex vendor application software.

Redesigning for Downsizing

The larger IBM shops tend to be the least interested in downsizing applications. Once a shop has invested tens of millions of dollars in hardware, and an order of magnitude more in software, change does not come easily. The cost reduction of consolidation seems more attractive than downsizing.

This resistance can be justified in many ways. A shop investing that much in central processing probably has a very good reason for centralizing. The investment implies commitment; staff have invested in technical understanding and the shop in tools. This type of shop often has such high overhead that the hardware cost is less significant.

At the same time, the larger IBM shops are the most committed to DB2. It seems that DB2 and downsizing do not mix that well. The goals are in direct conflict. DB2 strategy tends to direct the larger shops into

- Mass application conversion
- Client-server (cooperative processing) applications
- Large-scale projects

rather than downsizing. This implies that a large shop will not expect the industry support structure such as development tools.

The DB2 strategy is clear. The large shops have tremendous inertia. The goal of IBM is to enable "pure blue" distributed processing when the infrastructure is available. The only justification for most of these shops to downsize would be to off-load peripheral applications. This would happen only if a SYSPLEX could not support the full application load.

Summary

Downsizing is the use of smaller computers for standard applications. The price advantages of smaller computers is substantial, and the software prices drop correspondingly. Since these smaller computers have the power of a mainframe of a few years ago, it seems intuitive that downsizing will work. Downsizing is an enormously complex issue.

The problem is that consolidation and centralization have had a much better record of success than distribution and decentralization for company-wide computing. Downsizing to move a totally departmental process off central computing can work, if the interfaces are clearly defined. Downsizing as a corporate strategy will work only if there is a politically strong central design group.

The most common downsizing scenarios relating to DB2 applications involve smaller DB2 shops with weak central services. A common tactical situation is downsizing applications off of an overloaded mainframe.

Review Question

1. Should a downsized application be run on the same network that is used for office automation?

Answer to Review Question

1. A downsized application should typically be run on the same network as that used for office automation. In most cases it is unrealistic to add a completely new network for operational systems.

The problem with this type of configuration is the conflict in network management cost, capacity, and facilities for these distinct application types. The reasonable approach is to slowly and carefully plan for the integration of these systems.

Chapter 33

Repository Manager/MVS, AD/Cycle, CASE, and DB2

What Is the Repository?

Repository Manager/MVS is an IBM product with a long history. Conceived in the late 1970s for maintaining a hardware inventory, the repository was a database program to manage operations relating to that inventory. That would alleviate some problems in managing the system, and allow a consistent interface between applications relating to those data. IBM successes have always been system level, and "The Repository" seemed a means of consolidating the system information.

Simultaneously, IBM customers were grappling with the same issues at a business level. The independent vendor solutions to the problems of application design were conflicting, and no particular standard evolved. This meant that any shop looking to improve the application development and maintenance cycle was trapped. Each shop had to mix and match from a collection of incomplete tools with inconsistent interfaces. This forced programming tool makers to constantly reinvent basic tools at high cost and to the detriment of new function. Everyone lost.

The effort and cost would be high, and the risk would be enormous. Each shop would put together a collection of tools, often patching in makeshift interfaces. "Software development automation" seemed to be taking root only in specific niche markets such as real-time applications.

At the same time the status quo was a failure. Application development cost was escalating. Backlogs of applications to be produced were increasing. Other platforms were showing lower development costs. Users were turning everywhere to fulfill demands not met by central MIS:

- PC systems managed some data.
- Departmental computing came into vogue.
- *Infocenters* developed to do light computing tasks.
- User departments began hiring programmers directly.

This change in the data processing world rightly panicked IBM. The cheaper hardware sells in a commodity marketplace with lower margins and less brand loyalty. IBM cachet is totally dependent on the viability of the large central mainframe. Mainframe cost can be justified against smaller platforms only if the applications run on them are smoothly integrated. The integration uses the power of the machine to provide a centralized management resource. Most IBM customer applications were poorly integrated, making them tempting targets for downsizing.

At the same time, customers were complaining about application backlogs, poor application development facilities, and the lack of means and standards to integrate their applications. IBM was under pressure both to "enable" integration and the building of large applications and also to ease the general application development process.

IBM seized on the tool being built to solve the specific hardware and configuration issues to integrate the user environment. This was not a complete solution; the product is a back-end tool requiring user interface tools. IBM, with its justifiable insecurity about user ability to deliver user-oriented tools, was forced to review the market and find vendors to work with.

The mainframe synchronous terminal interface and the cost of graphics processing made a PC-based front end an obvious solution.

The initial vendors IBM chose were

- Index Technologies (now part of Intersolv), then the market leader in CASE drawing tools
- Knowledgeware, a glamour player attempting an integrated CASE product
- Bachman, a vendor with focus on expert systems to assist in analysis of database structures and physical database design

Other vendors were later added to address more technical niches, such as AS/400 and front-end development.

The repository at that time was a database engine that needed a program to execute. It processed a business model that defined the data processing and data flow issues and the relationships between them. IBM originally designed the business model, to the discomfiture of the CASE business partners. Later versions were built combining some elements of the partners' business models with the initial IBM model. The Repository Manager business model was not complete as of late 1991.

Intersolv

Intersolv became an AD/Cycle partner because of the early success of their product, Excelerator. This was a very early CASE product that was very successful in an immature marketplace. Excelerator was the ultimate low-end product.

Most of the competing products in the CASE arena in the mid-1980s centered on Digital Equipment's VAX computers. This was a niche market, but a significant one. The VAX users tended to be more technically sophisticated than the mainstream. The development projects involved tended to be complex technical projects, often involving real-time processing.

That environment was ideal for CASE. The project style required rigorous management controls. In many cases these were Department of Defense contracts or subcontracts, or projects for industries that were heavily involved with DOD, such as aerospace industry applications. The methodology for this type of project was rigid from two aspects. The design was done by rigorously following a development methodology (e.g., Ward-Mellor or Gane-Sarson), and the management was intense and involved voluminous status reports and paperwork.

This environment developed very specialized CASE tools that would ease various aspects of the development process. The tools would use the power of the minicomputer to develop large bubble diagrams corresponding to the chosen design methodology. The tools could spew out the appropriate reports, or even interface directly with management planning tools. The human interface was fun — large, very interactive screens and pointing devices. The high cost of these tools could be justified against the enormous costs of an integration project.

The IBM world at the time differed radically. Development methodologies were dismissed in most large sites with the comment: "You want standards? . . . We have dozens of them." The majority of shops had no methodological development standards, and most of the rest had standards that were often ignored or that mutated between departments. Computing power was provided by large IBM mainframes geared to batch or transaction processing but awkward at conversational and graphical computing. It could be also offered by IBM personal computers, capable of simple processing but also slow and awkward as graphical processors.

The CASE tools available did not match the IBM environment. Excelerator fit into that environment very nicely. It had very minimal requirements and facilities. Whereas most vendors had understood that for CASE to be effective it must assist users in following a rigidly followed methodology well, Index took the low road.

The idea was: the wonderful improvement in product can be provided only when it follows a specific methodology, but who cares? We can build a tool that uses existing hardware that will allow for minor improvements. There will be less of a culture clash, and less sales resistance.

Excelerator grew out of the limitations of the IBM PC, but could not evolve easily because of that same functional limitation. The next few years should be an exciting time for Excelerator users, as the newer Excelerator-II product attempts to support the activities CASE proponents attempt.

Knowledgeware

The IEW product is a weakly interconnected integrated CASE (iCASE) product. The goal of the product is to support either the entire application life cycle or those parts of the life cycle that the user wants to automate. Several major development and diagramming methodologies are supported.

There are several problem with this approach. Being an integrated CASE product implies rigorous compliance to a development methodology. (CASE is simply a means to automate aspects of the methodology.) But presenting an "all things to all people" approach conflicts with the desire to use the CASE tool as a validation and compliance analysis mechanism. IEW is forced to allow weak and inconsistent models.

The number of Knowledgeware customers and their visibility make this an important product. There are an enormous number of add-on products from third-party vendors. There is a large base of developers and modelers who understand the techniques of this product. The broad coverage and large installed base make this package a secure middle road.

Bachman DBA Workbench and Designer Workbench

The Bachman tools had several clever premises. One is that most application development effort is actually spent trying to figure out what the existing application is doing. Most application development these days is reimplementing applications with additional function. This is a valid argument.

Another premise is that artificial intelligence can be used to automate a very restrictive technical area in a design process. This again makes sense, and the Bachman tools often stand alone in giving evidence of intelligence among CASE AI products.

The problem with this scenario is that unlike IEW or Excelerator, the Bachman DBA tools serve a very restricted niche market. The rationale for a company to buy several workstations is generally a logistics rather than a technical issue. There is a much smaller market for the Bachman DBA products than the mainstream CASE products.

CSP and AS: The IBM Application Implementation Environments

CSP has a special role in the development world. It is the IBM strategic product for application development. The product is a development workbench, using a COBOL-like language. Applications written in CSP can be moved fairly easily between SAA platforms. The CSP application development capabilities are currently rudimentary, but ease the effort in testing applications.

CSP is significant in providing a standard other than COBOL for application specification. The CSP *External Source Format* (ESF) is becoming one of the few means for transporting an entire application as a single entity.

AS is a stillborn product, never having established a niche and never justifying itself. It is not long for this world as a pallid mainframe imitation of PC-based tools, unless IBM decides to resurrect it.

CASE and DB2

CASE and DB2 have grown up together. DB2 has some level of data dictionary embedded in the product: the system catalog. Heretically for a database management system born in the 1980s, DB2 does not include CASE or dictionary-based development facilities. This is even though most of the gains of other database management products have been due to integrated CASE facilities rather than the relational model.

Thus, DB2 understands its role in CASE very clearly. It is part of the engine that drives the applications built in CASE. Sometimes it provides the engine managing the data for the CASE tool. It never competes with any CASE product function, and therefore has little to lose in battles over methodology and application lifestyle.

DB2 Issues in CASE

Is the DB2 catalog a data dictionary?

The DB2 catalog provides information about the database structure. Specifically, it contains the information entering DB2 through DDL, DCL, and the bind process. The only user information the DB2 catalog will normally contain is free-form character string comments added to describe user-accessible DB2 objects, and the name fields: the CREATOR, CREATED BY, and the LABEL. (It is possible to create dummy objects solely for documentation; this is occasionally done with the ALIAS and SYNONYM statements.)

SAA, Systemview and DB2

IBM is a large corporation, so large that the various products it develops are built in isolation from one another. This has allowed the creation of many tactical successes. The cost of developing an application independently is an order of magnitude smaller than that of building the application under strict central guidelines.

It has also protected the IBM market: since it is not uniform, it would take tremendous resources to compete against the broad range of systems. This has also been a disaster strategically — the lack of uniformity means that any application shared between systems has to be rebuilt for each platform.

This process has allowed IBM to gain expertise at developing low-level operating system functions: there were always a lot to build. Almost nothing came out of the application software side — despite IBM being the largest developer of application software in the world.

The resources were being spent in redundantly building the same functions into different platforms, building nonstandard interfaces between the platforms, and building bridges between the various platforms and interfaces. IBM has been losing ground on the function (external) level to vendors like DEC, whose emphasis on standard scalable hardware allowed a smaller software investment to show more result.

The competitive environment has required that IBM reduce software costs and provide better function. The strategy IBM chose was to design a standard set of interfaces. SNA had been successful on the networking side — so an architecture seemed the valid solution. This would allow IBM to build interfaces to personal computers that were needed as knowledge work became popular, large-scale computers could manage complex tasks, and the architecture would provide a scalable solution from the $5,000 piece of hardware on the desk to the multi-million-dollar central computer.

The new strategy was integration. If IBM could get in on time, there would be such a wealth of software based on its architecture that the competition would be pushed to niche markets.

Summary

We are in the midst of complex machinations by IBM to justify large central computers. Repository manager/MVS is intended to share design information in the largest shops. Systemview is a sharing facility for run-time information about operating the computers.

Review Question

1. What are the benefits and consequences of a more restrictive business model?

Answer to Review Question

1. A more restrictive business model makes the tools easier to integrate. The structures are very clearly defined, and the interfaces are natural. A more strict model eases the development of applications that conform to the model.

A less restricted model is more flexible. Existing applications and models can be easily added. The interfaces are less strict. The entry cost is lower. There is less need to conform. The disadvantage of a less strict model is that there is less room to grow. The ease of migration to a less strict model is the cause of the lack of growth potential.

Chapter 34

Application Reviews

Design Reviews

Design reviews are a vital part of quality assurance for applications. The review process is totally reactive; a review session should not be a post-hoc redesign session! If well done, design reviews can help produce:

- **A cheaper product.** The review process can weed out errors early, and reduce the effort of rework.
- **A better-managed process.** Explicit entry and exit criteria for design reviews define the state of an application very clearly.
- **A more efficient product.** Performance issues can be identified and controlled earlier.
- **A better-documented product.** Review inputs are explicit components of the documentation of applications. Documentation is done up-front.
- **A more consistent product**. If the reviewers are familiar with other applications and shop standards, deviation can be identified and managed.
- **A more accepted product.** Since design reviews can include more people in the review process, the application issues get aired. Users who are included become better informed. Getting more people involved can help "sell" the product, both publicizing features and creating a knowledge base.

- **No surprises.** Users who participated in design reviews and who review appropriate documentation will be less likely to ignore the application until after it is implemented. Requirements can be cross-compared from stage to stage of the review process. The entire process becomes a means to control the application.

These points all sound great. Most shops implement various aspects of the design review process. This review process is one of those things where there is a huge gap between going through the motions and working toward real goals. Many review procedures get diluted over time. Many shops see management and user support of the review process deteriorate over time. A review procedure that does not effect its goals is worse then none at all. It is sad to see a useful procedure turned into a parody of itself, and that sometimes happens to review procedures.

There are various styles of review procedures: software inspections, user moderated vs. application developer moderated reviews, etc. All methods work, somewhere, and if your style of review procedure succeeds in your shop, you have opted for a correct one.

A major issue relevant to any review process is following up: verifying that problems determined in the review have been corrected. This is a straightforward issue. A tricky variant of this issue is verifying that the process works. There should be constant monitoring of problems identified to see if they could have been solved at earlier stages of the development process.

Applications Size and Design Review

The most important consideration in defining the review process is application size. This is not a one-size-fits-all technique. Quickly developed applications would be incredibly burdened by a long, iterative review process. Very large-scale system integration projects cannot be reviewed in one fell swoop. Matching the review process to the context is a vital way of making reviews work.

This issue complicates two issues. First, the multiplicity of levels of reviews can make a shop's procedures a long, cumbersome, and often vaguely followed standard. Second, the review process is a combination of a technical process and a managerial process.

A malleable review format can often make technical sense for correcting development problems, but it operates at the expense of complicating project management. A rigid review procedure often makes managerial sense as a means of evaluating progress at the expense of diluting technical value. Of course, a review process followed lackadaisically will benefit no one.

A large application requires incremental reviews of several issues. The application design and development process should be reviewed. The capacity requirements should be reviewed. Application interfaces are often reviewed as a separate process.

The importance of goal-oriented reviews is a point worth repeating. Explicitly define the goals of your review process. Regularly evaluate the effectiveness of the process. This is the *only* means of preserving the value of reviews. There is nothing as disappointing as a mechanical review process that is done as lip service to a requirement with no results.

External Design Review and Business Issues

Business rule review differs from most review processes in that it addresses a higher level of application. That higher level qualitatively changes the format of the review procedure. It is important to note that in general, meetings with lower management tend to be analysis meetings, attempts to identify rules with staff that does not create them. Most business rule reviews at higher than middle management level become design meetings.

If the meeting will be at an executive level, it generally is unrealistic to attempt to manipulate the meeting toward a review process. The attendees tend to be less controllable than typical inspectors. It is unwise to have more than a single technician in this sort of meeting, and the technician can act as a resource in a passive role. The meeting is a business issues review, and should be controlled from the business management area. The best use of the business rule review is as a consensus gathering meeting. After a reasonable first cut of the business rules has been gathered, the model can be reviewed by the executives.

The most important benefit a physical design review can offer is a review of whether the technique used is appropriate for the circumstances. Too often in DB2 (and in fact in any newer technology) we see applications made clumsy because of the misunderstanding or ignorance of design approaches.

A common example is the sequential loading of a table using SQL INSERT statements. If this process is done regularly, it can be expensive. It further creates a nuisance for maintenance, since DB2 index structures disorganize rapidly during mass inserts. Simply having the program output a sequential file to be processed by the DB2 LOAD utility can often improve performance by an order of magnitude, and in the process reduce the batch window radically.

This overview must be the first consideration of any review. It is very easy to fine-tune a design immediately, ignoring the broader issues. Remember that tuning generally can confer a percentage improvement, while an architecture change can result in order-of-magnitude performance change. (Both types of changes may, of course, have a profound impact on application flexibility for future enhancements.)

Knowing when to jump up a level and understanding the implications of that change is a sign of technical maturity. Everyone attempting to solve a problem should remember the old rule: "The cause of problems is solutions."

It is important to understand the causes of the problems. Why are the wrong tools used so often in DB2 applications? The most common reason is the diversity of application types in DB2; it is an amorphous type of system. Most systems tools have a clear focus, and typically address a particular type of application or problem. Not so with DB2. Can expertise in decision support transfer into transaction processing? To some extent yes, but there are clearly important differences.

Distributed database and distributed applications have special problems. Distribution of data can result in

- Performance problems due to network and processor load

- Availability problems as many less reliable components are integrated together

- Maintenance and control problems due to the immaturity of the facilities to support the applications

Implementation Review

This is sometimes also called a project post-mortem. The idea is to analyze the effectiveness of getting the application into production. This can be the most complex logistical and managerial challenge in major applications that are immediately needed.

In some cases, typically large-scale projects, this procedure is used to review the entire project to identify problems. This review process has two major goals:

- To quantify the effectiveness of the techniques used in the project. This information could then be used to correct the techniques in future applications.
- To evaluate success in the initial mission. Many applications are implemented in production only to find they are ignored by users, underused, or missed the mark. Often, applications when finally completed are not exactly what was initially specified. (This may be intentional through changed or scaled-down goals, or unintentional because of miscommunication about application function requirements.)

DB2 Design Review

IBM has promoted the concept of the DB2 design review. Note that this is a "DB2 only" review, unusual in that it doesn't correspond to a managerial checkpoint — it reviews employment of a technology. This has been in reaction to performance problems customers created in early DB2 applications. The combination of new-style applications and unfamiliar technology needed support.

The idea of the design review is to plan for a successful application, with rational use of DB2. The strategy is for experienced DB2 designers to review the application design as presented by the designers. The goal is to allow designers less experienced in DB2 to gain from the insights of the more practiced. The emphasis is on performance issues.

This approach has several advantages. Because it is completely technical, this review process is insensitive to the design methodology used. External expertise (such as could be provided outside the specific department or company) need not understand the business or development approaches and can be used in this format. Clearly the best uses of this process are quantitative. A sample environment summary appears in Figure 34.1. An example of an summary of an application characteristics appears in Figure 34.2.

Context of an Application

What is the business mission?

How is the business organized?
- Business divisions
- Organizational interrelationship

Why is the application needed
- what does it do
- what does it replace
- how should the application affect users

Computer environment
- hardware and software context
- problem management issues
- major applications
- service level agreements
- Processor:
- Real memory size (in megabytes)
  - Real:
  - Expanded:
- Channel controllers:
- DASD:

Figure 34.1 Business environment summary form.

Application overview

Broad overview of application architecture
major subcomponents
transaction processing requirements
batch windows

How is it being built?
methodology
tools

Development plans
developers and their experience
major application checkpoints

Implementation strategy
phased or total implementation
security management
recovery/restart strategy

What are the (minimal/ideal) requirements for the application?

Figure 34.2 Application environment summary form.

The disadvantage of this approach is that it cannot usefully deal with the hard parts of the application development process. Application issues such as logical design issues, including logical database design, can only be reviewed through deep understanding of the business issues. Like all review procedures, a DB2 design review can evaluate and review; it cannot change. Like all design procedures, the design review can only be as effective as the preparation.

Chapter 35

Capacity Planning Reviews

This is an easy way to define how large your application is. ("Large" in this context refers to the application's ability to clog up the computer.) Large is a relative term, and most shops define it circularly. Many operate this way: A large application for your shop requires incremental capacity planning. A medium-sized application is one that is understood (by the participants) to require capacity planning. A small application is one whose capacity planning issues are ignored.

The objectives of capacity planning are to quantify the resource requirements for an activity. This information can be used to design the platform the application will run on, and to justify or reject application function based on cost to run. In some instances, capacity planning determinations (such as the duration of a batch window) will change application function. We will discuss these application reviews from the small to large.

Capacity Planning for Small Applications

A small application gets lost in the shuffle. If the application involves transactions that are not machine intensive (again a relative term) and are not frequently run, it cannot cause too much damage. The capacity planning for this sort of application is done in retrospect: how much of the relevant resources were consumed over time.

The exception cases for this type of application are those that present a new and unqualified face. It is especially useful to capacity review the first few DB2 applications. This both serves as an educational mechanism for the planning staff and prevents surprises, since DB2 applications can overrun expectations.

Capacity Planning for Medium-Sized Applications

Mid-sized applications are a complicated area for capacity planning. A complex capacity planning process is a nuisance, but these applications can still present capacity or requirement problems. A balance has to be maintained, and this only works through effective communication between the capacity planner and the application designers.

The standard strategy of mid-sized application capacity planning is to build an advance gross estimate of the application resource requirements. The nice thing about medium-sized applications is the small number of designers involved. This small group should allow an early development of a reasonably clear picture of the application requirements. Significant deviations can be identified and capacity planners notified.

In most shops, medium size is the standard application size. This has a profound impact on our ability to estimate resource requirements. The easiest way to plan for application resource consumption is to compare it to an existing application. Small applications tend to be idiosyncratic, and there tend to be too few large applications to get a basis for comparison.

If the applications compared are reasonably close in action, this benefits both sizes of the fence. The application designers have a clear function by function metaphor for the planning activity ("they are similar except . . ."). The capacity planners have hard activity numbers with which to work.

This matching process makes this size of applications special in two ways. First, capacity detail planning can be evaluated. Second, the capacity planning information is more useful then just for the application itself; the history becomes the source of future planning.

Capacity Planning for Large Applications

As application scope increases, capacity planning gains a higher profile. A large application is typically poorly understood initially; designers have only vague ideas of application externals or behavior, and to estimate resource requirements would be presumptuous. This is really a way to define a large application: It is an application that is initially planned with the designers having no clear idea of what the final programs will look like.

Large applications add layers of design *above* the levels of smaller applications. To a capacity planner, the later stages of large application development can look like a composite of many smaller projects (the application development process may seem like many smaller projects or may not, depending on the development methodology employed).

Thus, we have techniques available to predict the requirements of the final implementation stages of the application. Large applications tend to consume lots of resources, and require early performance planning. Luckily, programs tend to behave externally in very similar manners; likewise, programs tend to fit into simple buckets. We have to identify categories of activity and analyze expected activity into those categories.

A typical transaction categorization is shown in Figure 35.1.

Simple transaction:

a transaction that
does up to 10
direct reads (on average 5 I/Os).

Middling transaction:

a transaction that will
read up to
100 pages (on average 30 I/Os).

Complex transaction:

a transaction that reads
over 100 pages. To the extent
possible, detail each of these
transactions activity. (Figure 300
I/Os for these.)

Figure 35.1 An arbitrary transaction taxonomy.

Even in early stages of application design it is possible to roughly estimate processing characteristics. For example, you may be told: "We aren't sure what they'll do yet, but figure that out of about 200 transactions, 150 of them are straightforward, about 40 or so having to think a little, and the rest messy. Figure about 100,000 transactions a day, mostly the very simplest."

This tells us a lot. If the typical read involves 25 ms. of delay and tends to carry about 10 ms. of processor time with it we can "guesstimate":

- A typical simple transaction will take 125 ms. wait, 50 ms. CPU.
- A typical middling transaction will take 750 ms. wait, 300 ms. CPU.
- A typical complex transaction may take 7.5 s. wait, 3 s. CPU.

These are not all-inclusive buckets. DASD requirements have to be estimated early as well. The number of DB2 objects is also important. The size of the objects should be predicted, including the number of rows and insert, delete, and update rates. The types of batch activity (transaction apply processing, reconciliations, decision support, etc.) are all relevant. The object here is to guess, since that guess will provide a baseline, and something to adjust when we gain more insight.

It is hard to identify the phases in which iterative capacity planning should be done in a context-insensitive form (context here refers to the specific development methodology). The capacity planning tends to be fit into the other management checkpoints. An example list of these phases is: external design, logical design, physical design, coding. This is not necessary, but convenient for managing a large integration project.

It is important to emphasize that this iterative process is intended to build on the previous step in two ways. First, the preceding iteration resource requirements plan is the major input to the current step. The current step is not completely analyzed; instead, disparities between what was predicted in the previous phase and what was done are identified and corrected. Second, the iterations are self-correcting if used correctly. Each phase both refines the estimate (what? how much?) and helps us to identify why the previous iteration deviated.

Capacity Planning Design, Development, and Maintenance Activity

DB2 projects have a tendency to consume far more resources in development than in production. The activity in development — use of tools with intense resource requirements, large numbers of developers, and other factors in a large development project — makes capacity planning here a requirement.

It is much harder to capacity plan for any other kind of project. The problem in most cases is that programmer activity in a smaller project is not stable. In most cases this process is managed by maintaining a gross model of programmer resource requirements and allowing that much activity, and controlling programmer excesses through MVS scheduler priorities.

Chapter 36

Design of Batch DB2 Applications

Batch applications occupy a strange place in the world of DB2. On the one hand, batch is what DB2 seems best designed to do: decision support queries that take a half hour to process are effectively batch applications. On the other hand, batch applications are often held in low regard — and often developed by less qualified staff.

There are very different tradeoffs in designing batch applications. Understanding these is often key to developing the complete DB2 application. Batch processing is the workhorse of DB2 applications.

Relational Design Considerations

Batch DB2 applications differ from more traditional processing in one major aspect. DB2 applications should be performing set processing. The most common error in DB2 application development is treating applications processing data as if they were record I/O.

This user navigation loses the efficiencies DB2 can provide: lucid, terse programs, efficient and tunable query optimization, and read-ahead processing. In accepting the additional overhead incurred for these services but not using them we create applications that are the worst of both worlds: inefficient, unclear, and unmaintainable.

This view of the negatives gives us a clue to the goals of an effective DB2 batch design. Batch applications tend to be structured according to access structure (of course, transaction applications tend to be defined by transaction structure). The power of relational access facilities should drive the application to a very simple and clear structure.

Given a single goal, most programmers can design a good cohesive program to support it. Many batch applications are designed as "garbage bag" applications, supporting an arbitrary mixture of weakly related objectives (see Figure 36.1). It is unreasonable to expect a good design from these weakly coupled needs. Traditional programs could hide some of this clutter under the overhead of navigation and data management. Relational programs tend to make this mess blatantly obvious. At the very least the designer should sort out the objectives before attempting to integrate them.

That is not to say that a relational structures are a panacea. There is a powerful connection between data structure and

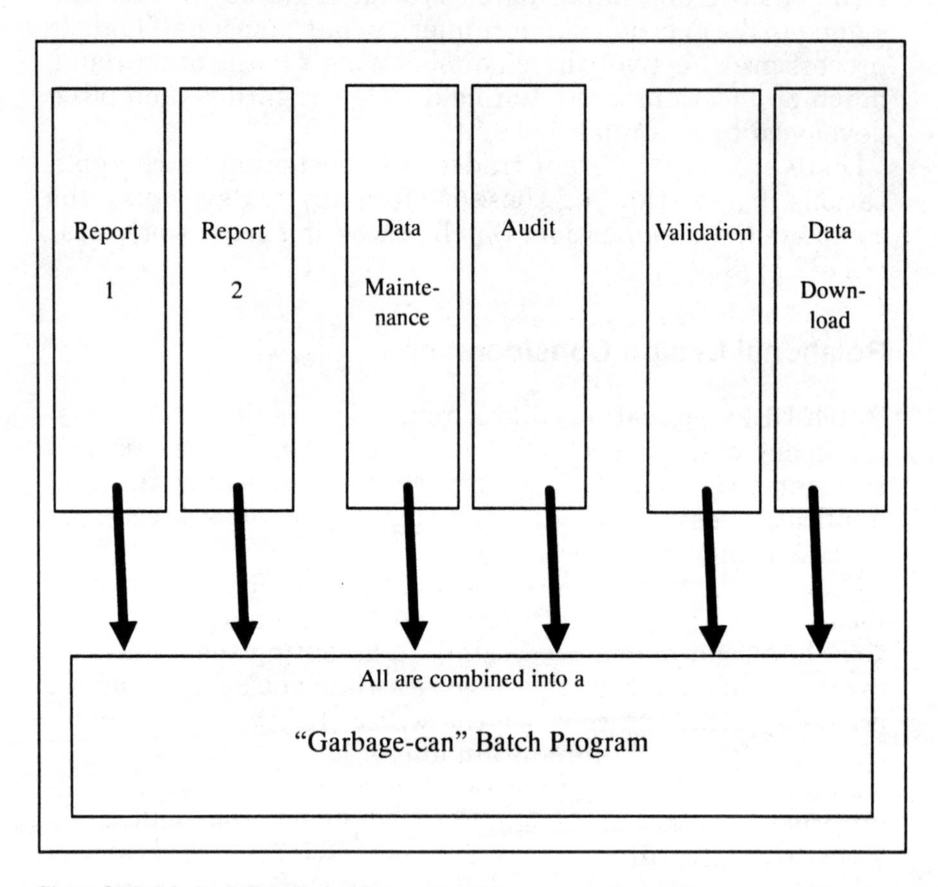

Figure 36.1 A jack-of-all-trades batch program.

access patterns inherent in a network data structure. We give that up for the mathematical framework of a relational system. In particular, there are clearly natural and unnatural SQL structures. Bill of materials and explosion processing (where a subpart record can contain subdividable subpart records) are common examples of recursive structures not amenable to set processing.

Many experienced DB2 designers tend to feel uncomfortable whenever much of the data semantics naturally is embedded in the data structure. Dynamic data structures are clearly not well supported in the SQL set calculus. The relational model can manage data that are recursive, but often does so by emulating nonrelational operations.

These structures can sometimes be redesigned to fit into the relational framework. This is an important consideration, since many of these structures are artifacts of the way we processed the information. This can sometimes provide valuable insight into a problem. At other times the relational redesign should be rejected simply because it does not naturally fit the way we think about the data.

Performance and Physical Design Considerations

Batch applications tend to process lots of data. Most do not have expediency requirements (e.g., subsecond response time) but instead are concerned with the cost of operation. An efficient batch program will smoothly process large amounts of data.

DB2 tables are loaded in cluster order, and utilities are run to keep them in that order. Many batch programs are required to traverse an entire table; common sense dictates that we prefer to process the table in the order it is laid out.

A case in point is match/merge processing. If this is done between tables it should normally be done internally by DB2. If the merge is between DB2 and an external data set, we may have the option of presorting the external data to follow DB2 cluster sequence. This can in turn reduce I/O by orders of magnitude.

Often there is a major physical design consideration that should be given to the choices of external vs. internal sorting. This is generally a batch programming issue, since most of batch processing is match/merge processing. DB2 is significantly less efficient then an external sort in some situations:

- If large amounts of data are involved, very efficient external sorts will be much more efficient than DB2 internal sort: cheaper, faster, and more easily tunable. A million rows or more can justify external sorting.
- If there is a need to maintain a stable bufferpool, large-scale DB2 sorting may have to be avoided.

But remember that arbitrarily rejecting DB2 sorting is a poor programming practice.

The natural presumption is that there is inherent order in the data retrieved from DB2, normally using an ORDER BY clause to force the issue. Since external sorts are very cheap, processing often consists of applying sorted external data to DB2 data retrieved in cluster order.

Most designers have some implicit cutoff point where they will choose between direct data selection and traversing the entire file. For many DB2 designers this cutoff (for large tables) is under 10 percent of the entire table. That is, if the application will process one-tenth of the entire table, read the entire table; if fewer data are processed read the specific rows on a piecemeal basis. This roughly corresponds to DB2 optimizer rules in choosing between tablespace scan and index search.

Process Data In or Out of DB2?

This is always a tough question. As a consultant I feel it is often poorly answered: many applications seem to arbitrarily unload DB2 data and process them using traditional sort merge logic. Many applications avoid this awkwardness by complicated, unnatural processing within DB2.

The first principle in deciding whether to unload DB2 data to process it as a sequential file is: don't. Don't even consider this option. DB2 can effectively support almost all application processing. Only a clear, demonstrable performance issue can make this option viable.

Minimizing Batch Windows

DB2 is a powerful and often slow tool. Many applications include requirements for off-line processing which should be done in as small a window as possible. Other applications, such as batch processing of ad-hoc queries, also strive to reduce their turnaround time. How can we speed up DB2 processing?

We are in luck. The cornerstone of the design of DB2 is to provide a facility that will be capable of sustaining growth in power as more, faster CPUs and I/O devices become available. Also, DB2 architecture is based on the concept of cheap (or at least lots of) memory. Thus we generally have a hardware out — get a bigger machine, **I**nstall a **B**igger **M**emory.

Understanding how DB2 exploits its hardware resources is a foundation for effective physical design of your applications, and of management of DB2 itself.

Let's see what happens when we do a trivial activity in DB2. For example if PHONEBOOK is defined:

```
CREATE TABLESPACE TSPHONE
IN MYDB
USING STOGROUP SG01
CLOSE YES
```

```
CREATE TABLE PHONEBOOK (
LNAME     CHAR(20) NOT NULL,
FNAME     CHAR(10) NOT NULL,
TELNUMBER DEC(10),
NUMBER    SMALLINT,
STREET    CHAR(10),
CITY      CHAR(10),
STATE     CHAR(2),
ZIP       DEC(9)
PRIMARY KEY (LNAME, FNAME)
IN TABLESPACE MYDB.TSPHONE
```

```
CREATE UNIQUE INDEX XPHONEBOOKLNFN
ON PHONEBOOK(LNAME, FNAME)
USING STOGROUP SG02
CLOSE  YES
```

```
CREATE INDEX XPHONEBOOKTEL
ON TABLE1(TELNUMBER)
USING STOGROUP SG02
CLOSE  YES
```

and we would like to perform an indexed read of a single column on a single row in a batch application:

```
SELECT LNAME
INTO :LNAME
FROM PHONEBOOK
WHERE TELNUMBER = :TELNUMB
```

If we assume no previous history that will help our efforts DB2 must perform these tasks (assumptions are that the user has already connected with DB2, has been authorized, a read includes some structural integrity checks of the data, we will ignore locking issues for the time being, and DB2 has selected an index scan of a three-level index for this static SQL query). The effort involved in this processing is staggering. Figure 36.2 shows an example of this work. This overhead of this intense processing is actually what makes batch processing so appealing.

```
OPEN XPHONEBOOKTEL indexspace
   (and read 2 header pages,
      wait for completion)
READ XPHONEBOOKTEL root page
   (and wait for completion)
search root page for value 2025553214.
READ XPHONEBOOKTEL non-leaf page
   we identified
   (and wait for completion)
search non-leaf page for value 2025553214.
READ XPHONEBOOKTEL leaf page we identified
   (and wait for completion)
OPEN TSPHONE tablespace
   (and read 2 header pages,
      wait for completion)
READ TSPHONE page we identified
MOVE the LNAME field to the user address space
NOTIFY the program to continue processing
```

Figure 36.2 Processing required for an index scan.

Locking

A simple statement such as:

```
SELECT NUMBER
FROM PHONEBOOK
WHERE STATE = :STATE
```

will often devote half its instruction path to locking. This is a high-overhead activity. The effort takes place in the DSNMSTR started task in coordinating the locking and in the IRLM started task managing the locks. We can eliminate that entire path by simply locking the table beforehand. If the PHONEBOOK table had been defined with LOCKSIZE TABLESPACE, we would only have a single IRLM interaction in the beginning.

Summary

Designing DB2 batch applications requires sophistication. Poorly designed batch DB2 applications which should take minutes often take hours. Designing these applications requires understanding of how DB2 accesses data and the logical capacity requirements for the application.

A common tendency in batch application design is combining all functions in a single module. The goal is to process all data in a single pass. This strategy has poor results in DB2, especially when the module requires maintenance.

A difficult choice in designing batch DB2 is determining what should be done inside of DB2 and what should not. Sorting large amounts of data can be done either in or out of DB2.

Review Question

1. Can a batch update application run concurrently with transaction processing?

Answer to Review Question

1. Yes, if the batch application commits work frequently. This can be done by designing batch update programs that simulate transaction processing. This means frequent COMMITs.

The batch program should not use the SQL LOCK TABLE statement. The plan should not be bound with the ACQUIRE(ALLOCATE) or RELEASE(DEALLOCATE) parameters.

Chapter 37

What DB2 Can't Do

DB2 is a powerful, multipurpose database management system; it is the most successful mainframe product in history. Some would have us believe that it can do anything. Studying the database management systems deficiencies will give us insight into both how we should best use it, and what IBM's strategy is for it in the future.

Distributed Processing

There is an obvious deficiency in current DB2 version 2.3; it only provides limited DB2 to DB2-distributed database support. The ultimate goal of tables partitioned across heterogeneous machines with automatic shadowing and site-independent work units seems very far off. Most DB2 version 2.3 applications using the distributed data facility right now are test applications, with only sporadic cross-environment demands.

Complete implementation of distributed database features in DB2 (and across the SAA line) will not be available until the mid-1990s. It will take even longer before we see common DB2 applications that use the full arsenal of distributed processing features. This has forced IBM into a cooperative processing strategy.

DB2 is very well positioned for distributed database services. Coordinating a work unit between two sites is no different than coordinating a work unit between DB2 and CICS — which is an existing feature. (Coordinating a work unit between *n*-sites is significantly more complicated.) The problems start when we look at systems in general, rather than at an isolated application work unit.

IBM has de-facto conceded the isolated application and turnkey systems market to lower margin vendors. The IBM philosophy dictates centralized computing. Current systems supporting businesses grow over time to become interlaced networks of interacting systems. The degree of dependency between these components requires applications that rigidly enforce a schedule, including scheduled availability. The implication then is that either everything is available or nothing is available.

The number of potential breaks increases dramatically as we interconnect systems — the foreign system may break down or the network connecting the two may fail. IBM cannot endorse a move to distributed databases until it can provide a stable distributed applications platform.

Cooperative processing then is a philosophy of providing cheaper, better, and more powerful user interfaces — but keeping the sensitive parts centrally managed and controlled. DB2 is clearly being positioned as a centralized server for this type of environment. This is what some articles imply when they describe MVS as being repositioned as a database machine.

Unnatural Relational Database Structures

When relational database was *the* buzzword in the press, physical design issues were considered the big bugaboo. The standard response to "that would be to slow" was that the relational structure was a logical representation (for clarity and mathematical rigor of presentation) and the underlying data structure would be the efficient network database model.

It is fascinating to see the what has happened in the interim:

- Relational databases have lost the "representation of data" battle in the press to object-oriented techniques that offer no mathematical structure and, instead, deal with the psychological issues in managing projects.

- Network implementations of relational structures have been a tremendous flop. The relational front ends built over network databases seem to offer the worst of both worlds: bad performance and incomplete function. The

> relational systems built from scratch have avoided the complexity of providing complex function over multiple data structures. Almost all are based on the single model of balanced-tree indexing of saturated data files.

There are clearly some areas of data management that are handled very poorly in relational database systems. These break down into two groups. There are some representation problems, where the relational set constructs are awkward in expressing a data relationship. The general purpose internal data structure of relational database management systems performs poorly in specific instances.

This leaves us with a DB2 having very limited physical database design facilities, which perform poorly in some circumstances. (Be careful: in many cases DB2 is blamed for performance problems caused by the designer.) Other database management systems built on more simple platforms than MVS provide some solutions. Ingres has tried to be a hero on the data management front by also offering hashed files. Many of the minicomputer-based relational database

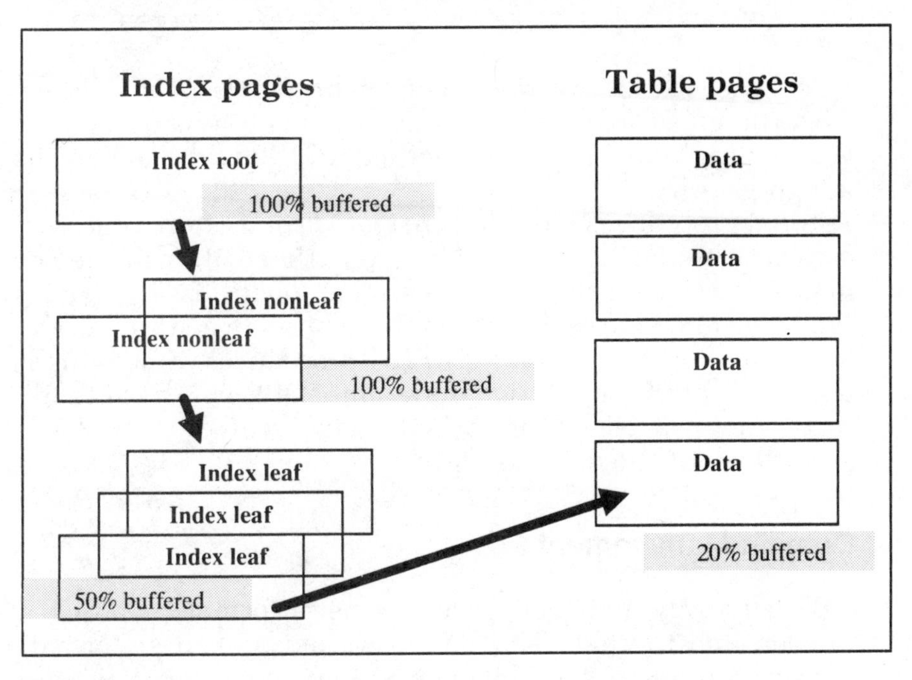

Figure 37.1 The I/O cost of a random access.

management systems provide various forms of stored procedures that allow the database designer to build more efficient centralized access modules.

Will DB2 provide hashed access to data? The overall DB2 architecture seems to be the issue. DB2 was designed based on a cost model of lots of cheap memory, which allows I/O reduction through large buffer areas. A typical DB2 data access path involves a three-level index, of which the top two levels are already in memory, and there is a 50:50 chance that the third level is in memory as well. The data is probably not buffered. The path and I/O likelihood are shown in Figure 37.1. In this figure, the top two pages are always buffered since they are accessed frequently. There are a lot more index leaf and data pages, but often data are accessed in patterns or sets that correlate to the data blocked on a single page. Thus, in this example we are performing

```
0 index root +  0 index nonleaf + .5 index leaf +
0.8 data page = 1.3 reads to randomly access a row
```

I/Os for each row we read. This figure corresponds closely with the effort for hashed access. Thus, we have to assume that adding a hashed access method to DB2 is not going to be a high priority.

Stored procedures have demonstrated their effectiveness on a variety of platforms. It seems likely that DB2 will thus be forced to respond and provide similar facilities. Repository Manager/MVS currently attempts to provide a stored procedure capability by invoking REXX procedures. Since this is unreasonable for operational systems, DB2 will have to (directly, not via REXX or CSP) provide real programmable procedures at the database level.

Domain Management

DB2 currently manages data in generic formats: character, integer, and the like. The objects we place in these formats have a more restricted range. For example, a salary field may be stored as an integer, but the field is more restricted. There are no negative salaries; the second digit of a USA area code is always 0 or 1.

This kind of processing has been traditionally the venue of application programs, but they are notorious for allowing inconsistent values to be stored. It makes sense to provide data value management at a central point. Dr. Edgar Codd's structural extensions to the relational model require domain value management at the database manager level. While referential integrity can theoretically manage domains, this is impractical. Consider the domain FLUNKY — defined as all employee numbers not equal to 00000001. We could copy all employee numbers except the boss's to another table for referential integrity checking, but it would be expensive and require application change.

DB2 designers realized this. DB2 was released with some inchoate facilities to validate data: EDITPROC, VALIDPROC, and FIELDPROC. These are exits that will call an assembler module that can validate the data. These are too flawed to be taken seriously. The assembler programs that run in a DB2 (privileged) address space are dangerous, hard to document, and hard to maintain. A code problem in one of these exits may corrupt the entire DB2 system. The exits add significant additional overhead to DB2. Ultimately, the fact that the exits were designed for system programmers rather than for application programmers and the rate of creation of new DB2 tables made these exits untenable.

DB2 has already capitulated to the requirement that it manage quality of data by introducing referential integrity. DB2 will have to provide a domain management feature for the same reason — popular demand. We can presume this will consist of a catalog-managed facility to describe valid values for data. These can include data ranges (e.g., a flight must be between 10 and 30,000 miles), and lists of valid values (e.g., a primary color can only be yellow, blue, or red). The values would be stored in an extension to the DB2 catalog through new data definition language statements. A new check utility would be needed to validate existing data against these values.

Image Processing and Large Objects

There is a fundamental deficiency in the DB2 architecture. It is poor at managing large unstructured chunks of data, such as are needed in image processing, voice processing, and other dealings with BLOBs (Binary Large OBjects). DB2 manages data on the page level, and is very effective in buffering objects that fit into 4K pages. DB2 only has two logical buffering sizes, 4K and 32K. Even the 32K pages are handled as a stepchild to the glamorous 4K pages. For example, reading a 32K page actually is processed as eight sequential 4K page-read requests. Most BLOBs are far larger than this (typically 50K and larger). Thus, DB2 forces us to break our large objects into smaller ones. BLOBs are not amenable to standard logging mechanisms — they are large and will serialize the system as users wait for them to complete logging.

These types of applications will force IBM's hand. The world is demanding these kind of applications, and if DB2 cannot manage them, then other systems can. This will result in dramatic changes in DB2. The data engine will have to manage arbitrarily large chunks of data. Presumably this will take place in hiperspaces on MVS/ESA systems (i.e., in extended memory where it will not interfere with other applications). More efficient I/O management of these objects is also required — implying that we will see cheap storage in the form of optical disks used to store BLOBs and fast I/O for large objects.

The current change logging mechanism is effective for transaction processing, but DB2 will be forced to introduce additional mechanisms to manage these large, basically static BLOBs. This will likely take the form of storing the BLOBs as nonlogged objects, and the log containing the before and after version BLOB data set name, rather than the before image and after image. This will probably require additional sophistication at the controller level (e.g., an enhanced 3990) and additional function in data management (probably requiring some enhanced System-Managed Storage).

24-Hour Operations

One of the forces that pushed customers into rejecting IMS has been the product's inability to manage extended operations well. Business requirements for the slightest change often required either a delay or intentionally stopping IMS. DB2 was required to address that need.

To some extent it succeeds. DB2 can allow ad-hoc queries, sometimes even on operational data. DB2 will allow some physical structure changes (such as adding a column to a table) even while the applications using the structure are active. DB2 does not support 24-hour, 7-day-a-week nonstop applications well.

The product deficiencies belong to two categories. One is effective recoverability. DB2 was designed to constantly validate consistency throughout its' operations. In the case of a read, it will validate the page structure. When it restarts, it will verify the consistency of the system. This process can take hours for an active DB2 system that has not been stopped for months. This delay is partly caused by an installation-defined checkpoint frequency, but is also very dependent on DB2 checking each open data set.

This long time to restart is incompatible with typical requirements for long-scheduled availability systems. This forces sites with round-the-clock applications in DB2 to partition their database systems by creating a separate DB2 subsystem to manage 24-hour applications. This lets DB2 do less work during recovery — at the expense of breaking the centralization promise we made when we started using DB2.

The other problem is more profound. DB2 manages data kept on secondary storage. Data structures tend to get disorganized, and access to the data gets less efficient. DB2 provides utilities to reorganize the data, but at the expense of taking the data off line.

IBM has been giving the round-the-clock availability issue high priority. MVS over the past few years has become a capable platform for round-the-clock operations. CICS and IMS/DC are not the limiting factors. DB2 will be forced to respond to user requirements and reduce the start-up time DB2 takes.

The data set reorganization issue is more profound. The requirement for availability is there, but DB2 file structures (especially index growth algorithms) are predicated on the frequent reorganization. DB2 has supported tables partitioned in different files (tablespace partitions and indexspace partitions) based on key value ranges. This is clearly going to be a future means of allowing the occasional file reorganization, by forcing off line only a specific key range of data.

DB2 is building shadowing mechanisms (that is, the ability to propagate updates to a file at intervals) to be used in distributing data. These same facilities can facilitate building a temporary copy of a table to be used while the original is being reorganized. This would additionally require a behind-the-scenes capability of flushing buffered pages of the inappropriate version of the data set. This facility would actually allow regular applications to be run in a round-the-clock fashion.

The only other easy option is to use a future model of the 3990 controller to provide the same service. Even current models of the controller can keep double copies of data sets (3990-3 duplexing). Functions could be added to allow tablespace copy while logging changes. If the controller could logically switch data sets it would provide the same functionality as the shadowing process, and off-load the effort from the central processor.

DB2 Security

DB2 security mechanisms are functional, but independent of the site security management facilities (in IBM's view RACF). This means that many sites have a security group managing TSO and RACF security, another managing IMS security, and DB2 DBAs forced to control DB2 security because the other groups refuse to assume responsibility. DB2 is thus under pressure to integrate its security with RACF.

DB2 has to rethink its security mechanism for some other reasons. Distributed database requirements will probably make further demands on DB2 development. The current direction is site-independent management of security. Large, centralized shops will have a hard time adjusting to this type of structure. Distributed locations (with no programmer or operations presence) will need some centralized support to manage such issues as application distribution and security.

IBM may abandon this area to independent software vendors, but it is unlikely. IBM has to keep *all* the centralizing mechanisms in a shop to prevent loss of shop control. This implies that they will offer some form of centralized management of the resource.

The options available include using Repository Manager/MVS as a front end to enterprise-level security management. This would truly centralize security administration, and solve some RACF problems in interfacing with other products and reporting. This seems like an ideal solution from the application design end; the business security requirements could directly drive the actual security management. The problems with this approach are the limited near-term penetration of the repository, and internal IBM resistance to front end, non-systems-level solutions that could open the door for other vendors.

DB2 security could be integrated into RACF. This would most likely take the form of new RACF security types corresponding to the existing DB2 security structure. (It would be unreasonable to expect the RACF database to move to DB2 since RACF must function even when DB2 is not available.) This would allow RACF administrators to manage DB2 security, but provide no growth direction. Evaluating the likelihood of this scenario is complicated by the lack of announced security direction — especially for PCs.

PS/2s under MS/DOS or OS/2 have too rudimentary security facilities to be serious candidates in a corporate DP strategy. At the same time PS/2s have a hardware security hook, the optional user password that is currently only used for power-on logon. Look for IBM to announce a more sophisticated security direction, needed in the short term to allow cooperative processing application security. This will likely give much insight into the security plans for DB2.

Effective Query Government

There is a basic problem in managing ad-hoc queries. The user will not know if the query will complete instantaneously or take days (yes, I have seen queries run from Tuesday to Friday with the user patiently waiting for the results). A broad solution to this problem is provided by the query governor in DB2 (version 2.1 and later, imitating a feature from QMF).

These governors can terminate queries that are doing an unreasonable amount of work. This can assist in managing the system, but will disorient the users. It is frustrating to run a query for 20 minutes, only to have the system terminate the request. This wastes both user time and system resources. A better solution would be to identify unreasonable queries before they are executed.

To some limited extent DB2 provides a solution. Even the earliest versions of QMF would display a "RELATIVE COST" value as a query was processed. (This estimate is calculated from the TIMERONS field that DB2 supplies in preparing a statement for execution.) The user could interrupt a query with a high cost estimate. The value of this field seems arbitrary, and it is generally ignored.

DB2 (in version 1.3) adopted the EXPLAIN mechanism, copied from SQL/DS. This identifies the access paths DB2 will use to process a query. The effort required to process the query is dependent on three issues:

- The selected data access path
- The system load, and relative priority
- Luck. If data you read is already in the bufferpool, your query doesn't have to do the I/O and will run faster. Also many queries are dependent on data values — until the data are read there is no way of identifying the final effort involved.

Even though users are demanding an IBM solution to these problems, we can expect IBM to avoid the issue so as to not damage its reputation with the problems associated with the luck factor.

Locking

Locking is a delightful mess in DB2. DB2 was initially designed as a decision support engine, and intentionally avoided addressing transaction processing issues. Careful, quality research determined that the decision support environment had fundamental problems with row-level locking.

DB2 planners decided that locking had to be very fast, or it would inordinately delay processing. On the other hand, choosing a fast internal locking method might complicate interfacing with other systems. The planners decided not to risk the ability to generalize services across DB2 environments, across CPUs and MVS systems, and across processor boundaries. A decision was made to use a more general lock manager from IMS (IRLM) and lessen the performance impact by block level "page" locking.

Later, market considerations dictated that DB2 be repositioned into the teleprocessing database management arena. The lock issue suddenly gained prominence. Locking was often the factor that lost DB2 sales. The worst lock offenders were the index pages — since transaction processing applications access data on the index level. Index pages have a high blocking factor. A partial solution was developed — splitting a page into up to sixteen parts to decrease the likelihood of collision. This gives us a manageable DB2 lock mechanism, and gives IBM respite before it provides row-level locking.

IBM has to provide row-level locking as an option, because the block-locking mechanism is destructive to certain types of applications. This forces designers to do things to improve performance (hampered by lock delay) such as pad data so that only one record fits in a block. This in turn destroys the whole premise of the DB2 architecture: effective data buffering. We should expect to see row-level locking soon.

Remember the choice of performance vs. future growth. This is the major issue here. Currently, many applications spend a quarter of their time performing lock management. If we increase the number of locks to be managed tenfold, we should expect a dramatic performance drop. This implies that IBM has two possible courses to take:

- The "nice guy" approach, building a fast internal locking mechanism and ignoring potential compatibility problems

- The "semi-solution" approach, where DB2 uses existing mechanisms to offer row-level locking — even if it is unusable in typical transaction processing for performance reasons

The latter approach has the advantage of providing checklist decision makers the comfort of having row-level locking, technicians the option of using this mechanism for very specific application needs, and IBM the ability to solve the CPU-load performance problem by selling a larger CPU.

As you see, I am tempted to assume that no new lock mechanism will be provided. Technical considerations aside, there has always been a strong aversion in DB2 development to row-level locking. On the other hand, DB2 development has been pushed on occasion (e.g., they had emphatically asserted that referential integrity was not in their plans) to provide functions. The jury is still out on this one.

Performance

DB2 is by no means a performance leader in database processing. Applications requiring transaction rates in the hundreds a second are rarely developed on DB2. Nor is DB2 a price-performance leader. The cost per transaction being processed by DB2 is high. This situation is acceptable to IBM, which positions DB2 as an engine capable of handling most loads (especially widely fluctuating ones), and is more concerned with marketing competitiveness than price competitiveness.

At the same time we should look at the competition. Only a few viable vendors are capable of delivering large-scale database engines. In particular, Tandem has developed a product (NonStop-SQL) that can deliver scalable high-transaction rates well.

Tandem has abandoned the general purpose database market to IBM, opting to concentrate on high availability transaction processing applications. Thus it is more of a danger to IBM chiefly when "true blue" shops are forced to look to Tandem because of outage concerns. The Tandem database management system offers reasonable transaction cost, scalable growth, and features such as row-level locking and utility processing concurrently with transaction activity and support for huge tables. Tandem traditionally is used as a complete processing system, but can be used as a back-end database machine, interfacing with IBM transaction processing software. The platform does not manage a diverse, changing work load well, and the available vendor applications are limited. The SQL is lacking in some features available in DB2, such as referential integrity.

Teradata offers a database engine to be attached to a front-end processor. This allows the device to be positioned as a "plug compatible" replacement for DB2 for certain applications. The engine can be attached concurrently to a variety of other platforms, such as other MVS machines, LANs, or many minicomputers.

Thus, Teradata can follow the IBM direction of centralized data management, and not require complete replacement of hardware (remember that mainframe computer growth is basically growth in existing installations). The platform offers very scalable growth and deals well with huge applications with huge amounts of data. The entry cost into Teradata machines is in the millions of dollars, the existing software base is limited, and Teradata SQL is missing some of the features in DB2 SQL, such as correlated subqueries.

These vendors are not going to take the market away from DB2, though they will nibble away at little pieces of it. IBM will respond to these kinds of vendor tactically, adding features required to remain competitive. This means that we will see an end to the 64-gigabyte DB2 table size limit — a factor that tilted some customers into other vendors' hands. A more virulent challenge is coming from the micro/mini world.

The players in this world include:

- Ingres — the technicians' favorite
- Oracle — the 500-pound gorilla
- Sybase — the glamour player

Each vendor has a strategy directly confronting DB2. DB2 has an child database product, OS/2 Extended Edition Data Manager (OS/2 EE-DM), looking to join in the competition.

Ingres attempts to supply function. Ingres started out on a UNIX base as an experiment in future database management capabilities. UNIX is a simple operating system, which allows experiments into areas of database capabilities to be done over a single college semester (where the equivalent project in MVS takes a year residency for several better qualified researchers).

The research roots (and easier platforms) have pushed Ingres into providing technical sophistication and delivering products with legitimate function. The expectations from any

Ingres function are very high. Thus the Ingres query optimizer is expected to deliver excellent path choice. In fact some features, such as understanding nonlinear key value distribution, have been adopted by DB2 (as the column RUNSTATS in version 2.1). The distributed processing feature is another facility where Ingres has led the marketplace.

The flashy features have secured Ingres' place in technical areas. At the same time the frequent updates, lack of sales and market acumen, inconsistent support, and its sale to ASK have alienated many potential business clients. IBM thus is following Ingres closely — as a technology guinea pig. In particular, Ingres is providing a model for effective optimization of distributed queries — a vital concern.

Oracle comes from a different background entirely. It was built on government money based on a perceived market niche. The company has been notorious for pre-announcing products, some of which never were delivered.

Other products it has delivered are technically suspect, such as the current distributed database offering that has no understanding of optimization issues. Currently, Oracle is the only player besides IBM in the database management world that can set market direction by itself. It has large market share, and is available on a host of hardware and operating system platforms.

Oracle attempted to compete directly with DB2 on MVS, a ploy that failed quickly. The current strategy is to coexist with and "wrap-around" DB2, by taking over the database management on all noncentral platforms. Oracle would still like to make a play for the central server for companies, but is attempting it on the cheap, through a joint venture building a server for the *n*-cube multiprocessor computer. The strategy seems appealing. The tasks a database manager does — sorting, comparing, and managing disk drives — are very amenable to parallelization. If the products succeed, they will provide a low-cost Oracle platform capable of sustaining very high transaction throughput. This must be considered a more direct threat to Teradata than to DB2. But if the *n*-cube platform takes off, it would probably start a high-end database transaction server cost war — which could certainly damage DB2's credibility if the cost difference became dramatic.

Sybase is in high gear in everything but profits these days. It developed in the standard Silicon Valley venture route, as a splitoff from a startup database machine company. The founders noted that the database machine looked a lot like a generic computer with a database manager running on it. The only difference seemed to be that the product was being sold as a means of centralizing the database's activity. This concept of a centralized, shared database, with other computers acting as intelligent displays seemed exciting. The resultant company was founded on the idea of a client-server database management model.

This model makes a lot of sense. Distributed database is hard. IBM has adopted the model as cooperative processing. The Sybase software is basically sound. The product is not in direct competition with DB2 yet, but has to be considered seriously in the near future.

The growth potential of DB2 is limited to the rate of processor power growth (we assume about 15 to 20 percent annually) and the number of processors which can be combined in a single complex (the limit seems to be 16 for the current generation of 3090s). As super-minicomputers become more powerful, can be coupled, and can deliver cheaper processing, their database managers become more viable. Sybase seems best designed to sustain a growth both in number of processors it can support and in more efficiently managed single processors.

DB2 can defend itself from this kind of onslaught in several ways. It can more tightly couple with the operating system, so that all MVS users will be forced into acquiring it. This strategy, much touted in the press, is good for DB2 penetration but ineffectual in guaranteeing that IBM mainframes with DB2 will be the central corporate data resource. IBM needs to maintain technical credibility.

DB2 can be made more efficient. This seems mandatory. IBM is betting the entire mainframe business on DB2. Thus, we must assume that we will see hardware boosts that allow DB2 to radically increase in power. (We can assume 30 percent annually, the rate that businesses tend to increase their processing needs.) We will also see a reduction in transaction cost, attempting to avoid the order-of-magnitude cost differential that would cause users to ignore the safety factors and reliability issues and abandon the product.

OS/2 EE-DM is the oddball in this equation. The database management system doesn't have a following yet, and it is already spawning off another server for the RS/6000. The mini- and microcomputer server market for relational database management systems seems to be saturated with mature products. Why introduce a new product into this arena?

In all likelihood the IBM of the early 1980s would not have opted for this scenario. Although IBM tends to wait until markets mature before invading them, it has been forced to concede most of the PC market to generic hardware vendors and does not expect to regain it. The strategy in fighting for a piece of the pie has to do with long-term database strategy, and IBM has no chance of early profitability here. IBM needs a glamorous nonclonable platform for two reasons: It needs to make money on the hardware underneath, and it has to maintain control of the centralized data resource.

The problem in controlling the data goes like this: If IBM doesn't have a distributed platform as an option on PCs, other vendors are going to provide them. Users at some point are going to need distributed database capabilities. DB2 will have to be opened up to non-IBM database managers, either by user pressure on IBM or through independent vendor programs. This will hurt the DB2 capabilities for functional growth because of the added complexity, and open the door for "plug compatible" alternatives. This factor combines with the new IBM need for software revenue to require a successful OS/2 EE-DM.

DB2 has been doing a remarkably effective job in increasing performance between releases. This has been provided through several means:

- Physical data structure, such as partitioned tablespaces (DB2 version 1.3), which can allow more efficient indexing

- Query processing mechanisms, such as using multiple indices on a single referenced table in a query (DB2 version 2.2)

- Query optimization, such as considering the CPU performance characteristics in selecting a search path (DB2 version 2.1)

- Data engine tricks, such as allowing the skipping of uninteresting blocks while reading ahead in a file (list prefetch in DB2 version 2.2)

- Underlying hardware/software, such as 3390 disk drives, or the MVS/ESA operating system
- Increased DB2 capability to multithread and path-length reduction, such as by providing latches to replace the slower catalog IRLM locking (DB2 version 2.1)
- Reduced lock contention, such as by reducing the blocking factor in index locks (index subpages in DB2 version 1.2)

We don't expect it to stop. Every two releases of DB2 have doubled the product power, half by hardware improvements and half by software improvements. There is currently no technical reason for this trend to stop. There might be marketing issues that slow the growth in the near future.

The reasoning goes like this. Sales of improved hardware are predicated on the marketplace capability to absorb them. In an expanding market we tend to see dramatic growth as increasing capacity needs are satisfied. If the market stabilizes, the demand for increased power will decrease — and the cost of providing the incremental improvement to fewer consumers will rise. We will thus expect IBM performance improvements to correlate to (but lag behind) economic trends.

Glossary

bufferpool

DB2 provides for four pools of memory pages that the *system administrator* can configure. These pools allow *staging* of reads and writes. The pools BP0, BP1, BP2, BP32K are associated with DB2 data spaces by the CREATE TABLESPACE, CREATE INDEX, ALTER TABLESPACE, and ALTER INDEX statements.

database maintenance

Managing the data in files by running standard utility programs to copy and reorganize the data to allow recovery and efficient processing.

data space

A general term for DB2 data sets, both *index spaces* and *TABLESPACES*

DBD

The Database Descriptor, contains the data definition information from the DB2 catalog in a tree (hierarchical) structure. The DBD is automatically changed whenever *DDL* is executed.

DDL

Data Definition Language, the *SQL* statements that create and drop objects.

domain restriction

Limiting (some or all types of) processing to data in qualified data value ranges.

EDM, EDMPOOL

The Environment Descriptor Manager, a buffer area that is used to support the *skeleton cursor tables* and *cursor tables* for application plans and *DBD*s.

high availability

An application that has unusual requirements to be functional during the specified service schedule (q. v.). Note that high availability does not imply an extended service schedule.

high scheduled availability

An application that has a small (or no) planned outage schedule.

index space

The file or files an index is stored in. Index space definition is part of the CREATE INDEX statement.

information hiding

Allowing each information user access only to the data it requires. This prevents accidental misuse of data.

inquiry only

Availability of the data viewing components and the restriction from use of the data updating facilities of the application.

log apply

Forward recovery of a file by updating a historical copy of a file using journaled update transactions.

MTBF

Mean time between failures, the average amount of time an application is functioning.

MTTR

Mean time to repair, the average amount of time used to restore an application to service.

outage

A scheduled or unscheduled removal of an application from service.

real time

Processing involving tasks that must be completed within a defined, short period.

recovery/restart

Solving problems that terminate an application and allow it to continue processing.

recycle

Stop and restart. DB2 currently requires recycling when it supports complex data requirements but must be capable of quickly restarting after a problem causes it to be stopped.

resilient application

An application that is capable of some degree of recovery from software or hardware failures.

restricted service

The availability of partial application function, such as inquiry only (q. v.).

service

The full availability of an application.

service schedule

The planned availability of an application.

shadow database

A method of allowing database maintenance by maintaining multiple copies of the data, and temporarily detaching a single copy when database maintenance need be performed.

SQL

Structured query language, the language used to interact with DB2. SQL is divided into *DML*, *DDL*, and *DCL*.

staging

Staging I/O is a means of reducing the read or write delay in an application. Staged reads are data read into buffers before they are needed. Staged writes allow applications to continue processing before the data are written to the actual destination.

system administrator

The technical support manager of DB2. System administrators are generally responsible for controlling the aspects of the system that cross application lines. There is a security level SYSADM for administering DB2.

tablespace

The physical instantiation of tables in DB2. Consists of one or more files called partitions.

tablespace partition

The physical subdivision of a tablespace used to store tables in DB2. If the tablespace in not partitioned, this is the same as the tablespace; if the tablespace is partitioned, each partition contains a key range of data established in the (required) clustering index definition.

tablespace partition file

The VSAM file used to store tables in DB2. This differs from *tablespace partition* when the partition size exceeds the VSAM maximal file size.

24-hour application

An application that is available 24 hours a day (includes applications that have scheduled nondaily outages).

24/7 application

An application that is available 24 hours a day 7 days a week (includes applications that have scheduled nonweekly outages).

24/365 application

An application intended to be available with no scheduled outages.

update

Unless otherwise qualified, refers to any DELETE, INSERT, or UPDATE processing.

Index

A

B

C

D

E

F

G

H

Q

R

S

T

U

V

W

X

Z